WHAT READERS SAY
Comments on the previous edition (published as Land of the Canyons)

"Your photography guide to Utah and Arizona is TERRIFIC!! We found it invaluable!"

—*Marjorie Carr, Ada MI*

"The book proved to be INDISPENSIBLE since there was no way that we would ever have found some of the locations without it. The information was accurate and sufficient for us to find every location we went looking for. The tips on lenses and lighting also proved useful."

—*Robert Robson*

"I recently traveled the 'Grand Circle,' with photography as my focus and your book was an INDISPENSIBLE part of my photographic itinerary. The proof is in my prints. I used your advice with respect to place and time, etc., and you were on the money. I RECOMMEND your book to many people on my trip. It's exactly what I was looking for."

—*Michael Ryan, Bogota, NJ*

"Awesome book, packed w/places to visit for the adventurous! The majority of suggestions are off the beaten path and a little adventurous, which I prefer. The author pays a lot of attention to photographic concerns, which helps immensely if you are a photographer, but you need not be to benefit from this book. This book is PERFECT for getting ideas of places to visit. I would definitely recommend this book for anyone visiting the Southwest, who wants to visit places you've only seen in photography magazines. YOU WON'T BE DISAPPOINTED!"

—*Regina Hugo, posted on amazon.com*

"I recently read and re-read your guide and it was INDISPENSABLE on my southwest Utah trip. It has also wetted my appetite to explore all the places in the book and I am recommending your guide to several friends."

—*Ross Martin, Seattle, WA*

"Your book is a MUST reading for anybody who is going to the Colorado Plateau. I have recommended and given copies of the book to many of my friends. Your description was in wonderful detail which would entice more people to visit the Colorado plateau."

—*Jerry Rosenfeld, Huntington Woods, MI*

"Just a line to let you know my wife & I made a trip out to Arches & Canyonlands this past fall. Your book proved INVALUABLE."

—*Martin Kullen, Stoughton, MA*

"I really enjoy your book and use it often. I RECOMMEND IT to everyone who asks about photographing in southern Utah."

—*af*

"I really appreciate your books on Photographing the Southwest, and they have been INVALUABLE guides."

—*Sharon Kocher*

"A fine little volume, with black-and-white photos and lots of concise information for exploring and photographing the southwest."

—*Los Angeles Times*

"Every Canyon Country traveler will appreciate having this handy guide along. It will lead you to the most exciting and photogenic spots in the American Southwest."

—*The Black Rabbit Catalog*

"Laurent Martrès has really outdone himself with the release of these two new photo/travel guides. If you are a serious photographer of the Southwest, you've GOT TO HAVE these books!"

—*Robert Hitchman, Photograph America Newsletter*

PhotoTripUSA™

Photographing the Southwest

Volume 1

A guide to the natural landmarks of Southern Utah & Southwest Colorado

by Laurent Martrès

GRAPHIE
INTERNATIONAL, INC.

Photographing the Southwest – Volume 1
A guide to the natural landmarks of Southern Utah & Southwest Colorado
Copyright © 2002 by Laurent Martrès. All rights reserved.

All photographs are by Laurent Martrès, Copyright © 2002, except where noted.
Cover photo: Pillars of the Earth (Arches Nat'l Park) by Laurent Martrès

Also available:
Photographing the Southwest – Volume 2: Arizona & New Mexico
ISBN 0-916189-09-0
Images of the Southwest – Vol. 1 CD-ROM ISBN 0-916189-10-4
Images of the Southwest – Vol. 2 CD-ROM ISBN 0-916189-11-2

Published by PhotoTripUSA™
An imprint of

GRAPHIE
INTERNATIONAL, INC.

8780 19th Street, Suite 199
Alta Loma, CA 91701, USA
info@phototripusa.com
Visit our web site: http://www.phototripusa.com

Printed in the U.S.A.

DISCLAIMER
Some of the locations described in this guidebook require travel through remote areas, where footpaths and 4-wheel drive trails can be difficult, even dangerous. Travel at your own risk and always check conditions locally before venturing out. The author and publisher decline all responsibility if you get lost, stranded, injured or otherwise suffer any kind of mishap as a result of following the advice and descriptions in this guidebook. Furthermore, the information contained in this guide may have become outdated by the time you read it; the author and publisher assume no responsibility for outdated information, errors and omissions.

Publisher's Cataloging-in-Publication

Martres, Laurent.
    Photographing the Southwest / by Laurent Martres. --
1st ed.
    v. cm.
    Includes bibliographical references and index.
    CONTENTS: v. 1. A guide to the natural landmarks of
Southern Utah & Colorado -- v. 2. A guide to the natural
landmarks of Arizona & New Mexico.
    ISBN 0-916189-08-2 (v. 1)
    ISBN 0-916189-09-0 (v. 2)

    1. Southwest, New--Guidebooks. 2. Landscape
photography--Southwest, New--Guidebooks. I. Title.

F787.M37 2002   917.904'34
                QBI02-200026

PREFACE
by Tom Till

Tom Till

I've often said that the Colorado Plateau is a place where two divergent forces, the world's best light and the world's most interesting landscapes, seamlessly combine to create a photographer's paradise. Having been lucky enough to travel worldwide in pursuit of landscape and nature imagery, and also lucky enough to have lived my entire adult life in canyon country, I believe I have the standing to make such a claim, although anyone who has spent much time here knows my words to be utterly true.

As I looked at the places mentioned in the text, I was flooded with a lifetime of memories of the great times I have had exploring, hiking, jeeping, river running and making photographs in the Four Corners area. I was fortunate, beginning in the 1970's, to be one of the first photographers to visit the Subway in Zion National Park, to cruise around the White Rim in Canyonlands without a permit, and to be the only photographer in Antelope Canyon for weeks at a time.

Photographers coming to the area now have a challenge I never faced in those early years: other photographers. Over the decades serious photography has become one of the major activities pursued by visitors to the region. As such, we have an increased responsibility to leave the land as we find it, behave ourselves around other photographers and visitors, and place the integrity of the land above our desire to create images. After you leave this magnificent place, you can also provide a valuable service and help insure its survival as a viable ecosystem by supporting national and local environmental groups who lavish a great deal of needed attention on the preservation of our spectacular deserts. These groups include The Sierra Club, The Grand Canyon Trust, The Southern Utah Wilderness Alliance, The Nature Conservancy, and The Wilderness Society.

I congratulate Laurent Martres on the fine work he has done with this book, on his own wonderful photography, and on his mission to give many other photographers a forum for disseminating their great work on his website. In this regard, he is unique among established western landscape photographers.

Photographing the Southwest will be a helpful tool for me when I return to many of my favorite haunts in the future, but I'm also glad that an infinity of canyons, arches, ruins, springs and secret places have been left out of this book. These places are the true heart of the wilderness desert southwest. They are available to all who push a little beyond the established scenic hot spots, and all who are willing to risk equipment, creature comforts, and at times, life and limb. It's all worthwhile in pursuit of the magical light that calls us onward around the next bend of the canyon.

ACKNOWLEDGEMENTS

As with any book of this scope, many individuals have contributed one way or the other to a better experience for the reader.

First and foremost thanks to Philippe Schuler, whose careful editing of the manuscript and numerous enhancements to its contents have contributed to a much better book. Philippe—who shares with me an intense passion for the Southwest—co-wrote several sections and added informative textual and pictorial content throughout the book. He also spent countless hours verifying the relevance and accuracy of the practical information, as well as restructuring the presentation to make the book a better read.

Tom Till's wonderful photography has consistently inspired me. Tom kindly wrote the Preface to *Photographing the Southwest* and some of his photography is also featured in this series.

Sioux Bally, of Heartstone Arts, lent her considerable artistry to designing the cover, as well as the anchor pages of each chapter. Sioux also helped me select the images to illustrate the book, sparing me the heart-wrenching process of eliminating some of my favorite pictures.

Patricia Joy designed the layout and style sheets.

Carol Bowdoin-Gil edited the material in the first and second editions of Land of the Canyons, the precursor to this book.

Julia Karet edited new material in this edition.

Julia Betz, Director of the Powell Museum in Page, AZ and Mike Salamacha, Bureau of Land Management (BLM) wilderness ranger in Kanab, UT corrected the Around Paria chapter.

Scott Walton contributed valuable advice and co-wrote some material for the Grand Staircase–Escalante chapter.

My photography partners Gene Mezereny, Denis Savouray and Philippe Schuler and my wife Patricia accompanied me on many trips to the Southwest. Thanks, Patricia, for being so patient and tolerant of my early morning departures when we travel together and for letting me go on all these solo trips.

Thanks to Esther Kemper for her unwavering confidence and encouragement.

Finally, thanks to all the photographers who have kindly contributed their talent to enrich the pictorial content of this book: Gene Mezereny, Lynn Radeka, Denis Savouray, Philippe Schuler, Kerry Thalmann, Tom Till and Scott Walton. Visit the www.phototripusa.com web site to find links to their own websites and learn more about their work.

ABOUT THIS BOOK

Welcome to *Volume 1* of *Photographing the Southwest*—a photographer's resource to the natural landmarks of southern Utah and Southwestern Colorado.

The scope of this book is to document natural landmarks from a photographic perspective, primarily those that are preserved under some form of tutelage, such as Federal agencies, State, County or Tribal authority. Some of these landmarks are well known, but many are off the beaten track and have largely been ignored by more traditional guidebooks. Most are easily accessible and will provide you with unforgettable images and memories.

Some human activity is also covered in the book, but it is essentially limited to pre-Columbian dwellings and rock art. This is due to the fact that cliff dwellings and rock art are tightly integrated into the landscape and can be interpreted as an extension of the natural world. I believe most landscape photographers would agree with that.

On rare occasions, mention is made of more recent sites due to their proximity to natural landmarks. However, other forms of human activity which greatly contribute to the essence of the Southwest, such as architecture, modern native Americans crafts and rituals, rodeo, etc. are outside the scope of *Photographing the Southwest* and are purposely left out.

If you're not a photographer, you'll find in this book lots of information that more traditional guides leave out. The most beautiful angle and the best time of the day to view a site are equally as valuable for seeing with your own eyes as for photography. This book is for everyone with a passion for the Southwest.

Photographing the Southwest is a resource, rather than a guidebook. It supplements other, more traditional travel guides with specialized photographic information. The information is arranged by large geographic areas. Locations whose photographic interest is particularly impressive are listed under these main headings. It also describes how to get there, as well as how and when to get the best shots. It purposely leaves out logistical concerns such as restaurant and hotel accommodations as there are already more than enough books on that subject.

Formerly published as *Land of the Canyons*, *Photographing the Southwest* began as a location resource for photographers interested primarily in the Colorado Plateau. The First Edition was essentially distributed over the Internet and in a few specialized stores. It garnered extremely positive feedback but remained a cult product owing much of its reputation to word of mouth on Internet newsgroups.

While the Second Edition greatly improved layout and added numerous locations and images, it didn't fundamentally change the scope of the book. What it did, however, was reach a much broader audience through channel distribution. With increased sales came a flood of reader mail from all over the world and numerous requests for additional coverage of outlying areas of the Southwest.

As I watched *Land of the Canyons'* Third Edition grow into a 450-page behemoth, I knew the time had come to split the work into two more manageable volumes. Volume 1 covers Southern Utah and Southwestern Colorado, while Volume 2 covers Arizona and New Mexico.

In addition to all the new areas covered in *Photographing the Southwest*, both volumes include a large number of new sites located in the territory previously covered by *Land of the Canyons*, as well as new commentary and advice concerning previously visited sites.

The chapter on photography has been greatly expanded, despite my initial reluctance to dispense this kind of advice. This chapter is common to both volumes. While I hope you'll benefit from the advice if your are a beginning photographer, my primary goal remains to provide you with a comprehensive location resource with which you can unleash your very own photographic talent.

Coverage of pre-Columbian sites has been significantly increased and reflects a growing interest on the part of the public for exploring the heritage of native Americans and interpreting their rock art. As Val Brinkerhoff, photographer of *Architecture of the Ancient Ones* puts it: "Visit one ancient dwelling site and you're likely to be drawn to experience another, and another, and another."

With these two greatly expanded volumes, my goal is to give readers from all over the world the best practical information to photograph the Southwest. I am committed to continue improving the quality of this information over time and to bring you additional material in Volume 3 (Southern California & Nevada).

I believe you'll enjoy discovering the infinite photographic possibilities of the Southwest and make some truly amazing discoveries in the course of following the recommendations of this book.

May this book bring you a slew of new ideas for your creative photography of the Southwest.

—*Laurent Martrès*

Important Note:

Two companion CD-ROMs containing the images of each volume and many more, are available:

Images of the Southwest – Vol. 1 Southern Utah & Colorado ISBN 0-916189-10-4
Images of the Southwest – Vol. 2 Arizona & New Mexico ISBN 0-916189-11-2

Each CD-ROM is a companion to its respective book (Vol 1. or Vol. 2). You'll get the photos from each book, plus many more—a total of 500+ high-quality images, all in full color, royalty-free for your personal use, arranged by chapters just like in the books. This is an excellent way to "pre-visualize" the sites—an indispensable part of quality photography. Windows/Mac compatible.

Look for a rebate coupon at the end of this book or visit our web site: http://www.phototripusa.com

TABLE OF CONTENTS

Dawn on the Earth – Dead Horse Point SP

Chapter 1

INTRODUCTION TO THE SOUTHWEST

A BIT OF GEOLOGY

Introduction

<u>*Note:*</u> this chapter is common to Vol. 1 and 2 of *Photographing the Southwest*.

What makes the Southwest so special is its amazing geological origins. The sedimentary layers of the Colorado Plateau were deposited, one after the other, in horizontal strata which were subsequently subjected to erosion by the various elements—wind, rain, and river action—forming fantastic and captivating scenery.

In no other part of the planet does there exist a similar concentration of such singular and varied geologic phenomena. Here the work of erosion manifests itself in such diverse forms as the great depth and enormity of the Grand Canyon, the tight corkscrew shape of Antelope Canyon, the stupendous spans of Arches and Natural Bridges, the incomparable coloration of Bryce Canyon, the fantastic gargoyles in Goblin Valley and the otherworldly dunes of the White Sands and Great Sand Dunes—all this to our great enjoyment.

This chapter does not pretend to be a course in geology. I do not have the expertise for that and the reader can no doubt research this in greater depth himself. For a superb, yet very approachable, in-depth exploration of the geology of the Southwest, I invite you to read two books: F.A. Barnes' *Canyon Country Geology* and Thomas Wiewandt's and Maureen Wilkes' *The Southwest Inside Out*. Even if you don't have the time nor the inclination to do so, a minimum of geologic knowledge will permit a better understanding of the striking terrain and how it is not merely an inanimate mineral world, but a monumental product of perpetual evolution.

The knowledge of some basic geologic features will enrich your experience of the Southwest enormously:

❒ the step-like structure of the Colorado Plateau which falls in successive stages towards the southwest;

❒ the various sedimentary layers of the land;

❒ the faults and promontories that fracture and raise the relief of the plateau;

❒ the role of the principal waterways in forming the landscape;

❒ the geographic location of the various mountain chains of the plateau;

❒ and finally, the deserts' ecosystems.

The Grand Staircase

The Grand Staircase starts at the Kaibab Plateau, to the north of the Grand Canyon of the Colorado. The limestone bed of the plateau, 225 million years old, is the first step of the staircase.

The Chocolate Cliffs, a brown color, form the second step. They are found at the south entrance to Zion. The Vermilion Cliffs, of a deep red hue and between

165 and 200 million years old, form the third step. They are found scattered along an imaginary line from St. George to Page. Without a doubt, the most beautiful examples are found along Hwy 89A where they appear on the horizon, seen from the viewpoint at Horseshoe Bend.

The White Cliffs, which appear white in strong sunlight but are really an ocher color, are between 135 and 165 million years old. They can be seen along the southern part of Hwy 89 in the vicinity of Mt. Carmel. The Gray Cliffs, 120 to 135 million years old, form the base of Bryce Canyon and are only visible with great difficulty as they are cliffs in name only. Their soft, friable nature causes them to form an almost worn out tread on the Grand Staircase. Finally there are the Pink Cliffs, 50 to 60 million years old, that form the top step of the Staircase of which Bryce Canyon is the most representative example.

During your travels across the plateau, you will cross and re-cross these steps of the Grand Staircase. Yovimpai Point, at the southern tip of Bryce Canyon allows you to view the Staircase in its entirety from a single vantage point.

Sedimentary Layers

A knowledge, however superficial, of the sedimentary layers that form the plateau will provide a better opportunity to get the most from your visit to the area. All these layers are uncovered, in one place or another. The geology of the Southwest is like an open book and all you have to do is read it—it couldn't be simpler.

A few formations constitute the majority of those, which are most commonly photographed:

❏ the ancient beige Cedar Mesa sandstone of the Permian era, which forms the spectacular spires of the Needles and Maze districts of Canyonlands as well as the bridges and canyons of Natural Bridges NM. It is also seen throughout the Cedar Mesa plateau from Blanding to Hite and down to Mokey Dugway.

Many sedimentary layers are exposed in Capitol Reef

❏ the salmon-hued de Chelly Sandstone, which is formed from ancient sand dunes and found in Monument Valley and Canyon de Chelly.

❏ the dark brown and red, strangely-striated Moenkopi, found throughout the Colorado Plateau, but especially well-represented in Capitol Reef.

Formation / Average layer thickness	Era	Where is it found?
Claron formation 600 ft	Tertiary	Bryce Canyon
Mancos Shale 1000 ft	Cretacean	Capitol Reef
Dakota sandstone 300 ft	Cretacean	Capitol Reef
Morrison formation 400 ft	Jurassic	Arches, Capitol Reef
Summerville formation 300 ft	Jurassic	Goblin Valley, Arches
Curtis sandstone 250 ft	Jurassic	Goblin Valley
Entrada sandstone 800 ft	Jurassic	Arches, Goblin Valley, Cathedral Valley
Carmel formation 650 ft	Jurassic	Capitol Reef, San Rafael Reef
Navajo sandstone 1000 ft	Triassic	Zion, Escalante, Arches, Rainbow Br., Capitol Reef
Kayenta formation 350 ft	Triassic	Arches, Island in the Sky
Wingate sandstone 400 ft	Triassic	Dead Horse Point, Capitol Reef, Colorado N. M.
Chinle formation 600 ft	Triassic	Island in the Sky, Capitol Reef
Moenkopi formation 1000 ft	Permian	Natural Bridges, Capitol Reef, Fisher Towers
Kaibab limestone 300 ft	Permian	Grand Canyon, Capitol Reef
White Rim sandstone 250 ft	Permian	Island in the Sky
Cedar Mesa sandstone 1500ft	Permian	Natural Bridges, Needles, Maze
Cutler formation 1200 ft	Permian	Monument Valley, Fisher Towers
Honaker formation 3000 ft	Pennsylvanian	Shafer Trail, Needles

Sedimentary layers of the Colorado Plateau

❐ the outrageously colorful Chinle formation, soft and crumbly, forming numerous badlands throughout the Plateau.

❐ the highly polished, intense red Wingate sandstone essentially forming the core of the Island in the Sky and Dead Horse Point. It is also found in the Escalante drainage, at Capitol Reef, Little Wild Horse Canyon and the Colorado Nat'l Monument. It assumes a wild animalistic quality when striated by desert varnish, reminiscent of a Tiger's fur. It makes fantastic background for photos of cottonwoods in spring and autumn.

❐ the grayish-red Kayenta sandstone, with its characteristic horizontal layers.

❐ the ever-present Navajo sandstone, encountered everywhere on the plateau. It is often whitish, with occasional hues of red and pink and is best represented by the minarets of Zion, the domes of Capitol Reef and the fantastic slot canyons near Lake Powell and the Escalante River.

❐ the superb Entrada sandstone, star of some of the best photos of the American West, finely grained and terra cotta in color; it appears dull under the midday sun but glows a brilliant red during the golden hour. It can be found in hard form in Arches, Cathedral Valley, and on the north shore of Glen Canyon, and in a softer, friable form in Goblin Valley or Behind the Rocks.

❐ the colorful Morrison formation, found everywhere in the Southwest; it is the material of many badlands photos, a good example being the Painted Desert.

Other Tectonic Phenomena

The geologic structure of the plateau is further complicated by innumerable fractures and upheavals caused by volcanic eruption, earthquakes and other tectonic movements of the earth's crust which have shaped the Southwest. A general understanding of the theory of continental drift will be helpful in understanding these phenomena. The Waterpocket Fold, the Moab Fault, the Cockscomb and the Comb Ridge, to name but a few, illustrate dynamic zones affecting the geology of this region as they alternately raise or lower the sedimentary layers.

Rivers

To the north, three principal waterways feed the plateau: the Colorado, the Green and the San Juan rivers. However, many others play an important role in the ecosystem of the Southwest and merit mention for their esthetic qualities:

❐ the Virgin River, which represents for many their first contact with the Southwest while following its superb gorge between Las Vegas and St. George and which forms the extraordinary Zion canyon;

❐ the beautiful Sevier River, that snakes through the Paunsaugunt Plateau to the west of Bryce Canyon;

❐ the Little Colorado River that feeds into its big brother of the same name

Flash flood raging

and which forms beautiful meanders at the edge of the Grand Canyon;

❐ the Paria River, traversing the Vermilion Cliffs and forming the most spectacular and deepest gorge of the plateau, that of Paria Canyon;

❐ the Escalante River, draining numerous watersheds before emptying into Lake Powell and which forms innumerable canyons that would take a lifetime to explore;

❐ the Fremont River, meandering through Capitol Reef and providing awesome autumn scenery on its way to the Dirty Devil;

❐ the Dirty Devil River, which carries waters from the Wasatch Plateau and the San Rafael Reef and joins the Colorado River at Hite, at the northern end of Lake Powell.

In central Arizona, the Verde, the Salt and the Gila River drain waters from the Coconino plateau. In arid New Mexico, the Rio Grande and the Pecos are the major waterways. The Rio Grande provides a wonderful riparian environment and birders and nature photographers should plan a visit to Bosque del Apache to photograph the spectacular bird life.

Needless to say, there are hundreds if not thousands of smaller water courses, washes and creeks all over the Southwest. Many become dry in summer but can be awakened into raging walls of water during the monsoon season. Extreme caution must be exercised when wandering along washes at that time.

Mountains

The main mountain ranges of the Colorado Plateau are laccoliths, formed by magma uprisings pushing horizontally and vertically through the thick layers of sandstone. At altitudes of 10,000 feet and visible for miles around, they serve as focal points and enrich the trip as you learn to recognize them. It is possible to measure progress as you travel by observing these mountain chains, adding an extra dimension to just reading the map. For example, as you descend from Moab on US 191, the La Sals are on your left. A few minutes later, the Abajos appear directly in front of you and a bit to the right. You'll reach them in the area of Monticello and you'll leave them behind near Blanding. In Monticello, Sleeping Ute Mountain is in full view to the east. By the time you reach Natural Bridges National Monument, the Abajos are already well behind and to your right. The characteristic flat dome of Navajo Mountain is in front of you and the Henrys are silhouetted to the left. Traveling the roads of the Southwest, you will rapidly become familiar with these landmarks, just like a seafarer sailing from port to port.

To the south, most of the mountains are either volcanoes or volcanic in origin. The sacred mountains of the south, Mount Taylor and the San Francisco Peaks, as well as the Gilas, Superstitions and Chiricahuas are the result of intense volcanic activity. Several dormant volcanoes can be found in northern Arizona, near Flagstaff, as well as in New Mexico, west of Albuquerque.

Deserts

Two great deserts span the area covered by this book: the bone-dry Great Basin to the North, warm and dry in summer but cold in winter, and the lush Sonoran to the south, very hot in summer and mild in winter.

A large part of the Colorado Plateau is located in the Great Basin Desert. Nowhere is the contrast between these two diverse ecosystems more evident than on I-17 between Flagstaff and Phoenix. In less than two hours, the scenery changes from the classic high plateau fare of Juniper pine and chaparral, to a rich landscape of creosote bush, brittlebush and multitudes of cacti. Travel in spring and you'll be greeted by millions of colorful Mexican poppies on a solid green carpet. Temperatures in the Sonoran desert can exceed 120° F; perhaps more importantly, they often approach 200° F on the ground, which makes the area a no-no for summer exploration. Many people, perhaps too familiar with the Mojave Desert between Los Angeles and Las Vegas, fail to realize how rich the Sonoran desert is; in fact, it harbors over 1,500 species of plants and is home to a wide range of fauna. Needless to say, this diversity contributes to the attraction of the Sonoran, and greatly enhances its appeal to the photographer.

FLORA AND FAUNA

The Southwest is, by definition, an arid country, limited in types of vegetation and animals. The photographer will not find a great variety of animals. Deer, antelope and rabbits are the mammals most frequently encountered by the roadside and they tend to be most strongly concentrated in the heart of the National Parks and Monuments where they are protected.

There are always mule deer, squirrels and chipmunks begging for a piece of bread on the main park roadways and near the Visitor Centers; an unfortunate habit reinforced by visitors who want to capture the moment on film, despite numerous official warnings not to feed the wildlife.

Deer and antelope are found in herds from autumn to spring, and it is not unusual to see them in large groups by the side of the road. Even in summer, your chances of seeing deer are very good. You should be extremely cautious when driving at night to avoid collisions with animals.

The Southwest has a great variety of flora

You will also have the opportunity to observe eagles, falcons, buzzards and the omnipresent ravens. At nighttime, it isn't unusual to spot a great-horned owl in your headlights—an impressive sight.

Snakes, scorpions, spiders? Yes, they are here, but the visitor would have a hard time finding them, especially in the daytime. Rattlesnakes present little danger as long as you don't alarm them and they'll usually give you advance warning of their presence. Just be cautious of where you step and pay attention to where you place your hands when scrambling around the backcountry. Large stones and holes in the rock serve as a refuge for these cold blooded creatures during hot summer days. I'm sure you've read all this advice before, but you may not have read these two little-known facts: venom injection is actually rare, even if you receive a bite; however, in the unfortunate and statistically small chance that you've become injected with venom, you should be aware that there is a scarcity of antivenom in the Southwest and that a full treatment usually requires 20 vials, at approximately $1,000 a vial. Better carry medical insurance. Scorpions are present in Southern Arizona and New Mexico and are known to inflict an extremely painful bite. Be cautious at night if you're camping out. Black widows are extremely shy creatures and present no danger. If you live anywhere in the southern United States, you learn to live with them. Brown Recluse spiders are also extremely rare, but I know two persons who have been bitten, including my wife. The bite is nasty, creating necrosis of the local skin tissue and taking months to heal. In case of trouble, call the Poison Control Center at (800) 362-0101 in Arizona or (800) 432-6866 in New Mexico.

The southern part of Arizona is home to an extraordinary desert flora: saguaros, senitas, chollas, organ pipe cactus, ocotillos, as well as wonderful poppies and other wildflowers. When they bloom in spring, it's a festival of color. Photographers should pay particular attention near chollas (a.k.a. teddy bear cactus), as their spines have a remarkable propensity to jump into your skin at the slightest contact, and they are extremely difficult and painful to remove.

To the north, juniper trees are ever present despite the arid climate. Cottonwoods line up streams and dry washes. They bloom an intense green in mid to late April and turn yellow and golden in mid-September to late October. Aspens and Bristlecone pines can be found at higher elevations. All help considerably in making spectacular photography.

A BIT OF HISTORY

Ancient History

In the Southwest, man is very small, while space and time appear immeasurable. Even multiplied by a hundred, what are a few thousand years of known history in relationship to the slow mineral transformation of this Earth, in successive waves, from volcano to mountain, from river to canyon or from ocean to desert? The ruins of the Fremont and Puebloan—or Anasazi—cultures, dispersed over the plateau, are eloquent testimonies to the vulnerability of the human condition when confronted with implacable nature. In contemplating their abandoned pueblos, sheltered under the immense sandstone cliffs, one cannot help but ponder how fragile their protection really was and what a tenuous hold life has here.

The Fremont populated a geographic zone situated to the north of an imaginary line that passes through Capitol Reef extending to the Great Basin in the west and the Rocky Mountains in the east. The Puebloans inhabited the Four Corners region, so-called because it is the junction of the boundaries of Colorado, New Mexico, Arizona and Utah.

The Puebloans are almost always referred to as Anasazi, a term meaning "the ancient enemy" in the Navajo language. As a matter of fact, the Navajo migrated to this land much later and bear no genetic or linguistic relationship to the Anasazi. The Hopi, Zuni and other tribes to the south of the Grand Canyon are direct descendants of the Anasazi and Fremont and prefer to be called Ancestral Puebloans—based on the style of their dwellings. I will, therefore, use the term Puebloans throughout this book. These ancient ones disappeared rather mysteriously around 1400 AD. No one knows with complete certainty what caused their disappearance. It is not completely correct to talk about "disappearance," however, as there is ample proof that the Puebloans migrated to the south and were gradually absorbed by the Hohokam, Sinaguan and Mogollon (pronounced "mug-ee-yon") cultures. Three theories are frequently advanced for what we shall call the collapse of their society: the first presumes that a large meteorite struck the area, blotting out the sun, and rendering the land incapable of growing crops and, therefore, making it uninhabitable for many years. The second postulates a radical climatic change around the beginning of the 14th century causing increased erosion with the same result—decreased harvests. The third theory rejects geophysical causes but is similar to the second in that the consequences were the same. This theory places the responsibility for increased erosion and the disappearance of topsoil on the intensive system of agriculture practiced by the Ancestral Puebloans, which eventually exceeded the capacity of the system to sustain their needs.

Petroglyph critters & footprints

Although the answer may elude archeologists, the remains are ample testimony to a well-established social order that was able to assure subsistence and artistic production of great merit. Numerous artifacts discovered on the sites attest to this, in particular the baskets, pottery and fabrics. A visit to Navajo National Monument, the Anasazi and Edge of the Cedars State Parks, the Chapin Museum in Mesa Verde and the Museum of Northern Arizona near Flagstaff is strongly recommended for a better understanding of the human history of the Southwest.

Archeological Sites Etiquette

Rock art and ancient dwellings are a most precious heritage of Native American Indians and humanity at large. They are obviously extremely fragile and when not protected, are often the unfortunate subject of vandalism. When photographing rock art and ruins, the first and foremost rule is don't touch. Natural oils from human skin can and will affect glyphs and paintings. Even though a slight touch may only remove a minute amount of pigment or sandstone, when you multiply that by many years and many visitors it will eventually lead to irreparable degradation of the art. Much worse than that is the use of chalk or crayon to enhance or highlight the art for photographs. It compromises the integrity of the art by becoming a permanent part of the design and paves the way for others to add their own mark, thus destroying the precious heritage forever. This is a sad an irresponsible act, which I have observed too many times on otherwise beautiful rock art throughout the Southwest. The Black Dragon (see San Rafael Reef chapter) is a prime example of such misguided alteration. Another reprehensible practice is the wetting of rock art with water to accentuate contrast and texture. Needless to say, you should not cut, chip, or try to remove rock art. The Antiquities Act protects rock art and infractions are subject to very high fines. It is our responsibility as observers and photographers of our era to treat it properly so that it may be preserved as a testimony to those who came before us and for the benefit of future generations.

Some of the best places to admire and photograph rock art are Horseshoe Canyon, the Maze, the San Rafael Reef, the San Juan River area, Sego Canyon and Newspaper Rock. The most outstanding unprotected ruins are located in the Cedar Mesa area. Fortunately, most of the best ancient dwellings are under the protection of some governmental, state or tribal agency.

Recent History

Modern native Americans, early Spanish explorers, Mormon pioneers, ranchers, cowboys, uranium miners, adventurers... the history of the settlement and exploitation of natural resources in the Southwest by native Americans and diverse groups of Europeans is fascinating. Much has been written about it by infinitely better qualified authors and I invite you to discover more about the recent history of the Southwest by reading a short, eclectic—and necessarily biased—selection of works, ranging from factual to fiction, which I describe in the Other Recommended Reading section at the end of this book.

Nevertheless, I'd like to present here a brief compendium of seminal events that shaped the history of this Land:

❏ the Spaniards' explorations: their first foray occurred in 1540, two decades after Cortès' brutal Mexican campaign, when Hernando de Alarcón sailed deep into the Gulf of California and encountered the Colorado River delta. That same year a young Lieutenant in Coronado's army, by the name of García López de Cárdenas, stumbled onto the Grand Canyon with the help of local Zuni scouts. Juan de Oñate, first governor of the region, searched the land extensively—but in vain—for routes to the Pacific Ocean. Expeditions were abandoned for almost two centuries until 1776, when two Franciscan friars, Atanasio Domínguez and Francisco de Escalante went looking for a northern route to link Santa Fe to San Francisco. Their extraordinary five-month long expedition "discovered" many of the Canyon Country sites described in this book.

❐ the first mappings: first by Escalante's cartographer Bernardo de Miera; then by Alexander von Humboldt and later by John Fremont: these successive mappings of the Southwest opened the way for trade and provided the groundwork for the next wave of explorations;

❐ the American explorers: Gunnison, Beale, Seatgreaves, Macomb, Newberry, Wheeler, Hayden and the greatest of all: Major John Wesley Powell all led remarkable expeditions to then uncharted regions of the Southwest, helping to open new routes for the railroad and new settlers;

❐ the Mormon influx: the massive and extraordinarily courageous migration of the Mormons from the Midwest, under extremely inhospitable circumstances, established Utah's Caucasian farming communities and ranches;

❐ the Indian wars: a sad period of our history during which the U.S. government fought, defeated and deported Native American tribes, with people like Kit Carson, Cochise and Geronimo emerging as leaders on both sides of the fence.

WHEN TO VISIT

The Southwest can be visited year-round. Each season possesses its unique charm and presents various advantages and disadvantages.

Summer monsoon storms make for sublime skies, occasional rainbows, soft lighting due to the haze and spectacular sunsets, but there is a high price to pay for that. It's the busiest time of the year on the roads and in the parks. In the last two decades, foreign visitors en masse have also discovered the American West, in organized tour groups or as individuals, crowding the roads and parks, not to mention the motels. In the most popular places, in particular at Grand Canyon Nat'l Park, reservations become indispensable and need to be made in advance to guarantee a place for the night. This can create a serious obstacle to the flexibility of your itinerary by imposing a measure of control on your evening's destination.

The intense heat is not generally a problem in the car or on short walks, but it can become a powerful factor on long hikes. Summer is also the time of frequent afternoon downpours with all the risks they entail, especially when visiting the numerous canyons described in this guide. Additionally, dirt roads are often closed by water runoff.

Insects can pose a problem in certain areas, particularly at the beginning of summer when deerflies and biting gnats or "no-see-ums" will attack your skin relentlessly. Unfortunately, it is impossible to predict when and where they will hang out in a particular year.

Finally, the days are at their longest and this allows you to cover a lot of ground and see lots of sights. On the other hand, this can considerably limit your photographic opportunities during the day when the sun is high in the sky and your shots will be way too contrasty and without nuance. Also bear in mind that the angle of the sun is at its highest in summer. There is a no such thing as a "golden hour" at the height of summer, merely fifteen minutes of very good light after sunrise and before sunset.

Waterfalls appear during springtime

Narrows see few visitors in winter

Autumn is the best time to discover the Southwest. It's still warm, but the heat is less ferocious. The days are still long, but less grueling. The students and a large part of the population have returned to work and school after the Labor Day holiday. The motels empty out. Prices lower to a reasonable level, the parks are not as congested and parking near the panoramic vistas no longer requires you to drive around for half an hour to find a spot. Also, insects will not make your life miserable.

Fall colors begin in September in the high country and in early November at lower elevations. October and November are absolutely marvelous in Zion or Capitol Reef as the foliage changes and a new, multi-colored palette of ochers and reds appears with a less-defined illumination than in summer. Strong rains are relatively rare, but at high altitude locations such as Cedar Breaks or Bryce, snow is possible.

Finally, the sun rises and sets at a lower angle and the "golden hour" lasts quite a bit longer than in summer.

Winter is the off-season and offers exceptional possibilities to enjoy the surrounding tranquillity at incredibly low prices. Also, winter's short daylight hours, as well as the low trajectory of the sun on the horizon, are a blessing to the photographer.

With a bit of care to dress warmly, the dry cold is not disagreeable, though it can make camping less attractive. Winter storms often bring rain or heavy snow to the higher elevations and can last two or three days. However, a snowfall in Bryce can be an absolutely magical experience when, with these alternate periods of beautiful weather, the air attains an unequaled purity and the sky is an intense blue. By the same token, there are few clouds in the sky and it can be tough to come up with spectacular photography including much sky. Nonetheless, unobstructed views such as those one sees in Canyonlands or the Grand Canyon, to give but two examples, reveal extraordinary distances when there is no pollution, as is rarely the case in the Grand Canyon in summer.

Large animals descend from the mountains and are frequently and easily observed in the valleys. The only major inconvenience is that certain sites become inaccessible, particularly the North Rim of the Grand Canyon, Cedar Breaks, the Narrows of the Virgin and sometimes the trails of Bryce (at least without adequate equipment, for these last two).

Spring is a magnificent season, although the weather can be very unpredictable. You are as likely to encounter stormy, wet days as warm and sunny weather. Precipitation is frequent in March and the rivers and waterfalls are at their highest. High peaks are still snowbound, greenery is sprouting, the trees are leafing out and wildflowers bloom everywhere. Displays of wildflowers in the Sonoran desert in a good year can be overwhelming. Spring is definitely the best time to visit southern Arizona and New Mexico's mountains and deserts. It's also a great time to visit the canyons of the Escalante, when cottonwood trees explode an intense green and temperatures are still tolerable. However, beware of high water levels, which may make it impossible to wade.

The days are getting longer and the prices are still not as expensive as during the height of the season. Insects can also present a great nuisance. No-see-ums, fond of blood and penetrating everything and aggressive deerflies are to be found along the watercourses and in the washes. ✿

Magical pools of the Subway

Chapter 2

SOME PHOTO ADVICE

SOME PHOTOGRAPHIC ADVICE

Introduction

I do not make any assumptions throughout the book about your level of ability with respect to photography. Whether you are an enthusiastic beginner or a seasoned pro is irrelevant. We all perceive the world somewhat differently and bring back a different vision from our travels, unless of course one purposely sets up to emulate someone else's photography (there is nothing wrong with that as long as we keep it as a hobby). This book is essentially a location resource, but in the process of describing the locations, I also give you basic facts that will assist you in being better prepared, based on my own experience of having been at these locations many times and under different lighting circumstances. Experienced photographers need to be patient and understanding, whenever I dispense advice that may seem basic to them. Drawing from the feedback I garnered from the past two editions of this book, I know what the majority of my readers want and I try my best to provide this information.

Film vs. Digital

The technology of traditional film and camera equipment is very mature and there is little room for other than esoteric improvements, with little noticeable impact on image quality. Whatever improvements the industry will come up with in terms of optical construction and quality will automatically benefit digital technology, as any optics can be used on a digital SLR accepting interchangeable lenses. As far as film is concerned, there is still progress being made in terms of lower grain and better color, but with most R&D funding now going to digital, it's unlikely that there will be any breakthroughs. Traditional film-based photography is bound to become obsolete at some point, although it will coexist for quite some time with digital photography. The digital camera industry, on the other hand, has a bright future; it is only in its infancy and we will see spectacular progress in the years to come. There are currently three stumbling blocks that will soon be overcome: CCD size, storage limitations and battery life. Current CCDs produce digital files that are adequate for the Internet or 8"x10" prints, but insufficient for big enlargements and commercial photography. However, it's only a matter of time until much larger CCDs are developed. Storage is an issue if you want to shoot and save lots of high-quality images during a trip. There is a variety of storage media that will evolve or disappear. No doubt autonomous storage devices will become a necessity. In such a rapid growth industry, today's latest toy can become obsolete in a matter of 18 months. Until more efficient storage devices are developed, you'll be hard-pressed to do without a computer on the road in order to download and archive your images.

Barring that, you'll need to review your work every night on the LCD and discard anything that isn't a "keeper" to make room on your removable storage. Batteries are also a problem in the field, as digital photography requires a lot more energy to power the camera, store the file, pre- and post-visualize images on the LCD, etc. All this should evolve rapidly and become easily adopted. One tremendous benefit of digital photography in its current stage is to allow long telephotos to act as if they were even longer. This is due to the fact that the actual footprint of a CCD is smaller than that of the film window; as a result, a 400mm lens gives you in effect the magnification ratio and perspective of a 500mm, while maintaining the same aperture. This is a tremendous boon for photographing wildlife, but it is also a welcome benefit to landscape photographers. Note: the photographic advice dispensed throughout this book is geared at traditional photography, which is still the dominant force as I write this.

The Middle Way

At least for the foreseeable future, there is an excellent alternative to all-digital by combining traditional argentic photography with digital scanning. This method yields remarkable results, as long as you keep away from low-quality consumer scans. If you only want to produce a small quantity of large prints, you can give your images to a professional digital lab, to be scanned on a drum scanner or on Pro Photo CD. The latter technology isn't very well known because Kodak never really pushed it very hard. It's too bad because it yields excellent results at a very minimal cost. As of this writing, you can get Master Photo CD scans for less than a dollar. Pro Photo CD scans—offering higher dynamic range and resolution, and required for medium and large format—can be had for six Dollars for 18MB and ten dollars for 72MB scans. Pro Photo CD scans performed by a good lab will let you make big high-quality enlargements. Pro Photo CD was originally intended for viewing images on a TV screen. This proved to be a complete bust, as people didn't have the patience to wait for an image to load slowly on their screen. As a result of this original intent, Photo CD scans have a certain amount of haze that needs to be removed in an image editor before they can become usable, but they are usually easy to correct and sharpen. An additional benefit is that negatives—which are traditionally hard to scan—scan extremely well on Photo CD. Drum scanning without question yields the best quality, but at a much higher price. Consumer film scanners have improved tremendously, both in terms of resolution and dynamic range. With the arrival of 4000dpi CCDs, they are now becoming usable for enlargements in the 11"x14" to 16"x20" range. They remain difficult to use for negative film, however. Mid-range scanners such as the Imacon Flextight do a fantastic job, but their price point of ten thousand dollars—although cheap in comparison to a drum scan—is still out of reach for most people. Flatbed scanners with transparency adapters are extremely convenient, but they are adequate only for small prints and web use. Their advertised resolution is often way optimistic and they do not yield razor-sharp scans despite what the ads would like you to believe. I consider them totally unacceptable at this time for exhibit-quality work.

Prints vs. Slides

This used to be the question that popped up the most in discussions about photography; lately, it has been superseded by the film vs. digital debate. The bottom line is that it is possible to obtain excellent results using each medium.

In the past few years, print film has largely overcome the handicap of poor quality that it had compared with positive film. Modern emulsions, incorporating micro granulation technology, are remarkable and perfectly suited to small automatic cameras equipped with slow zoom lenses, used without a tripod during a pleasure trip. The capacity of negative film to capture nuances and forgive exposure errors can be very useful in many instances. That said, the quality of your prints would ultimately depend in large part on your choice of photo lab, unless you scan your negatives and do your own inkjet printing. Concerning print film, I recommend a speed of 400 ISO for general use and 800 ISO for slot canyons if you shoot handheld. The grain on these new, fast emulsions is totally invisible on a standard format print, and barely noticeable on large format enlargements. This speed advantage is crucial when working without a tripod, especially in the slot canyons where it becomes possible to work with considerably shorter speeds. Also, exposure can easily be corrected in the lab during the printing process. If you are not satisfied with the results, you can ask for a reprint accentuating red, yellow or orange, over or under exposing the print to reduce shadows and bring out detail. Finally, the ease with which you can show your prints to friends and family is self-evident.

Color transparencies, on the other hand, provide high quality results and are more true to life but impose many more constraints than color negative film. In the first place, correct exposure is absolutely critical. This effectively excludes the use of color transparency film in point & shoot cameras that do not allow for manual exposure compensation—and few do. In addition, you lose at least one stop by comparison to the exposure range of negative film and you must constantly concern yourself with keeping the contrast between light and dark areas to a minimum. Finally, although slow color transparency emulsions have almost non-existent grain, this becomes very present at film speeds above 200 ISO. All these factors make it necessary, in a number of circumstances, to use a tripod if you want to shoot transparencies. This can be a nuisance for many who are on a pleasure trip, but it will go a long way toward quality results.

Ninety-five percent of professional photographers use transparency film; however, this is largely dictated by the needs of magazine editors more than personal choice. Transparencies can be immediately examined on a light box and, with a good loupe, the editor can judge the qualities and faults of a first generation image. A printed photo is already a second-generation image, which makes it impossible to ascertain how it will reproduce in a magazine. However, these considerations need not concern the amateur. For him, choice of film is essentially a matter of taste and the effort he is ready to put out to show his photos.

Lab Prints vs. Inkjets

This is another raging debate and I'm not sure that there is a clear winner, although inkjet prints are bound to become preeminent within a few years. I now look somewhat fondly on my early years with argentic photography, having processed my own film and prints since I was eleven years old. In the mid-seventies, I became an early adopter of the Cibachrome system to process my own color prints. I have been producing inkjet prints for several years now—on consumer-level printers—and I have never looked back. New long-lasting inks, archival paper and miniaturized nozzles allow you to create stunning enlargements from digital scans at a surprisingly low cost. Print longevity, which used to be an issue in the early days, is no longer a problem. Who wants to keep the same print on the wall for years anyway? Besides, you can always reprint. For big enlargements, professional-grade inkjet printers—such as the vaunted Lightjet—are the way to go, albeit at a price. I'm looking forward to the day I'll be able to produce my own 16"x20" or 20"x20" on my own printer and at a reasonable cost. I have no doubt that this time will come soon.

What to take on your Trip

Throughout the book, the 35mm format is used as a standard to describe which lens(es) will work best. Medium and large format photographers should have little trouble converting this reference system to their own needs.

You will notice that I do not talk much about equipment throughout the book. That is essentially because equipment is not a deciding factor in the quality of your photography. Light, the ability to "see" and an eye for composition are much more likely to affect the results than simply pointing an expensive camera at a well-known landmark and shooting.

❏ The camera body is at the center of your photographic equipment, although it is not the most important component in terms of results. Modern camera bodies offer a tremendous amount of functions—too many in my opinion. Some of these functions are nonetheless useful, if not indispensable, if you want to go beyond simple snapshots. Reflex (TTL) vision is helpful for precision framing, although many people are just as happy with a rangefinder. Aperture-priority mode is essential to maximize depth of field—which you'll also be able to test if your camera has depth-of-field preview. Aperture compensation allows you to manually correct exposure under difficult lighting circumstances. Exposure bracketing is very useful to guarantee correct exposure for those critical shots. An all-metal lens mount is also recommended over polycarbonate if you're planning on changing lenses often. One function that has completely vanished on entry-level camera bodies is mirror lockup. This is sad because it has been scientifically demonstrated that pictures taken with the mirror up have a higher count of lines per millimeter, which in turn produces sharper enlargements. A rangefinder camera eliminates the mirror shock problem, but it has its own limitations.

❏ Lenses are the most important components of your equipment. Optical quality of the "glass" is crucial in producing quality results. Prime lenses used to be better than zooms, but high-end zooms are now equally as good and are extremely practical, both in terms of speed, weight and even protection of the mirror and internal mechanism from dust and wind. Stay away from low-cost consumer zooms, they yield disappointing results. A bright zoom covering 28mm to 105 or 135mm works well in the Southwest. If you take a digital or analog point & shoot camera, be sure not to settle for 35mm or 38mm at the wide end. It will be insufficient in the field. You'll find yourself using a wide-angle most of the time. Needless to say, a super wide-angle (24mm or less) and a long telephoto (200mm and above) will significantly enhance your potential for original shots.

Wide-range zooms (28-200mm and 28-300mm) are deservedly popular for travel photography, but be aware of the fact that they are very soft at their telephoto settings. They are adequate for small prints up to 5"x7", but do not expect high-quality enlargements.

One new development that offers a lot of value to the photographer on the go is the emergence of gyro-stabilized zooms and long telephotos. This technology allows you to gain at least two stops, which may be enough to forego a tripod in non-critical 35mm landscape photography. While this doesn't completely obviate the use of the tripod, especially to maximize depth-of-field, it offers much better sharpness at speeds in the 1/30th and 1/60th range. It allows, for example, to quickly capture fleeting moments—a furtive ray of light or a rainbow—with increased chances of getting good results.

As for doublers, which generally come with a 1.4x and 2x factor, only use prime models in conjunction with high-quality lenses to get good results. A factor of 1.4 is less radical and less detrimental to overall picture quality.

Whatever lens(es) you end-up buying, do not try to shave a few dollars. Too many people buy an expensive body, then equip it with a mediocre consumer zoom lens. Major manufacturers always have two or even three lines of lenses: a consumer line, a so-called "prosumer" line and a high-end and more expensive line. My advice is to buy a cheap body and the best possible lens for your money. It will result in sharper, higher contrast pictures, with better colors.

❏ I do occasionally recommend the use of filters, not to enhance but to compensate for the shortcomings of film. I'll leave the enhancements up to you.

A UV or Skylight 1B filter will protect your lens without diminishing quality, but use them with caution on a zoom lens. Due to their complex optical construction involving the use of many elements and groups, zooms are particularly prone to flare—the phenomenon of light entering the lens and causing unwant-ed reflections. I do not personally use such filters, relying instead on my lens shade to protect the lens, but this advice is not for everybody.

A graduated neutral-density filter (or ND Grad) is an essential piece of equip-ment, especially if you shoot transparencies. It will help keep contrast in check and open up shadow areas. Split neutral-density filters work great when the sep-aration line between lit subject and shadow is very obvious, but these instances are rare in Canyon Country. By all means, use a high-quality filter. Cheap ND grad filters are not neutral and will give a nasty color cast to your skies. In my opinion, you'll be better served by a 3-stop filter than a 2-stop. Also, a model you can slide up and down on a holder is more flexible than a simple screw-in filter.

A mild warming filter such as an 81A, KR 1.5 or Nikon A2 is also a most important filter. It is useful under many circumstances, but most particularly in the shade to get rid of the blue cast and when photographing under a strong sun. It adds a slight warm punch to your images, without introducing a color cast. These filters work very well in the Southwest.

Most books and articles enthusiastically endorse the use of a polarizing filter, or "polarizer", as a vital piece of equipment to carry in your bag. I am not so

Photographing the Southwest is sometimes full of surprises

enthusiastic and I recommend that you use your polarizer with moderation. If you have high-quality, contrasty lenses and shoot on a highly saturated film, such as Fuji Velvia or Ektachrome VS, you won't need one most of the time. Used indiscriminately, a polarizer may turn your skies too dark; also, in combination with a wide-angle lens, the polarizing effect could become too strong, resulting in light falloff in one corner of the image. I use my polarizer mostly to eliminate glare on foliage, streams or various textures, but I generally keep it in the bag in broad daylight unless the sky is full of nice fluffy clouds. If you use a rangefinder, carry a pair of polarizing sunglasses and look straight into the lens to see the effect, then apply the proper amount of exposure compensation for your particular filter (1.5 to 2 stops), based on experience. It is also not too hard to use an ND grad with a rangefinder with a little bit of practice.

❒ A shade is very instrumental in preventing flare. Be sure it is designed for your lens to avoid the phenomenon of vigneting, which is light falloff in the corners of your image. This is particularly nasty on blue skies.

❒ Now we come to what I consider the second most important piece of equipment after your lenses: the tripod. A tripod is an almost indispensable item for landscape photography if you shoot transparencies. Good slide film is inherently slow and doesn't lend itself well to handheld photography. A tripod also allows you to compose your images more carefully. If you have never used a tripod before when shooting landscape, you'll be surprised at how it can improve your photography. Unfortunately, there is also a big price to pay when you have to carry a 4 lbs tripod on long hikes, especially if some scrambling is involved. Carbon fiber tripods are very expensive, but they shave a couple of pounds from an otherwise heavy tripod. I recommend using a headless tripod and buying your own ballhead. I personally use a combination carbon-fiber tripod and magnesium ballhead.

❒ The natural companion of the tripod is fortunately very lightweight: a cable release is essential to avoid camera movement when releasing the shutter. A good quality one costs only a few dollars more and is much nicer to use than a small flimsy model. If you don't want to bother with one, you can also use your camera's built-in timer release. There is one potential pitfall with the timer technique: someone may walk right in front of your camera by the time it's taking the picture. I can almost guarantee you that this will happen in highly frequented places, such as Antelope Canyon.

❒ Do not forget a pouch or camera bag. You shouldn't carry your camera and lenses without some form of protection. It is risky to switch lenses in an environment where dust and sand are always present. Be sure to protect your camera from the wind when changing lenses and to blow away dust every time you load a new roll of film. It's amazing how many frames can be wasted by dust-induced streaks. To take the Antelope Canyon example once again, there is always a fine dust suspended in the air, although you might not see it, and you run the risk of having lines across your entire film. A single speck of dust can ruin all your frames when you rewind. You should also carry a soft airbrush, with which to blow away dust from the lens and from the inside of the camera between rolls. Obviously, digital cameras are almost impervious to this kind of misadventure, but dust can also cause malfunctioning of the storage media.

If you carry several lenses, consider a photo backpack. It will also carry your tripod and your water bottles on long hikes.

If you are going to venture into narrows when the water level is high, you should carry your photo equipment in zip-lock bags. If your photo adventure involves swimming, a dedicated dry bag is a must to protect your equipment.

❏ If you use expensive, bulky or slow to operate equipment, such as medium or large format, I recommend that you take with you an auxiliary point & shoot camera with a good lens. It will prove invaluable for photographing difficult sections of trails or narrows. A small camera is also useful to shoot test images in places where you intend to come back at a later time for more serious shooting.

Photographing Slot Canyons

The range of perception of film is greatly limited in comparison with the human eye and it is impossible to reproduce on film all the nuances that we perceive. Variations of 5 or 7 f/stops are the norm in slot canyons and choosing the best exposure is not easy. Your task consists of perfectly exposing the part that most interests you within the limitations of the film range. This can be achieved in two ways: by carefully selecting your composition to avoid too many high-lights and minimizing areas in deep shadow, otherwise these shadows risk appearing completely black, especially on transparency film (note that you should never photograph light directly hitting a canyon wall); or by making an intelligent compromise between the various spot measurements obtained on those parts of the wall for which you want to preserve detail. In practice, I find that it is very difficult to overexpose in slot canyons. By increasing the exposure, either purposely or by accident, you will still get excellent images, albeit with a different gamut of colors. Short exposures yield a lot of yellow, as well as deep ochers, orange and red, while very long exposures introduce light and deep purple into the palette.

Photographing slot canyons may involve some very messy aspects

If you do not have a spotmeter, either handheld or in your camera, be ready to bracket heavily: easily said when you shoot 35mm, but almost out of the questions if you carry a view camera. You'll often have to add 1-1/2 to 2 stop overexposure to bring out the detail on the darker surfaces without burning the lighter walls. If you add too much, what could be a beautiful yellow light could end up totally white on that high-contrast slide film.

Try to find compositions that restrict the EV range to the smallest possible range, avoid all the brightly lit areas, concentrating instead on reflected light. Take plenty of time to frame your shots and even more time to take them. Use very small apertures and long pauses: let that beautiful reflected light seep onto your film. If you use an automatic camera, no tripod and fast film... and can hold your camera perfectly still, you can simulate a spot metering technique, by closing in on an interesting detail that is not too brightly lit and locking the exposure by pressing the shutter release halfway before moving back, recomposing and taking your picture.

Don't use a flash if you want to preserve the texture of the walls and the nuances of color created by natural light. However, the flash will give acceptable results if you are just taking shots of the family or trying to capture the general atmosphere of the canyon.

Knowing your equipment well is a must: not only must you be able to operate it without hesitation, but also you should be able to anticipate how your images will look. If there is one thing I have learned from my many visits to Antelope, it is that experience can play an important role in increasing the number of high-caliber "keepers" that you'll bring back from your visit.

For best possible results, have your film processed first, examine your results, learn from the inevitable mistakes and return to the Canyon.

Be prepared to deal with a steady traffic of visitors who are not necessarily interested in photography and will be in your way. Just be courteous and don't take yourself too seriously and you'll find that people will give you a wide berth. One consequence of such intense foot traffic is small particles of dust pervading the air, a phenomenon exacerbated by some photographers purposely throwing dust in the air to add dimension to the shafts of light hitting the floor around midday. Be sure to protect your equipment as best you can and give it a careful cleaning after your visit.

Photographing Dunes and Lava Beds

Sand and lava are two subjects that will assuredly fool your built-in meter and you may get very unpleasant colors if you use it. Many new automatic cameras have programs that supposedly compensate for specific lighting conditions; however, you will get better results by compensating the exposure manually based on the lighting conditions. For brown and red sand, you should bracket your exposure in small increments of 1/2 to 1-stop based on the effect you want to achieve. For deeply saturated red sand in the evening sun, try half a stop under and over exposure, plus whatever your meter says. For extremely white sand in bright daylight 1-1/2-stop overexposure works best; in early to mid-morning, late afternoon or when it's overcast, try 1/2-stop for scenics and 1 stop for sand patterns.

Lava usually doesn't need any correction, as it is more gray rather than pure black. If you want to make it darker, underexpose by 1/3 or 1/2-stop maximum.

I do not recommend that you shoot dunes and lava using print film—or any other bright or dark texture for that matter—unless your goal is to have them scanned professionally or to have custom prints made from the negatives.

Sand dunes can yield simple but effective compositions

Always pay close attention to your depth-of-field

Photographing Scenics including close Subjects

If your scenic compositions include a close subject, it is important to work with the smallest possible aperture (i.e. the highest settings such as f/22 or even f/64 if you shoot large format) to guarantee maximum depth of field. In essence, except under particular circumstances where you want to isolate a detail from an indistinct background, it is very disappointing to view a photo in which some parts are not razor-sharp. This becomes even worse if you enlarge the photo.

If you use a sophisticated autofocus reflex camera you may be able to visualize depth-of-field in the viewfinder. For critical landscape work, it is preferable to work with the manual focusing option and to set the distance not as a function of exact focus when viewed through the lens, but by using the depth-of-field marks of your lens creatively to maximize sharpness within the particular range of distance pertaining to your shot. Unfortunately many modern lenses, particularly zooms, lack depth of field marks and it is often necessary to improvise. Another way to guarantee sharpness and to maximize depth-of-field is by using the hyperfocal distance method. As an example, a 35mm lens focused at 10 feet at f/16 yields a sharp image from 5 feet (which is half the hyperfocal distance) to infinity. There are some handy charts you can buy for a few Dollars for every camera format. This method is a sure bet to create sharp-focused images from close range to infinity.

Of course, depth of field is equally as important when photographing close subjects without a scenic backdrop. When photographing rock art, for instance, be sure to position your camera parallel to the rock panel.

An entire book could be devoted to photographing close subjects with large format equipment, using tilt and shift to manipulate the focal plane, but this is outside the scope of this book.

Photographing Rock Art

Rock art tends to be quite contrasty; therefore it is prone to displaying a color cast when photographed with highly saturated films under strong reflected light. Puebloan ruins, often tucked inside deep alcoves, bring the danger of reciprocity failure, particularly for those who shoot large format.

If you shoot under strong reflected light, you are bound to have an exaggerated amount of red on films such as Fujichrome Velvia and Ektachrome VS. If you shoot in dark areas, Velvia will tend to give you an excess of green. In both cases, a slightly lower contrast film such as Fuji Provia will better serve you. The latter offers the finest grain of any slide film as of this writing and it is well suited to accurately reproduce the delicate textures and subdued golden browns of rock art. Another benefit is the added speed of the film; with large format, an exposure of 30 seconds is common in low light situations. With an additional one stop, you can reduce this to fifteen seconds, thus limiting the color shift. Large

Wolfe Ranch petroglyphs – low contrast film yields softer results with rock art

format photographers have the advantage of being able to change plates to match a particular lighting situation. 35mm and medium format photographers must be more careful with the kind of film they load before shooting rock art and small ruins. If you shoot negative film, these problems do not really affect you.

More on Exposure

If you are working with slides and wish to obtain the best results without concerning yourself too much about determining the right exposure, take five different shots at 1/2 stop intervals—i.e. two on either side of the setting you think is correct. In the case of negative film, this is useless since the density of the highlights and shadows can easily be altered during the printing process. Negative film tolerates up to 2 stops of overexposure fairly well, but does poorly with underexposure. If you are a perfectionist, you can always take a second shot with one stop of overexposure—it is useless to try more. If you are using a digital camera, you have the advantage of seeing the results immediately on your LCD; while this is not very precise, it gives you at least a starting point.

There is also a somewhat complex technique consisting of pre-exposing an 18% gray card before taking the actual shot on the same frame. This has the effect of reducing contrast and bringing out more detail in the shadow areas. As you can imagine, this is rather cumbersome to implement within the framework of a pleasure trip.

Attention should also be paid to the reciprocity failure characteristics of your film, especially if you are using a tripod and slow film. With exposures of several seconds, certain slide films display a tendency towards incorrect exposure and you risk having underexposed shots. There are reciprocity failure tables for the major brands of film on the market. Unless you are taking exposures of four seconds or more, you shouldn't have to worry about this.

Some Advice on Composition

Composition is fortunately not an exact science, or art would be the domain of engineers. Rather, it is a subtle blend of classic established rules, specific properties of your subject and, last but not least, you own artistic sensibility.

While I can't help you much with the last two, I think it's worth it to briefly go through a bit of advice that applies to the highly mineral universe of the Southwest:

❒ before you even think composition, remember that lighting is everything in landscape photography; however well composed it is, an image is rarely attractive unless it has interesting light;

❒ remember the rule of thirds, to avoid an unaesthetic horizon line smack in the middle of your picture as well as to avoid a centered main subject;

❑ resist the urge of trying to squeeze too much of a grandiose panorama onto a small picture (Grand Canyon, Island in the Sky, Needles Overlook and Mokey Dugway are prime examples.) Results are almost always disappointing due to the lack of a center of interest, unless the sky is exceptionally interesting. Even so, your image will be more interesting if you zoom on a small portion and include some of that beautiful sky.

❑ fill most of the frame with your main subject. Too many secondary subjects become indistinguishable on a small picture, even though they look good to the naked eye.

❑ include an interesting foreground (juniper tree, flowers, rocks with an interesting color, shape or texture) and put your main subject slightly off-center when it is distant. This will give great depth to your image and reinforce the feeling of presence. Make sure the foreground is really interesting, not just a fill in.

❑ by the same token, be ready to break this rule if no interesting foreground is available. I'd rather see a distant view than an image where the bottom two thirds are filled with an excruciatingly boring subject.

❑ always think depth and presence. Some imposing formations may appear smallish on your image if you do not include a reference object to provide a sense of scale (trees, human silhouette, trail, etc.)

❑ rethink preconceived ideas about telephotos. Long telephotos serve three purposes: extracting details from the landscape, making a subject stand out through creative use of bokeh (the unsharp area in a photograph) and compressing the perspective. The compression effect makes your photographs appear rich and dense by allowing several planes to cohabit on the image. This is very effective with the Southwest's grand landscapes.

❑ super wide-angle lenses give great results with very tightly framed close subjects, (rocks with interesting colors or texture, shapes in sand dunes or badlands, trees or bushes...) by accentuating—or even esthetically distorting—the graphic, geometric or even abstract properties.

❑ be mindful of shadows, especially when using slide film, and use an ND Grad filter if necessary. So called "golden hour" photography is great but what appears to you as a simple shaded area may look completely black on film. Under some instances, it's unavoidable, but try to limit the black areas to their minimum by framing tightly or use an ND Grad filter.

❑ above all, be constantly on the lookout to spot photogenic details around you—rock texture, natural elements with abstract shapes or uncommon colors, reflections or transparent views, interesting vegetation, tracks or leaves on the ground, framing close to ground level, etc. Results are often a bit of a crapshoot. Some of these images won't make it, but others may yield beautiful, original compositions that will make a welcome departure from your "grand landscape" images.

A few non-technical Tips

There is another less palpable, but nonetheless vital ingredient to good land-scape photography: you must possess unbridled love for nature and feel a strong emotional connection with the land and your subject. The act of photographing should be an extension of that love, to record the memories and share with others the joy of being there. If your fascination with camera equipment or the physics of photography take precedent over your love of nature in an unbalanced way, it is doubtful that you'll ever achieve great results. Your craft may become technically excellent and you may acquire a nice portfolio of shots to show off, but you won't be able to communicate emotions that weren't present in the first place. Most people I know who seriously pursue photography of the Southwest have this love of the land within them, but I sometimes meet folks who are more interested in the act of photographing than in enjoying the beauty around them. Over the years, I have taken pleasure in asking people whether they would do a particularly strenuous hike to a beautiful spot if they had to leave their camera at home. I have had a few people flatly—and honestly—tell me that they wouldn't. This isn't necessarily a criticism; photography doesn't have to equate to love of nature to be enjoyed as a hobby. I do say, however, that simply being there, qui-etly enjoying the place and the moment is far more important than bringing back a few pictures.

Another important axiom of good landscape photography is that it rarely hap-pens by accident. In all probability you'll need to visit a location several times, to see it under different light, perhaps even in different seasons—perhaps even a few times without a camera—to start pre-visualizing your image, refining it as you observe, think, feel and draw on your past experience to anticipate a change of light or a break in the clouds. Your best images—those which carry the most emotional content—will be the result of careful planning and pre-visualization.

Finally, with your future image in mind, you'll rise early—make that very early—drag your sleepy body inside the freezing car. You'll drive on the edge of your seat to the now familiar location, peering at the darkness to spot deer on the road through the partially frozen windshield, nervously glancing at the clock and worrying about the changing light on the horizon. Perhaps you'll be chewing on a hard power bar between nervous sips of coffee, to warm you up a bit and get your mind in gear. You will walk to your location briskly, plant your tripod firm-ly, ready-up filters and lenses. You will wait, floating in a dual state of serene peace and nervous anticipation.

And then, the exhilarating moment will happen: the miracle of sunrise, the serene and benevolent apparition of light, basking the landscape in surreal hues of yellow and red, the joy of solitude, of communion with Mother Earth.

But there is no time for reflection; there is a job to be done, photos to be taken. And now the adrenaline kicks in, you are totally focused. You shoot like a mani-ac, oblivious to everything else but your subject, annoyed if someone else sud-denly shows up, and you shoot and shoot until the incredible light finally becomes a little too bright, a little too crude. And when you're done, you smile and bask in the deep feeling of joy that overtakes you, as you feel one with this place you love so much, and you linger a while to make the feeling last, letting the sun warm you up, your body still weary from lack of sleep. Now it's time to head back to the trailhead; and as you walk back, you let your mind wander and play like a puppy. You're proud and ecstatic at having experienced this cosmic moment. You've done something good. You suddenly become part of the great brotherhood of early rising nature lovers; unbeknownst to you, you have just bonded with the fly fisherman in Montana, the ice fisherman in Minnesota and the deer hunter in Idaho!

The Southwest is prime territory for nature abstracts

Months later, you sit in your living room and pull out that big, majestic enlargement and you grin happily at the beloved landscape basking in the morning sun, as if Scotty had just beamed you up out there.

With a little bit of experience in your craft, the wonderful photographic memories you'll bring back from such incredibly poignant and invaluable moments are what you'll be fond and proud of reliving and sharing with others.

Photographing in National Parks

If you consider the content of this book, you'll notice that the majority of the sites I describe are located inside National Parks and Monuments. Now, consider for a moment the amount of visitors going through our parks each year. Some of the most popular parks see a couple million visitors per year.

Most people carry some form of camera and all are eager to capture memories of their trip, using the glorified icons of the West as a background. National parks have become incredibly recognizable through movies, advertisements, postcards, park literature, and coffee table books, not forgetting the many guidebooks such as this one. No wonder people want to show that they've been there. The glorification of the West in turn creates a desire to accumulate photographs as trophies, what with cheap film and fun digital cameras. Cast me the first stone, for I'm one of them. The main difference is that I have developed an addiction for being there—with or without a camera. In view of the massive onslaught of people in relatively concentrated areas, we must ask ourselves what impact we are collectively having on the land.

So far the National Park Service has maintained the view that photographers—whether amateurs or "professionals"—should be treated as any other visitors. There are no specific restrictions imposed on us. Some large-format photographers talk of a certain stigma attached to carrying a tripod and bulky equipment in remote places. I carry a tripod at all times and I have never felt like I was being singled out in all my interactions with park rangers. So should we worry? I personally don't think so. The National Park Service once floated the possibility of requiring a permit from "professional" photographers, but the idea was later abandoned. My credo is that we, as privileged visitors to pristine areas, should act as good citizens and be mindful of the environment, least our impact on the land forces more closures of sensitive areas.

One area where more closures appear unavoidable is backcountry roads. Rumor has it that several roads in Grand Staircase-Escalante Nat'l Monument will be closed in the future. There is no doubt that vehicular access outside of asphalted roads has the potential for causing a lot of damage—not only when vehicles are driven irresponsibly, but also because of sheer numbers. Let's face it, only ten years ago, the term SUV wasn't part of our everyday vocabulary. Today, light trucks and SUVs are the fastest-growing segment of the automobile market and they are the vehicles of choice for visiting the Southwest. We must do everything we can to tread lightly, on foot and on the backroads to avoid damaging the land and preserve it for generations to come. ✿

The Zion Narrows (photo by Gene Mezereny)

Chapter 3

AROUND ZION

The Great White Throne from Angel's Landing (photo by Scott Walton)

ZION NAT'L PARK

Located at the head of the line for many visitors coming from Los Angeles and Las Vegas, Zion is frequently the first national park visited by travelers making the "Grand Circle" of national parks in Utah and Arizona. It's a spectacular introduction to the discovery of the Colorado plateau.

For the visitor with little time, the park consists of essentially two parts: the canyon and the plateau.

The canyon is deeply cut (between 2,000 and 2,500 feet), which doesn't make for easy photography because of the great contrast between the sunlit summits and the valley plunged in deep shadow. In the spring of 2000, the NPS has instituted a mandatory shuttle service to reduce the congestion and pollution in the canyon's interior, thus putting an end to everyone's misery trying to find a parking spot at the popular locations. The service is running smoothly and will deliver you and your camera gear to the location of your choice in the canyon in a much healthier frame of mind. From early April through the end of October, private vehicles are not allowed on the Scenic Drive. Shuttles normally run from 6:30 AM to 9:30 PM and leave every 6 minutes during peak hours; however they leave only every 30 minutes in the early morning and late evening. The trip to the end of the canyon takes 45 minutes. Note that the Visitor Center's parking lot is usually full by mid-morning; in that case, you must first take another shuttle from Springdale to the Visitor Center. While in Springdale, you should make it a point to visit Michael Fatali's gallery for a look at his beautiful and inspiring images.

If you are visiting by car outside the mandatory shuttle season, you can travel with the sun as it crosses the valley and harvest a great crop of photos. If you travel by motorhome, note that there are parking restrictions in the canyon and you will need an escort to go through the tunnel on Scenic Byway 9.

If possible, the most interesting way to arrive in Zion is by way of the plateau from the east entrance, since the views are particularly spectacular coming from Mt. Carmel. In addition, illumination is best in the morning at the principle viewpoints of the plateau.

If you follow this advice, you have two possibilities: visit Zion at the end of your "Grand Circle" or make a detour through Kanab. In practice, spending the night at Kanab is very feasible if you leave from Los Angeles in the morning. If you leave from Las Vegas, you are only three hours from Zion and you'll be hard pressed to resist the attraction of starting from the canyon.

I will begin our visit at the plateau, but the choice is up to you. In any case, the universe of Zion will not disappoint you.

Checkerboard Mesa

A short distance from the east entrance station, you'll find the viewpoint of Checkerboard Mesa, one of the most celebrated views in Zion. The prow of the mesa is inclined at a 60° angle and is striated like a baguette fresh out of the oven. Checkerboard Mesa appears best in mid-morning until the beginning of the afternoon, with the sun on the left. If you come from the canyon, you will be against the sun after noontime.

Checkerboard Mesa in Winter

The view of Checkerboard Mesa is a classic and it's difficult to take an original shot even by changing the viewing angle. It is mostly the unusual cross bedding of the Mesa, more than its own beauty, which makes for the interest in this photo. From the parking between the entrance station and the mesa, Checkerboard Mesa can be photographed at just about any time of the day. A medium wide-angle to standard lens will work best; from the pullout right at the base of the mesa, you'll need a 20mm to 24mm. A 20mm will allow you to shoot upward while framing pine tree needles. Walking in the direction of the Canyon, you'll find a small hill to your right. This makes an excellent vantage point at Sunset to shoot the East Temple silhouetted against the evening sky. A medium zoom will be helpful in fine-tuning your composition.

Rock formation typical of the Zion Plateau

The Zion Plateau

All of the southwest area of the park, on Scenic Byway 9 between the east entrance and the tunnel, is absolutely spectacular and offers numerous photographic possibilities. It is without doubt one of the most fantastic landscapes you'll encounter. The rock walls, some white, some pink, some red, possess extraordinary rounded forms, whereas the summits are ornamented like minarets. A sculptural sensuality emanates from this topography that defies the imagination. The ground switches from polished to checkered within a very short space. Stone tumuli scorched raw by the wind, burst forth here and there from a ground alternately smooth and lined. It's an incongruous landscape, kneaded, molded and painted as if by some crazy pastry-chef. Just past Checkerboard Mesa, you'll see some really interesting eroded hoodoos on the north side of the road, looking a bit like submarine kiosks. It is well worth stopping there to photograph them with a wide-angle to normal lens. About 2 miles from the entrance, you'll come upon a landmark dear to photographers: a little pinion pine growing on top of one of these eroded sandstone shapes. There are a couple of pullout spots on the south side of the road and the tree is about 150 yards to the south.

Canyon Overlook Panorama

Coming from Mt. Carmel, you reach this viewpoint from a parking spot located just before the entrance to the tunnel. The trail is about a mile long, round - trip. The viewpoint overhangs the Great Arch—which is in fact an alcove—that you can see and photograph while descending the switchbacks leading into the valley. From this often windy viewpoint, you'll gain a superb view of the entrance to Zion Canyon. Pine Creek and the switchbacks of the main road are visible below, but they only become sunlit in mid-morning during the summer and the middle of the day in winter. Very early in the morning,

Submarine rock on the Zion Plateau

you can isolate the West Temple and the Towers of the Virgin with a short, 85 to 100 mm, telephoto by concentrating on the golden rock face and eliminating the problematic shadow areas. By the end of the morning, the walls are basking in direct sunlight and have lost their relief. Of the park's three high observation points (Angel's Landing and Observation Point are the other two) this one is by far the most accessible, but unfortunately it's also the least spectacular.

Towers of the Virgin

At sunrise, this is the most beautiful panorama in Zion. If you love beautiful lights on rock walls, you won't be disappointed. The sun penetrates the valley through the Pine Canyon fault and bathes the summits of the temples in a warm gold light. Station yourself directly behind the Zion Museum and mount a 35mm lens. This will allow a tight framing of the West Temple, the Sundial, the Temple of the Virgin and the Altar of Sacrifice and keep the shadowy zone at the bottom of the photo to a minimum. A graduated neutral density filter is

The Towers of the Virgin from behind the Museum

mandatory in order to maintain detail in the shadowy zone and to conserve the vibrant red and gold color of the high walls. If you don't have one, you can also crop your image into a panoramic format later on. You'll have a good thirty minutes before the sunrays irradiate the summits with so much light that the shot gets lost. If you are spending the night close by, in Springdale or in Zion, this sunrise vista is a must. Note that even during shuttle season, you are allowed to drive as far as the Museum and park there.

Court of the Patriarchs

Zion Canyon reveals its entire splendor as the sun climbs over the surrounding peaks and your first stop should be to view the Court of the Patriarchs. You'll get the best results between sunrise and mid-morning. At the end of a short trail, you arrive at an unrestricted viewpoint where you can photograph the Patriarchs with a wide-angle lens. A 24mm is essential to include all three summits, but you can also get equally good results with a 28 or even a 35 mm, though you won't be able to fit in more than two of the Patriarchs. Finally, a short telephoto lens will let you isolate them individually.

Emerald Pools

The Emerald Pools, especially the lower one, are heavily visited and can be reached by a trail of a little over a mile, round-trip, from the Zion Lodge. Or you can take one of about 2 miles, round-trip, from the Grotto parking lot. Add another mile round-trip if you decide to hike to the upper pools. For most visitors, the attraction of this spot rests in the water droplets raining on you from the main wall of the lower pool—a great source of fun for all. In summer, you'll find it quite pleasant to rest under the maple trees and bask in the fine mist of water enveloping you. For the photographer, there are several interesting images waiting. I recommend that you come via the middle trail, by turning left past the footbridge near the Zion Lodge. After having negotiated the switchbacks, you'll gain superb open views of the southern part of the canyon from about halfway up the trail. As you reach the pools, you'll also cross an open area with a nicely polished rock surface, affording a really nice view looking down toward the lodge. Walk down toward the lower trail. There are some very good spots at the edge of the trail leading under the cascade, although your back will be against the wall and you'll need a 24mm to frame the entire waterfall. The waterfall is best photographed in spring and summer or after a rain. The upper pool is another mile round-trip and leads to a true cascade with a year-round flow.
  As the walk to Lower Emerald Pools isn't hard, consider going either before (from the Lodge) or after (from the Grotto) Angel's Landing. The walk to the Upper Pool is a bit harder.

Angel's Landing

Because of its central location, this is the most beautiful view of Zion Canyon but to access it will require good physical condition and a lot of exertion. Above all, heights must not make you dizzy. You'll start your ascent from the Grotto parking lot, following the steep switchbacks of the West Rim Trail before reaching the welcome shade of Refrigerator Canyon. Scaling another series of switchbacks, you arrive at the first viewpoint, Scout Lookout, where you have an exceptional and very steep view of the upper part of the Canyon's meanders as well as of the Temple of Sinawava. The last five hundred yards require a lot of effort as you painstakingly move forward up a stunning trail, which is more of a rock flank. Chains are anchored in the rock for use as handholds. The round-trip from the Grotto is about 5 miles. The vista from the top of Angel's Landing is sensational and well worth the effort. You can see the entrance to Zion Canyon opening up to the right, while in the center you get a breathtaking view of the Great White Throne. To the left, the canyon meanders toward the Temple of Sinawava.

Photo advice: ascend in late afternoon to get the best lighting. You'll need a 24mm to frame both the Great White Throne and the Canyon.

Time required: 3 hours round-trip. Caution: the end of this trail is not recommended for anyone prone to vertigo. If you have any doubts, skip the end and stay at Scout Lookout, which also offers nice views of the canyon to the north and east. Don't wear sneakers on this hike; you'll need excellent traction.

Zion Canyon from Angel's Landing

<u>Nearby location:</u> at Weeping Rock, where a short trail leads you behind a curtain of water droplets falling from the rock face, the end result of a two-year voyage through the porous rock. Twenty minutes should be enough for a brief visit. I find Weeping Rocks particularly interesting in winter when the seeping water forms a long ribbon of icicles reminiscent of fine lace.

Temple of Sinawava

This remarkable area, located at the end of Zion Canyon, is one of those special spots that evokes a mystical and spiritual connection with nature. The happy traveler, intoxicated by the succession and variety of the panoramas of Canyon Overlook, the Towers, the Patriarchs and brief glimpses of the Great White Throne, attains a sort of nirvana when reaching the Temple of Sinawava. The Pulpit rises in the middle of a cove formed by the river. As a result of the twists and turns of the canyon, its lighting is mediocre in the morning and evening but by pacing yourself along the Scenic Drive you can time your arrival for early afternoon, which is the best time to photograph it. Directly from the parking lot, you'll have reflected light striking the pulpit on the parking side and with a bit of luck, some nice direct light on the other side. I find that a normal lens to very

The Pulpit at the Temple of Sinawava

short telephoto works best to photograph the Pulpit from the parking lot. Another good location is from the last bend of the road before your reach the parking lot. A short telephoto will let you capture the green cottonwoods, the reddish pulpit and in the background the darker walls of the canyon. In late spring and early summer, a waterfall will be active in the background.

Further on, the 1-mile long surfaced Riverside Walk (unfortunately as crowded as Los Angeles freeways at rush hour) leads to the Gateway to the Narrows, the entrance to the Virgin River Narrows. The trail, which follows the bank of the Virgin River, offers magnificent views in the spring and early summer, as well as later in autumn when the foliage changes color. At about the halfway point, you'll go past a small cascade worth photographing if it is full.

Virgin Narrows

It's an unforgettable memory to go up the Virgin Narrows for an hour or so or until you reach the confluence with Orderville Canyon. The principal interest of the narrows, compared to other more accessible or perhaps more photogenic locations, resides in the fact that you are almost constantly immersed in the Virgin River, often up to your knees and sometimes higher. Out of season, the Virgin River is glacially cold or its water level is too high, so it is recommended that you make this journey during summer. Unfortunately, if you do, you won't be alone and will also run the risk of flash flooding. At the entrance to the

Narrows, there is a signpost warning of the potential risks of flash floods and rating the danger for the day. Permits are not required for day-hikers, but the Park Service strictly forbids walking the narrows on days when a storm is threatening. You can rent a dry suit, as well as Neoprene socks and canyoneering shoes to make the experience safer and more enjoyable, but a good pair of stiff hiking boots with firm ankle support will also do an

Exploring the Narrows

excellent job. Out of season, this equipment becomes absolutely indispensable (check Resources in the Appendix.) You should also consider carrying a walking stick to probe the riverbed for treacherous rocks or holes and to keep your balance if the current is strong. You'll find a stockpile of pretty rough sticks at the end of Riverside Walk, from which you can borrow.

Walking the Virgin Narrows can be a real pleasure, although it may be quite strenuous—especially when walking against the current. If this seems a bit too much or you don't feel ready to walk in cold water, don't despair. Later in the book, I will propose several relatively easy walks of similar interest and originality; some in narrows (see Paria Canyon, Buckskin Gulch and Coyote Gulch) and some in slot canyons (see Peek-a-Boo and Little Wild Horse Canyon). Don't miss reading the chapters concerning these extraordinary and lesser-known sites. Scores of visitors crowd the Zion Narrows while adventures and photographic possibilities abound elsewhere.

The complete descent of the Virgin Narrows requires two full days as well as preparations and logistics beyond the scope of this book.

If you are planning on hiking the Narrows in summer, keep in mind that the risk of thunderstorms is statistically higher after midday than in the morning.

Moreover, you'll find the Narrows definitely less crowded in the morning.

Since the introduction of the mandatory shuttle, the timing and logistics of a stroll in the Narrows in the high season is rather complicated:

You can no longer change into canyoneering gear at the Temple of Sinawava parking lot, nor can you leave your belongings in your car, then switch back when you come out of the Narrows for other hikes inside the canyon.

You'll need to leave properly equipped from the Visitor Center and return there with the shuttle in order to recover the equipment that you didn't take with you into the narrows (clothing, food, perhaps bigger and better photographic equipment) before returning into the canyon for other strolls.

This also militates for planning your visit to the Narrows in the morning, in order to leave time for other sites after midday.

One example of this would be to go as far as Orderville Canyon in the morning and do all your photography on the return trip, when the light is best. This will also put you at the Temple of Sinawava at an excellent time for good reflected light on the Pulpit.

Photo advice: from a photographic standpoint, one of the unique features of the Narrows of the Virgin River is the chance to take photos of yourself or your friends wading in the water, fording the narrows. To eliminate problems, a fast film is needed as the Narrows are very shady and it would be cumbersome to bring a tripod, unless you are very serious about your photography.

If you have at your disposal a small automatic camera, bring it in preference to a more expensive one. Just remove it from your pocket when an opportunity presents itself and the zoom will let you take excellent pictures of people. If all you have is a reflex camera, protect it in an airtight plastic bag. You will have to walk over slick rocks and it's easy to take a spill. I strongly recommend against taking expensive medium or large format equipment into the Narrows.

Time required: 2-1/2 to 3 hours round-trip from the Gateway to the Narrows to reach the junction of Orderville Canyon—the final destination for most visitors—but an hour will suffice to get a glimpse of the place and take some people shots if you are in a hurry. If you choose to explore Orderville Canyon, you can reach the first little cascade, usually on dry ground, in about 20 minutes.

The Great White Throne

It's preferable to see the Great White Throne on your return from the Temple of Sinawava, as you'll have to cut across traffic if you do it first (when the shuttle system is not in effect). It is without doubt one of the most recognizable symbols of Zion. Unfortunately, it does not allow itself to be photographed as easily as you would like. There are two vantage points; both situated on the right side of the road returning from the Temple of Sinawava. The first allows a rectangular framing of the throne between two walls of the canyon, which is quite mediocre. The second vantage point offers a more unobstructed view and much more leeway to play with the light, whether you keep to the perfectly satisfactory view from the road, aptly name Photo Point, or descend to the bank of the Virgin River. The best lighting is in the middle of the afternoon. Too early in the day, the canyon is shrouded in shadow and later in the evening it is backlit. It took me many visits to Zion to finally get the right light and a picture I was satisfied with. I shot it with a 17mm lens, but a 24mm will work too.

The Great White Throne from Photo Point

Kolob Canyon Viewpoint

The Kolob section of Zion is rather remote from the Canyon and many travelers pressed for time pass it up. That's a shame because the valley that follows the road towards Cedar City is very pretty. Also, the road through the park only runs about 6 miles before reaching the Kolob Canyon Viewpoint, making it a very short trip. All along the route, the view of the impressive red rock walls of

Double Arch Alcove towers over Taylor Creek

the Finger Canyons is remarkable. The detour is worthwhile if you decide to go up to Bryce by way of Cedar Breaks. But don't let it cause you to miss the road from Zion to Mt. Carmel, allowing you to cross the plateau. If you have to choose, the plateau should be the first priority.

Photo advice: the best time is late afternoon.

Getting there: take Exit 40 from I-40, 32 miles north of St. George and 19 miles south of Cedar City. The Kolob section is frequently closed in winter.

Time required: 1 hour round-trip from Interstate 15.

Taylor Creek

This is a very scenic and highly recommended hike to a fantastic photographic location: a vast grotto-like alcove, topped by two closed arches carved in a 2000 feet cliff. The trail is easy and suitable for families with young children. It is only 2.7-mile one way to Double Arch Alcove on a mostly flat trail. You will cross Taylor Creek dozens of times, but none of the crossings presents a challenge; in fact, you even end up walking in the shallow creek bed toward the end of the hike, which is a lot of fun.

The canyon walls and vegetation are splendid all along the trail and you'll pass two old cabins on your way. There is a patch of lush green grass and mosses at the back of the lower cave, which contrasts beautifully with the red rock. This is due to the presence of a spring seep. In the fall, you'll get the benefit of intense yellows and reds to complement your photos. Some very large pines and spruce trees grow above the first and second alcoves, adding a touch of green to your composition.

Photo advice: a 24mm or 28mm works best to encompass the entire rock wall including some vegetation at the bottom, the alcove and the two arches. Best photographed around midday under the reflected light from the opposite rock wall, which gives the alcove a fantastic orange and red glow.

Getting there: the trailhead is only 3 miles from the Kolob Section entrance on I-15 between St. George and Cedar City. This section of the park is frequently closed in winter.

Time required: 3 hours round-trip.

Crossing Zion by way of the Kolob Terraces

For those with time and a thirst for adventure and hidden corners, it's possible to cross Zion from north to south in a high-clearance or 4WD vehicle. You can start either from Cedar City or Kanarraville to the north or from Virgin to the south. The road is known as the Kolob Reservoir Road and is classified as a Scenic Backway. The northern part of the route, unpaved and in very poor repair, crosses privately owned land on the Kolob Plateau. It's difficult to follow because of tracks left by the pickups of local ranchers, but with a bit of close attention you can quickly locate the right one going to Kolob Reservoir by way of Blue Spring Reservoir and enter the park at Lava Point. The main attraction of this foray into the high country is in crossing the semi-alpine landscape and the solitude that one is sure to encounter there.

Photo advice: in the early evening, you'll have superb views of the Kolob Terraces lit by the setting sun with magnificent tall grasses in the foreground. Fantastic views abound between mile 8 and 15 from Virgin.

Getting there: take the Kanarraville exit on I-15, follow the Kanarraville signs south until you find the trail on your left about a mile from the off ramp, or from Virgin simply follow the Scenic Backway sign.

Time required: 3 hours. Make sure your vehicle is in excellent running condition and take supplies. I drove the 45 mile distance without encountering another vehicle. The road is closed by snow in winter.

The Subway

This is a fantastic location, but also a very hard hike, and if you are thinking of taking heavy photographic equipment, you'd better think twice, because you will feel it all the way and back. However, the surreal sight that awaits you at the end of the journey makes it all worth it.

The Subway is a narrow canyon that has been carved in a tunnel-like fashion by the waters of North Creek. In one curve made by the river, it feels like you are in a tunnel, except for a narrow opening at the top. North creek gently winds its way on the polished red rock under your feet, flowing over pools of azure and

Looking back toward the Subway (photo by Denis Savouray)

green; small cascades trickle down pour-offs and choke stones further up. The absence of light reinforces the crypt-like feeling of the Subway. It is a very haunting place indeed.

You'll need a permit to visit the Subway. It is not too difficult to come by because the NPS issues up to 50 of them each day. You can apply for your permit at the backcountry desk of the Visitor Center, up to two weeks prior to your visit. Overnight camping is no longer permitted inside the canyon. In summer, you might find serious competition for the permits from adventurous young people intent on a day of wading and rappelling. In other seasons, crowds are sparser and on a cold or overcast day you may well be the only soul venturing into the canyon.

Photo advice: regardless of the format you shoot, you will need a sturdy tripod because the light is extremely dim and you'll find yourself working with very long pauses: 8 to 30 seconds if you shoot slow film and want maximum depth of field. This is prime territory for reciprocity failure and you had better know the characteristics of your film and how it reacts to cool dim light. A warming filter would certainly help warm things up a bit, although the very cold blue-green light creates a very ethereal effect. At about Mile 4, you'll come to a small cascade that makes a nice picture. Just a bit further to the left is a large cave with mosses and other moisture loving vegetation. In between the cave and the bottom of the Subway, notice the crack in the bedrock on the canyon floor. The crack channels water from the creek at high speed, making a terrific picture.

Getting there: let me say first that this is a very long and difficult hike, which I do not recommend if you are not a dedicated hiker or photographer. You can reach the Subway from two different trailheads. The easiest way, at least for a photographer carrying equipment, is to go from "the bottom", a trailhead located about 8 miles north of the Kolob Terraces Scenic Byway turnoff in the town of Virgin. To call this entry "the bottom" is a figure of speech because after only half a mile of flat walking, you must negotiate a difficult descent down a steep gully. A walking stick or pair of trekking poles will make this descent as well as the whole day much easier. Once you reach the bottom, follow the creek up the best you can, crossing and re-crossing many times. Sometimes there is a visible trail, at other times there is none. It will be a challenge to keep your feet dry all the way but it can be done by detouring over the bigger boulders and crossing with the help of trekking poles. This "easy" way is a compromise which allows you to see only the lower part of the Subway, albeit the most spectacular one.

The other way, certainly more fun and adventurous, is to come from "the top", parking at the Wildcat Canyon trailhead and following the Great West Canyon for a while until it meets North Creek. From there, you'll need to rappel your way down several cascades and choke stones. You'll need a partner or two to make this trip safe and it is not recommended to take heavy equipment on this one. From the Subway, you can either retrace your steps or continue all the way to "the bottom" if you have arranged a car shuttle.

Time required: a very long day.

AROUND ZION

Smithonian Butte

An excellent way to get to Zion is by using the nine mile long Smithonian Butte Scenic Backway. Seen from UT 59 coming from Fredonia, the scenery is magnificent in all seasons with the Canaan Mountains to the east and the tall grass prairie in the foreground. However, it's on the Scenic Backway itself, going toward Rockville, that a surprise awaits you with an extraordinary view of the entrance to Zion Canyon. From the mesa, you can clearly see the Watchman to the right of the canyon entrance and the Towers of the Virgin to the left. Just before reaching Rockville, a short detour leads to Grafton, a turn-of-the-century ghost town resembling those in movie Westerns. As of this writing, Grafton is being renovated and it may lose some of its old charm.

Photo advice: from the highest point on the Smithonian Butte Backway, reached after about four miles off UT 59, the angle is just perfect for an early morning or late afternoon shot of Zion. The serrated ridge of the Smithonian Butte comes into view at this spot, looking much like the backbone of a dinosaur.

Getting there: on UT 59 coming from Fredonia or from Hurricane, the road begins about 15 miles to the east of Hurricane and comes out at Rockville, a mere 4 miles from the west entrance to Zion. It is marked by a small Scenic Byway sign. The otherwise excellent road deteriorates rapidly as it plunges toward Rockville and you'll have to exercise caution. Do not take this road after a rain, as it can be extremely slippery. Coming from Rockville, the road is not marked. You'll need to make a turn at a small sign marked Bridge Street from the main road in order to catch it.

Time required: a 45-minute detour off the main road.

Coral Pink Sand Dunes

This Utah State Park is really worth a detour, at dawn or sundown, if you happen to be in the vicinity. As its name indicates, these are sand dunes of a beautiful strong ocher tint. The extremely fine sand—Navajo sandstone ground and sifted by wind over and over again—becomes an extraordinary coral pink in the setting sun. The dunes are formed by hot air currents coming from the south and accelerating as they pass through Moccasin Gap, seen to the southwest of the viewpoint. These currents lose their speed when coming in contact with cold air masses forming above the Grand Staircase region and deposit sand in this area.

The dunes are spread out over a relatively small area, which makes it easy on the hiker or photographer. From the parking lot, you can quickly get to the summit of the two main dunes, which are not more than 40 feet tall. The surroundings are not exactly exceptional, but the White Cliffs to the north and the

Vermilion Cliffs to the south allow you to add some depth to these superb dunes. This park should not be missed if you are traveling with children.

Photo advice: the interest here is as much along the order of macro-photography than landscapes. Motifs created by the wind and the vegetation stand out from an interesting pink background. Out of season, you can get fantastic panoramic views of the dunes without any trace of footprints on their summits—something you'll be hard pressed to achieve in Death Valley or Colorado's Great Sand Dunes. Contrary to lighter colored sand dunes, like those of White Sands, it is not necessary to compensate by overexposing. A normal exposure will preserve the shadows and relief of the motifs on the sand as well as the beautiful ocher color. Try to be in position on the dunes at Sunset; you'll be treated to an unbelievably pink glow turning into a dramatic red during a brief but miracu-

In winter, Coral Pink Sand Dunes SP offers solitude and no footprints

lous last minute before the sun disappears behind the horizon. In early summer, there are nice big yellow wildflowers near the boardwalks, making good foregrounds for shots of the dunes.

Getting there: the park is located about 12 miles from Mt. Carmel on the Ponderosa/Coral Pink Sand Dunes Scenic Backway. Coming from Zion or Bryce, leave US 89 about 3.5 miles south of Mt. Carmel Junction. If coming from Kanab, exit US 89 about 8 miles north of Kanab. Signs mark the two routes, which are fully paved except for a small section to the south. Watch out for livestock, as they are free to roam along this route.

Time required: 1 and 1/2 to 3 hours.

Nearby location: tiny Pipe Springs Natl' Monument preserves a collection of buildings erected and used by Mormon pioneers in the last century. Pipe Spring began as a ranch, but was abandoned a few years later after the settlers were killed. It was subsequently used as a Mormon militia outpost and a fort was built to serve as a refuge for the farmers of the surrounding area. The interest is more cultural than photographic, but the site is right along the route and quick to visit. There is a short 0.5 mile interpretive trail that provides a glimpse into the geology and history of the Arizona Strip. The Monument is located in the middle of the Kaibab Paiute Reservation and the Visitor Center presents many interesting aspects of Paiute Indian culture.

Snow Canyon

Located just a few miles to the northwest of St. George, Snow Canyon State Park sees few visitors despite its proximity to Zion. And yet, Snow Canyon has plenty of interesting sights along its 7-mile long Scenic Road: lovely pink sand dunes, colorful sandstone cliffs ranging from white to deep red, spectacular cross-bedding alternating with black lava fields and great views from several easily-reached promontories. All this results in excellent photographic opportunities.

Photo advice: the park's diverse colors are best seen from the middle of the afternoon on. It is preferable to start from the South entrance, which is in the shade quite a bit earlier. After a brief stop to photograph the sand dunes, park near the campground and hike the Hidden Pinion Trail to the overlook, which offers a 360° panorama of the canyon. At the Lava Flow overlook car park, located 1.5-mile farther up, take the trail leading past the lava beds and ascending the West Canyon Overlook. From this easily-reached vantage point, you gain another great all-around view. There is some highly photogenic sandstone cross-bedding all around this overlook. As you drive back toward St. George on Hwy 18 after exiting the park, stop at the Snow Canyon Overlook for a great bird's eye view of the canyon. Look for the marked dirt road to the right, less than a mile after leaving the Scenic Road from the north entrance.

Getting there: leave St. George on Hwy. 18 towards Ivins and follow the signs to the Park.

Time required: about 3 hours to drive through the park and do the two recommended hikes. There are other trails begging to be discovered and a very nice campground for those who prefer a starry night over one of the numerous motels in St. George. ✿

Thor's Hammer under a fresh dusting of snow

Chapter 4

AROUND BRYCE CANYON

Bryce Amphitheater from Sunset Point

BRYCE CANYON NAT'L PARK

Bryce Canyon, along with Arches, is the park preferred by the majority of visitors to the Southwest, especially foreign visitors, who come from the four corners of the globe to admire it. The whole world, consequently, has seen images of Bryce and the name immediately invokes a geological phenomenon bordering on the supernatural. A case in point: a French software application generating virtual landscapes is named after this park and its publisher didn't have to explain the choice of name to the public. Happily or unhappily, its proximity to Los Angeles and Las Vegas makes access easy. As a result, just at the entrance of the park, there is a strong concentration of Disney-like tourist attractions. This phenomenon is reinforced by the presence of the sprawling lodging complex in the middle of the desert-like Sevier Plateau. It's unlikely that you'll find solitude or spiritual communion with the environment at Bryce, but you are sure to find a landscape that will hold you in a hypnotic trance the first time you lay eyes on it. It's a landscape filled with weird and incredible formations combined with remarkable nuances of light and saturated with color. It's understandable that visitors come from all over the world to see this spot and enjoy taking pictures there.

__Time required:__ to get the most out of Bryce, it's advisable to stay at one of the motels in the area so you can visit the park in the early morning hours and until sunset. It's also recommended that you take at least one hike on the canyon trails —an experience that involves a bit of effort.

Allow 2 1/2 hours by car to visit the amphitheater viewpoints and 2 hours to hike the canyon. If you don't have much time, go straight to Sunset Viewpoint. The Rim Trail running between Sunrise and Sunset Viewpoints and Inspiration Point is an easy walk if you don't want to descend into the canyon proper.

Early morning light on the Silent City

Sunrise and Sunset Viewpoints

Sunset Point is arguably the best spot to admire and photograph Bryce Canyon. It's also the most popular and you won't be alone. The view on both sides is excellent, looking towards Sunrise Point on the left or Inspiration Point and Bryce Point on the right. The Silent City is set back from the first viewpoint to the right of the parking lot. Mornings and late afternoons are excellent for photography. If your time is limited, Sunset Point is the best place to catch Bryce in all its glory.

Sunrise Point doesn't offer such a spectacular panorama on both sides and the formations are not as densely packed as those are at Sunset Point, but they are just as lovely. It's easier to isolate individual formations from Sunrise Point with a short telephoto lens, however.

Photo advice: you can be sure of one thing, all those magnificent photos of Bryce displayed at the Visitor Center or in the gift shop at Ruby's Inn were taken either early in the morning or late in the afternoon. If you arrive at Bryce during the middle of the day and only stay a few hours, you can't hope to come away with professional quality photos. The canyon's formations must have a warm light skimming their surface, whether from the back or the side, to bring out the relief and color. If you want to bring home high quality photos, you should be at one of the amphitheater viewpoints at dawn and use the rest of the morning to descend into the canyon. Watch out for overexposure, which will wash out the ocher, yellow and orange of the spires.

Inspiration Point and Bryce Point

Inspiration Point offers the best view of the extraordinary conglomeration of spires that make up the Silent City, situated in a recess to the south of Sunset Point. It's also possible to photograph the Silent City from Sunset Point. The Rim Trail between Sunset and Inspiration Point displays a constant stream of spectacular views. You can easily stroll it in about twenty minutes. You'll find the crowds much thinner at both Bryce and Inspiration Points, which could make your photography a lot easier in summer.

Thor's Hammer and other shining hoodoos (photo by Scott Walton)

Navajo and Queen's Garden Trails

To really absorb the magic of Bryce, a descent into the canyon is a must. By then you'll understand why old Ebenezer Bryce called this canyon "a hell of a place to lose a cow" as you take in the views, each more spectacular than the last. Many trails run among the hoodoos and take you right into the middle of these formations. Two of these, Queen's Garden Trail (about 1.5-mile) and Navajo Trail (about 2.2-miles) carry most of the foot traffic. This is due not only to their location in the amphitheater and their beauty, but because they are short and easy to reach. All the trails in the amphitheater are connected and you can make a loop using the Navajo and the Queen's Garden Trails, which shortens the entire walk to 3 miles. The Navajo descends from Sunset Point, passing by the famous rock chimney called Thor's Hammer and quickly arrives among the spires of Wall Street, which seem immense when viewed from below. The trek is short and not particularly difficult, except for the ascent on the way back. The Queen's Garden Trail begins at Sunrise Viewpoint and is rather short. It's not as steep as the Navajo and it's more frequented as well.

Time required: 2 hours for the entire loop, using the connecting trail. Begin at Sunset Point, it's both easier and more spectacular. Each trail will take about one hour to complete separately.

Note: these two trails are about 8,000 feet in altitude. It can be extremely hot and dry in the summer and it is imperative you carry a canteen of water, a sun hat and sunscreen. You can hike these trails in jogging shoes without many problems but use extreme caution, especially on the steeper parts. These trails are often snow-covered starting in October and continuing until the end of April. Descent can be extremely risky without the right kind of boots. Once inside the canyon, though, snow and ice are less of a problem and the going is not so steep.

Peek-a-Boo Trail

If you've enjoyed hiking the Navajo and Queen's Garden trails and are craving for more, you'll enjoy the Peek-a-Boo trail. In fact, time permitting, I strongly recommend combining the preceding walks with the Peek-a-Boo Loop; this adds another 4 miles to the walk (including the small connecting trail at the end of the Navajo Trail) for a total of 7 miles and approximately 4 to 5 hours.

The Peek-a-Boo Loop offers solitude as well as great opportunities for less cliché photography, particularly at the Wall of Wisdom and The Cathedral. In addition to the beauty of the circuit, its variety makes it interesting, with many small switchbacks, passages close to the edge of the ravine and a couple of very short sections dug into the rock. On the other hand, it is a bit of a roller-coaster and often dusty because of the twice-daily commercial horseback rides. It is better hiked clockwise.

If you don't feel like tackling the whole loop on foot, consider a horseback

Wall Street section of the Navajo Trail

ride. The half-day "Complete tour of the canyon" leaves at 8AM and 1PM each day, during the high season. You'll need to reserve at least the day before (See On the Go Resources.) Take the 8AM tour if you can.

Fairyland Viewpoint and Trail

You'll find the Fairyland Viewpoint at the end of a spur road to your left, between the Park entrance and the Visitor Center.

Visitors, who tend to congregate around the more famous viewpoints near the amphitheater, frequently neglect this one, as well as the trail of the same name. Fairyland is just as lovely and gives you a completely different view of the canyon and its formations. This part of the canyon is more wooded and more touches of green are sprinkled against the red and orange rock chimneys. If you lack the time to do the Navajo/Queen's Garden loop trail, try following the first 1,500 feet of the Fairyland Trail until you reach the promontory which you'll see a bit to the left of the viewpoint. The walk is easy and the view on both sides of the promontory is magnificent.

Yovimpai Point and Rainbow Point

These two viewpoints, at the southernmost tip of the park, appear very different from the amphitheater. You won't find similar scenery there. This is a superb alpine landscape and an interesting contrast after the amphitheater, if you have the time. The route climbs imperceptibly to the heart of a forest where pines and aspens blend. You'll find lots of wildlife here and an almost total absence of cars out of season. From Yovimpai Point, the view takes in all the steps of the Grand Staircase to the south. From Rainbow Point, close to 8,500 feet in elevation, you have a sensational, unobstructed panorama of the Pink Cliffs, the highest tread on the Grand Staircase. It's also a good chance to view some ancient bristlecone pines and take spectacular photos of the tortuous forms of these members of the world's oldest living plant species. Some of their cousins in California's White Mountains are 6,000 years old and still growing

Mossy Cave

This extremely pleasant trail, almost flat three quarters of the way and little frequented, was restored in the summer of 2000 after having been closed for a long time, due to partial destruction by a flash flood.

It follows a perennial creek meandering among a spectacular landscape of red spires, before reaching a deep alcove with green vegetation and, a few hundred yards further, a pretty little cascade. There are great shots of openings in the red spires, high above the trail to the right.

Getting there: on the west side of Scenic Byway 12, halfway between Tropic and UT 63 going into Bryce Canyon.

Time required: about an hour.

AROUND BRYCE CANYON

Red Canyon

Red Canyon, under the jurisdiction of the Dixie National Forest, is an excellent prelude to Bryce if you are coming from Zion. For the majority of visitors, Red Canyon usually means a quick stop along the side of the road to snap a few shots before continuing on to Bryce. That's too bad since Red Canyon has a per-

Red Canyon State Park

sonality all its own. Its formations are definitely different from those of Bryce. For off-season visitors, arriving in greater numbers all the time, it's a first-rate alternative to the icy, snowbound trails of Bryce.

Among the variety of available trails, the easiest and most pleasant is without doubt Pink Ledges, a loop of about twenty minutes, starting from the Visitor Center and passing several extremely esthetic viewpoints. The trail is very easy and a perfect alternative for those who don't want to tackle the Navajo/Queen's Garden loop trail.

Much more difficult is the Birdseye Trail, located down from the Visitor Center. This trail climbs steeply to the heights and contains some superb vistas. The contrast between the abrupt halt of the angular formations and the peaceful valley of the Sevier below is interesting to observe.

For longer hiking, the Cassidy Trail, upstream from the Visitor Center, offers the hiker in search of solitude a pleasant stroll far from the crowd in a lovely, steeply banked canyon bordered with trees.

Photo advice: in adapting to the angles of the sun, the light is as good in the morning as in the afternoon. If the sun is very strong, be careful not to under-expose the red rock if you use a matrix-type meter. Conversely, take care not to overexpose the rock. A setting of a half stop on either side should be enough to assure a perfect exposure. The east side of the Pink Ledges Trail is highly recommended for photography.

Getting there: either by Scenic Byway 12 from Bryce or by way of the splendid Scenic Byway 89 connecting Bryce to Panguitch following the course of the Sevier River.

Time required: about 1/2-hour for the Pink Ledges to 1-1/2 hour for two trails depending on the amount of time you have.

Bristlecone Pine near Spectra Point in Cedar Breaks

Cedar Breaks National Monument

This National Monument resembles Bryce, though it presents some original formations. Cedar Breaks is laid out in the form of a vast, uninterrupted semi-circular amphitheater, deeper than Bryce is and equally as colorful. Does it merit a detour? Without hesitation, yes, for enthusiasts desiring complete insight into the national parks of the Southwest, but no, for visitors who only have a week to ten days to do the Grand Circle.

Cedar Breaks' location is close to 10,000 feet high and the summit is often subjected to extremely violent winds. It closes around mid-October because of heavy snowfalls and remains closed until late May. The plateau is less obstructed than that of Bryce, with some good-size prairies interspersed among the forest pines. Scenic Byway 14 between the valley of the Sevier River and Cedar City is absolutely lovely. In winter, the snowfields of Duck Creek are invaded by snow-mobiles, a very tempting sight if you do not mind the noise.

Photo advice: four viewpoints allow you to photograph the amphitheater along the 5-mile long Scenic Drive; each one is a bit different from the other. If you are pressed for time, Point Supreme is probably the best, as well as the most crowded. The Wasatch Ramparts trail is a nice walk with excellent late afternoon and evening views and allows you to photograph a rare group of very old Bristlecone pines at Spectra Point. If you can be there in July, you'll have great wildflowers in the meadows on the east side of the road.

Getting there: on UT 148 from Scenic Byway 14 connecting with US 89 to Cedar City or from Scenic Byway 143 connecting Panguitch with I-15. Coming from the north, you'll pass the ski resort at Brian Head.

Time required: 1 hour to 1-1/2 hour to cross the park and take a few pictures from the viewpoints. Add a couple of hours for a leisurely stroll on the Wasatch Ramparts trail. ✿

Reflections at the Wave

Chapter 5

AROUND THE PARIA

Fantastic hoodoos of the Rimrocks

AROUND THE PARIA

The Rimrocks

The Rimrocks is an outstanding area of badlands located north of US 89 between Cottonwood Canyon Road and the Cockscomb fault. It contains a large number of fascinating hoodoos, mushroom rocks and rock towers. The most prominent and accessible landmark of the Rimrocks is Toadstool Hoodoo, a spectacular sandstone spire, shaped a bit like the Seattle Needle with a larger rotunda at the top. The area around Toadstool Hoodoo offers endless photographic opportunities, at any time of the day. About 30 feet west of Toadstool Hoodoo is another prominent hoodoo, shorter and rounder. They are close enough to each other to make an oft-photographed duo. About 200 feet behind Toadstool hoodoo, near the cliff, is a series of striking rock-capped sandstone towers. Once you're done photographing Toadstool Hoodoo, follow the rim to the west for about 300 yards until you come to a recessed area, somewhat hidden on your right, containing several large white towers, capped with brown slabs of hard rock. I like to call this place "hoodoo central". This area is in deep shadow until late morning, which will give a strong bluish cast, so it is best photographed in late afternoon. Back on US 89, about a mile further to the west lies another recessed canyon full of spectacular white towers coifed with rocks. You can see this area with the naked eye from the Paria Contact station across the road, but it is best observed with binoculars.

___*Photo advice:*___ early morning and late evening both work well; there are plenty of formations so you're guaranteed to find some that will be correctly exposed regardless of what time of day you visit. Toadstool Hoodoo itself can be photographed successfully from different angles and under various light conditions.

Toadstool Hoodoo

Getting there: about a mile east of the turnoff for the Paria Contact Station, near milepost 20, there is a small pullout space and a cow fence on the north side of the road. The access is unmarked so you'll have to pay close attention, but there is an electric line running perpendicular to the road at that point. Cross the opening in the fence and follow the wash to the north for about 15 to 20 minutes. There is also a footpath running along the wash. Climb the low badlands at the end and the hoodoos will come into view. Despite the fact that the area north of the Paria Contact Station is fenced, it is all public land and can be explored on foot, at your own risk. This area is very fragile, so tread lightly.

It takes quite a bit of effort and route finding to climb to the other ledge, where the white hoodoos visible from the Paria Contact Station are located. It's best to go with a companion. Cross the fence north of US 89 opposite the ranger station's road and walk east to the mouth of the canyon. You'll notice that the canyon ends in three arms, follow the right arm though a slot canyon, then scramble up carefully to the ledge, where the hoodoos will come into view.

The White Rocks

The White Rocks is a lesser-known area centered around the Upper Wahweap Creek drainage, north of Churchwells. It consists of outstanding badlands, hoodoos and white capped towers. The soft white shale, remnant of an ancient seabed, is often twisted into remarkable shapes by erosion forces. It is a fascinating area to explore and photograph.

Photo advice: there are many different groups of hoodoos with a different orientation inside this wide area and it is impossible to recommend a perfect time of day as a whole. As a general rule, most of these hoodoos are in canyons and rincons and are in shade during the golden hour. If you want them in full sunshine, mid-morning or mid-afternoon is usually the best time. They can also be successfully photographed in the shade; they acquire a blue cast that can be easily removed in a digital darkroom. Do not use an aggressive warming filter or you will lose the pure white color of the towers.

Getting there: the easiest way to access the White Rocks is from the little town of Churchwells. Coming from Page, turn right at a red dirt road located 0.5 mile before Churchwells. It is BLM road 435 and is easy to miss. Follow it for about 3 miles until you come to a cow fence, with a gauntlet and reservoir to your right. The prominent landmark to the north is called Chimney Rock. From there, easy to spot tracks lead straight-ahead. Follow the less obvious tracks to the right, cross the fence at the rightmost gate and continue for less than a mile to reach the end of the canyon, an area which is great fun to explore and photograph. It is best photographed in mid to late afternoon.

For a more adventurous trip, you can also explore the Wahweap Creek drainage above Chimney Rock. From US 89, take Cottonwood Canyon Road for about 2 miles, turn right onto BLM road 431, then right again at the junction with BLM 430. Follow BLM 431 straight ahead. This is a fairly good road in the beginning, but it deteriorates badly after 8 miles. When you are just north of Chimney Rock, you'll see a dirt road to your right. Follow it southeast for about a mile. This one is a very rough road and a rugged 4WD vehicle is necessary. Park where the road ends and look for an easy entry into a canyon full of hoodoos to your right. To enter the Wahweap Creek drainage and see its amazing white hoodoos, continue all the way on BLM 431 until you descend into

Towers of Silence in the Wahweap drainage

Wahweap Wash. This is a difficult approach on an unmaintained road, which the BLM is considering closing in the future. A somewhat easier approach is to drive up Wahweap Wash from Big Water. Take the road heading northwest along the Fish Hatchery and follow it for a good 3 miles until you reach the Wahweap Wash crossing. If the stream is not high and you've got a high clearance vehicle, bear left and drive into the wash heading north for 3/4 of a mile until you reach a fence across the wash. Park there and follow the wash on foot for about 1-1/4 hour until you find the hoodoos at the foot of the left cliffs. There are three groups of hoodoos separated by a few hundred yards along the cliff.

Old Pahreah

Old Pahreah (aka Paria) is an easy side trip off US 89 between Kanab and Page, accessible to all passenger cars except after a rain. It is an area where history meets breathtaking Chinle formation badlands for a highly rewarding photographic journey. The very good dirt road starts innocuously enough but soon becomes roller coaster like as it straddles a narrow ridge dominating colorful badlands on the right side. As the road dives down into the Paria valley it is often washboard-like, requiring some caution. You'll soon arrive at the Paria movie set, now consisting of two newly reconstructed old-West buildings, originally erected in 1963 for the filming of Western movies. In 1999, the buildings were badly damaged during a flash flood, so the BLM removed all of them and rebuilt two new structures higher up, to make them impervious to flash floods. The old set used to integrate well into the landscape and made for nice pictures; it will take time for the new set to absorb the patina of time and look authentic. Further down the road, you'll find the Old Pahreah cemetery, the only remaining testimonial to human presence in the area. Take a walk through the cemetery; it is a very moving reminder of the hard life of the early settlers who tried to eke out a living in this desolate area. Still further, you end up on the banks of the Paria. Across the river is the actual location of Old Pahreah, but nothing remains standing. You can hike about a mile down river to the area called the Box, which cuts through the

Old Paria movie set (Photo by Philippe Schuler)

western side of the Cockscomb before joining Cottonwood Canyon Road.

Photo advice: in the vicinity of the cemetery or the movie set, take some time to explore and photograph the amazing badlands—some of the most colorful you'll ever see in the Southwest—especially in the warm afternoon light. If you are lucky enough to have a dark stormy sky, with streaks of light falling on the badlands, you'll be rewarded with amazing contrast and beautiful hues. If rain seems imminent, be sure not to linger in this area; even with a 4WD vehicle, you may not be able to climb back the steep ramp just past the movie set. Instead, take your pictures from the flat ridge to the left, immediately after the ramp. It has a splendid view looking down into the badlands.

Getting there: about 40 miles northwest of Page on US 89; at the Historical Marker, take the good dirt road (BLM 585) heading north and follow it for 5 miles to the movie set.

Paria Canyon

Paria Canyon is arguably the most famous classic hike of the Southwest. Most people take 3 to 5 days to hike the 38 miles from the White House trailhead to Lee's Ferry on the Colorado River. If you do not have that much time or are not inclined to backpack, you can also get a very good idea of what Paria Canyon looks like by hiking down from the White House trailhead. You can walk to the confluence of the Paria and Buckskin Gulch and back in a moderately difficult 15-mile round-trip. This will take the better part of a day, especially if you have to cross water holes once you reach the narrows at mile 4. The first few miles are usually dry most of the year, but you should expect some muddy areas further down. There are some outstanding features in Paria Canyon: at mile 2, you'll reach the Windows, an area of deep holes—small and large—carved by water and wind on both sides of the canyon. In the narrows, powerful Sliderock Arch at mile 6.7 makes a great picture. The confluence, at mile 7.3, is truly majestic.

Flash flood power!

Photo advice: as usual in narrows, it's best to be there at mid-day to take advantage of reflected light. The confluence of the Paria and the Buckskin offers really spectacular shots.

Getting there: take US 89 from Page (30 miles) or Kanab (43 miles) and turn off at the sign signaling the "Ranger station" near milepost 21. There, get the latest weather and trail information (also posted on the registration board when the station is closed), and, if chances of rain are slim, proceed to self-register and pay your day-use fee.

Unlike the nearby Coyote Buttes, there is no quota limiting the number of hikers into Paria Canyon and nearby Buckskin Gulch. The contact station sells an excellent map called *the Hikers Guide to Paria Canyon*, which is very helpful. Before embarking on such a long hike, however, you should consider the much easier and shorter trip into Buckskin Gulch from Wire Pass, described in the following section.

Wire Pass — Buckskin Gulch

This mini-adventure inside Wire Pass and the beginning of Buckskin Gulch will give a quick, but spectacular insight into the narrows of the Paria River area. These are, for many, the most beautiful and interesting narrows on the Colorado Plateau.

The visit will take half a day, including the drive, and can easily be arranged when traveling between Kanab and Page. You can also do the Cottonwood Canyon Road on the same day (see the Grand Staircase/Escalante Chapter) since this comes out just a few miles from the Paria Canyon ranger station.

Do not venture into Buckskin Gulch if bad weather is threatening. Once in the canyon, you won't be able to get out in case of flash floods. The enormous tree trunks lodged in the walls several feet above you testify to the force and height of the flash floods that can hit any time of the year, but particularly in summer.

The marked trail begins at the Wire Pass parking lot and follows the dry bed of the wash for about half a mile before arriving at the entrance to the narrows. The first narrows, a few dozen yards long, will give a little preview of what awaits you further on. Soon, you enter the true narrows of Wire Pass and move along between very dark walls, over a hundred feet high. Depending on how the last flash flood affected the canyon, you may have to scramble above choke stones as high as 8 feet at the first and/or second narrows; this may present a mild difficulty to some. You'll eventually reach the junction with Buckskin Gulch at 1.7 miles from the trailhead. Follow Buckskin Gulch downstream as long as you like or time permits.

Returning to the junction, go a little way up to the right into Buckskin Gulch instead of returning directly to Wire Pass. At this spot, Buckskin Gulch frequently contains water and mud-holes, and will give you a good idea of what the

The Confluence of Paria Canyon and Buckskin Gulch

narrows look like further down Buckskin Gulch and deep inside Paria Canyon.
   Photo advice: the narrows are generally rather wide, between 10 and 15 feet, with a narrow passage of about 3 feet at the entrance. They are also very high and therefore quite dark, except around mid-day. A wide-angle lens will let you maintain the depth-of-field and show the canyon's dimensions despite the wide aper-

ture you'll be forced to rely on. With a firm grip, it's perfectly possible to photograph with a hand-held camera using ISO 400 or 800 film. Refer to the advice on photographing narrows and slot canyons in the Photo Advice Chapter.

Getting there: from the Paria Contact Station turnoff, head west toward Kanab for about 4.5 miles (just past Milepost 26) until you come to a hard-packed dirt road branching off to the left when the main road makes a wide curve to the right immediately past the Cockscomb. This is BLM Road 700, better known as House Rock Valley Road. Be careful not to miss it, as it is not clearly visible when coming from Page because of the angle and the fact it is slightly downwards from the road. Using this well-maintained track, pass Buckskin Trailhead at 4.3 miles and continue for another 4 miles to the parking lot at Wire Pass. In summer, House Rock Road can be closed for a few days after a particularly strong storm.

Time required: 1-hour round-trip to get to Wire Pass from US 89; 3 hours in the narrows to really enjoy them.

Cobra Arch

Cobra Arch is a remarkable arch, in the shape of the lithe body of the snake of the same name, complete with checkerboard striations reminiscent of the serpent's scales. It is often visited by backpackers coming off Buckskin Gulch by the difficult Middle Trail. Photographers will want to take the more conservative approach of coming via Long Canyon Road, but that too isn't an easy affair. It's a long and difficult hike over rough terrain with no trail. Still the result is worth it, as Cobra Arch is truly unique.

Photo advice: Cobra Arch is best photographed in mid-afternoon, from its western side, to bring out the snake-like shape and texture of the arch.

Getting there: take BLM Road 750, also known as Long Canyon Road, which leaves from the Paria Outpost, 0.25-mile west of the Paria Contact Station turnoff. Inquire on the condition of the road first, as it may be impassable, especially in summer, due to sand accumulation or flash floods. The first five miles of this road are usually in good condition, but things deteriorate after that when the trail drops down and you must go through an area of deep sand in which you can get bogged down in some years. Park at the fence at Mile 8, sign the register and follow the fence line to the ledge overlooking the Buckskin. Using your topo map, make a route toward a large promontory visible two miles away. The route is very sandy and tiring and it will take between 1-1/2 to 2 hours to cover the 3.5 miles to the arch. Ron Adkinson has a detailed description of the hike in his excellent *Hiking Grand Staircase-Escalante guidebook*. It is very helpful if you are not adept at routefinding. If you feel uncomfortable going solo, you can also enlist the service of a private guide in Page; see the On the Go Resources chapter in the Appendix for both. Do not do this hike in summer when there is no shade and trudging back up in the sand is agonizingly slow.

The Coyote Buttes & The Wave

A few miles south of Buckskin Gulch lies one of the most extraordinary formations on the Colorado Plateau, an area of simultaneously gnarled, polished and twisted rock called the Coyote Buttes. Within its northern permit area lies

The fantastic "Wave", seen from the top

its crown jewel: the Wave—a magical place where the colorful sandstone gives itself to mind boggling psychedelic gyrations.

"Discovered" in some coffee-table books, videos and magazines in the early nineties and kept away from the limelight for a few years, this truly unique site has become a favorite subject for photographers from all over the world. It would be terribly sad if its growing popularity would reduce it to a cliché.

The Coyote Buttes are part of the Paria Canyon/Vermilion Cliffs Wilderness, jointly administered by the Kanab Field Office of the BLM and the Vermilion Cliffs Nat'l Monument (part of the Arizona Strip Field Office in St. George, UT). Concerns about widespread ecological damage to this pristine area has led to the establishment of a quota system in 1997, restricting visitation to twenty permits a day, evenly spread between the southern and northern permit areas of the Buttes. This means that only ten individuals can reserve a permit for the Wave on any given day.

This drastically low quota may or may not be revised at some point in the future after studies show what impact a steady flow of visitors has on the land. The permits are issued for daytime use only and overnight camping is strictly forbidden within the Wilderness area.

Obtaining a permit for the Wave is a bit of a challenge: first, it requires that you have access to the internet, as it is the only way your reservation can be processed; second the waiting list is such that you need to be very flexible when scheduling your visit.

Many people find the low quota system objectionable. I have no moral or scientific authority to pass a judgment, but I am quite happy with the present system. A limit of ten bodies a day seems indeed quite low at first glance. There are, however, several factors that weigh heavily in favor of keeping it that way. The vast majority of visitors come to the Coyote Buttes to see the phenomenal, but fairly small, site of the Wave and a concentration of visitors in this particular area not only could impact the fragile ecosystem but would detract from the enjoyment of the place.

Getting there: as mentioned earlier, you'll need to reserve your permit online well in advance by visiting the BLM web site at https://paria.az.blm.gov. Depending on the time of year (springtime being the peak period), you may have to reserve up to six or seven months in advance to find an empty slot. Travelling as a group—a maximum of six per group is allowed—further diminishes your chances of finding your date of choice. Be ready to make some major scheduling concessions.

For those who couldn't reserve a date on the Internet and are vacationing in the area, there is still a glimmer of hope: they can try for one of the four walk-in permits available each day for the next. These permits are handed out at the Paria Contact Station at opening time. If more than four people are present, the permits are drawn randomly. Do not attempt to go to the Wave without a permit. Access is often patrolled; if you got caught, you'd have to pay a hefty fine and face possible prosecution for trespassing on Federal land.

From the Wire Pass trailhead (see Getting there in the Wire Pass/Buckskin Gulch section), it is approximately 3 miles to the Wave. Count on at least 1-1/2 hours to reach the Wave the first time around, depending on your route-finding ability. Although some people fail to locate the Wave, it is not that difficult to find your way around, based on descriptions from guidebooks, web sites or friends or by looking for specific landmarks. Ask the rangers at the Paria Contact

The "Second" Wave

Some of the unusual patterns found at the Wave

Station to describe these landmarks before beginning your hike.

It is one place where a compass or a GPS could be useful, especially if you come back to the trailhead after dark. There are less obvious landmarks to rely on during the return trip and this is exacerbated if you are in darkness. In summer, you'll need plenty of water and adequate sun protection, as there is no shade along the way. Watch for possible thunderstorms (read the recommendations given to that effect on the BLM web site.)

From the trailhead, walk for about 10 minutes in the dry wash in the direction of the Wire Pass narrows. As you come to the sign indicating Buckskin Gulch, you'll notice an old jeep trail climbing to the right. Follow it to the plateau, sign the trail register and continue on the sandy path down to a wash at the foot of a slanted sandstone ridge. Climb up on the ridge and cross an easily located saddle, a bit to the left. Turn right past the saddle and walk south on the slickrock on the other side of the ridge, staying high on the slope. You'll soon come to a couple of large conical rocks; circumnavigate them on the left side. Soon after that, you'll come across the old barbed-wired fence marking the border of Utah and Arizona. From here, Top Rock—the ridge below which the Wave is nested—comes into view. Top Rock is easily identified by a long black crack running vertically in its flank. Once you have found Top Rock and its crack, you will have no problem reaching the Wave. Just walk cross-country in that general direction, staying high as long as you can on the slickrock slope until you come to a large wash; descend into it and climb the steep sand dune on the opposite side, near a small isolated tree. There, you'll reach a shallow gully leading in a couple hundred yards to the main entrance to the Wave.

At the Wave, avoid walking on the thin ribs and ledges of rock that make the Wave so special. You don't need heavy boots to walk to the Wave, so wear light-weight boots or sneakers that won't mark the rock. Also, be careful where you place your tripod. It is a privilege to experience the Wave and it's up to you to preserve it for those who'll follow.

Photo advice: first, let me say that although the main corridor of the Wave is the focal point of any trip, there is plenty of wonderful scenery around it. Do not concentrate exclusively on the Wave or you'll fail to exploit the tremendous pho-tographic potential of its surroundings. Be sure to bring lots of film because the Wave will strongly stimulate your creative juices, and you're not going to have another chance the next day, unless you have reserved on successive days, which is allowed.

It's possible to photograph at any time of the day. Some of the colorful rock formations located to the right of the main corridor leading to the Wave are best photographed in the early morning. Shooting at sunrise toward the Teepees is also very nice. There is a myriad of details all around the Wave that can be pho-tographed successfully throughout the day. The Wave itself can be photographed from just after mid-day. The heart of the Wave will be partially plunged in shad-ows as the afternoon progresses, generating potential contrast problems. Things get easier in late afternoon when a larger area is in shadow. Always avoid com-bining brightly lit and shadow areas on your images. To photograph the Wave itself, try many different compositions. Even though the site is small, varying the height and angle of the camera will yield very different results. Make liberal use of the different optics you've brought with you, even from the same spot. For instance, when photographing the Wave's corridor from above with your back turned to the big crack, you can either use a wide-angle to capture all the gentle curves or a medium telephoto to zoom-in on part of the striations and compress the perspective of the different waves. A mild warming filter or a polarizing fil-ter will give you pleasant results. I also recommend using an ND Grad filter to keep the sky in check when photographing the Wave's corridor from above.

Many visitors fail to see the surrounding area of the Wave. There is a tenden-cy to relinquish the desire to scout the area because one is so elated by the sight of the main Wave. Many people are also unaware of the existence of other fasci-nating subjects of the Coyote Buttes, in particular the back of Top Rock, where you can see more brain rocks, great cross-bedding, a high flat plateau with beau-tiful green trees and some beautiful arches.

If you don't want to explore much farther than the Wave's immediate area, I recommend the following loop, which will take you through several surrounding features. The loop is under a mile round-trip and can be done in about an hour. Of course, it can take much longer if you spend quality time concentrating on your photography. It is best done in late afternoon.

Leave the main corridor of the Wave, climbing toward the big crack on Top Rock. This brings you to a small plateau to the right with amazing "brain rocks" and incredibly colorful cross-bedding. This plateau may have large puddles of water after summer and in spring, making it photographically even more interesting. Some of the brain rocks have extraordinary shapes and color. Continue on this plateau toward the southwest and follow a 12-foot high slope of widely-spaced diagonal striations. Go around it on the left and, as you are barely more than 200 yards from the main Wave, you will arrive at what I call the Second Wave. This Second Wave consists of two exceptionally photogenic swirls of polished and striated sandstone. With its paler colors, the Second Wave can only be photographed successfully in late afternoon. You can easily scout this spot earlier in the afternoon and come back as your last stop before returning to your car. From the Second Wave, look down below toward the southwest and locate a cluster of small red buttes, one of which is a bit isolated to the left. Descend cautiously the 300 yards that separate you from the buttes. Cross to the backside of the buttes and you'll see to your right some photogenic red and white striations on the rock. To return to the main Wave, follow the red and white striations in a northerly direction and enter a small gully with a mixture of sand and rock. Follow it for a few hundred yards until you come to a dryfall, about 12-foot deep. Don't climb down the dryfall; instead, leave the canyon by climbing the small dune to the right, continuing in that direction and ascending the gentle slope until you reach the characteristic forms and shapes of the buttes surrounding the main Wave. You can then re-enter the main Wave through the narrow passageway on its west side.

Arches on the backside of the Coyote Buttes

Time required: at least 4 hours round-trip from Wire Pass to allow enough time for photographing the main Wave; up to a full day to include a side-trip to the North Teepees (see below) in the morning, as well as the above-suggested tour around the Wave in the afternoon.

The Teepees

The area known as the Teepees lies to the south of Wire Pass and east of the northern permit area of the Coyote Buttes. There are two distinct groups: north and south Teepees, both easily observed in the distance, on your way to the Wave. The Teepees are majestic sandstone outcrops eroded down to a conical shape reminiscent of Native American teepees, hence the name. What makes this area particularly attractive is twofold: views of the Teepee shapes from a short distance, but mostly its great potential for superb abstract pictures. Inside the North Teepees, you'll find sandstone swirls reminiscent of those around the Wave, although different in color and texture.

Photo advice: coming from Top Rock, you'll be on the west side of the North Teepees. You'll find photogenic pink and black striations at the base of one of the Teepees to the left. Walk around the right side of that teepee and you'll come to a narrow passage leading up to the heart of Teepees. There are some superb shots from inside and you can easily climb west to an open 'window' for a panoramic shot encompassing the South Teepees and Top Rock with part of your teepee. Even though the west face of the Teepees is better lit in the afternoon, I recommend that you reserve the best light for the short loop around the Wave described in the previous section. On the other hand, if the sky is cloud-covered I encourage you to head to the North Teepees and point your camera to the ground and the great sandstone sculptures and patterns.

Getting there: the Teepees are located on the east side of the Coyote Buttes, outside the permit area. Going around the permit area requires a difficult and fatiguing cross-country trudge requiring good routefinding ability and lots of ups and downs in deep sand. Your best bet for visiting the Teepees is to include them in the morning on the day of your visit to the Wave with your permit for the northern section of the Coyote Buttes. From Wire Pass, follow the path to the Wave (see above). At the bottom of Top Rock, do not climb the sand dune with the isolated tree, but circumnavigate to the left, continuing on the slickrock slope until your reach the eastern flank of the Coyote Buttes. From there, you can cut cross-country in a straight line on sandy ground. The distance from the east face to the North Teepees is only about one mile, but it is hard work.

Of course, you may want to visit the Wave first (I can't blame you) and do the North Teepees round-trip later in the day. In that case, you'll need to leave the main Wave in the direction of the black crack, but immediately turn left and ascend the slickrock until your reach a saddle from where you can descend the east face to join the previously described route. To avoid getting lost on the way

Follow me to the Teepees...   *Inside the Teepees*

back, return the way you came instead of trying to cut directly toward Wire Pass.

__Time required:__ from the Wave or from the base of Top Rock, allocate 2-1/2 to 3 hours to the round-trip for a thorough exploration of the North and South Teepees. ✿

Narrows in the Escalante drainage

Chapter 6

GRAND STAIRCASE–ESCALANTE

Circle Cliffs and Henry Mountains from the Homestead Viewpoint

GRAND STAIRCASE–ESCALANTE

Introduction

Officially designated a National Monument in 1996, Grand Staircase-Escalante encompasses a vast area between Capitol Reef, Glen Canyon and Bryce Canyon. Inside are three different regions: the Canyons of the Escalante, the Kaiparowits plateau and the Grand Staircase itself (see A bit of Geology in the Introduction). Crossing its northern side from east to west is Scenic Byway 12. This route passes through some of the most grandiose scenery in Utah and is always spectacular no matter how you approach it. The section between Escalante and Boulder is considered by many to be one of the most beautiful paved roads in Utah. An interagency regrouping the National Park Service, National Forest Service and Bureau of Land Management has the difficult task of managing this land and accommodating the diverse needs of resident farmers, ranchers, miners, loggers, visitors and others. The Monument's headquarters are located in the town of Escalante, which is also the site of half a dozen motels and B&Bs, making it an excellent base for exploration.

This chapter covers all the sites directly accessible from this side of the Monument, following SB 12 from east to west. Within this chapter, I took the liberty of making a few forays outside of the Monument per se, as a matter of convenience to the reader. Conversely, some sites located in the southern portion of the Monument have already been covered in the Around the Paria chapter.

Around Boulder on Scenic Byway 12

Boulder is one of the last communities of the West to have been linked to civilization with a road. Hwy 12 (today a Scenic Byway) opened in 1940 but remained partially unpaved until the mid-eighties. The section south of Boulder, which passes through vast expanses of slickrock, was finished in the seventies; the northern section, which crosses the forested area around Boulder Mountain was the last to be asphalted. Be sure to allocate plenty of time when driving SB 12; not only does this beautiful route have plenty of curves and ups and downs, but it has also numerous pullouts providing great opportunities to appreciate and photograph the awesome scenery.

In the hamlet of Boulder, the Anasazi State Park provides an interesting glimpse into the life and culture of the Fremont Basketmakers, who originally settled this region. The museum was entirely refurbished in 1997 and has many interesting interactive exhibits. Behind the museum, there is a replica of a typical Puebloan-type ancestral dwelling and the excavated ruins of the Coombs site with a partially reconstructed pit-house. Even if you do not visit the Museum, the State Park rangers are an excellent source of information for local hikes and the latest weather forecast. This is helpful if you want to explore the area without driving all the way to the Escalante headquarters.

To the north of Boulder, Scenic Byway 12 turns into a true mountain road while crossing Boulder Mountain—an ancient volcano over 50 million years old. Near the highest point on the road, you can photograph large groves of aspens.

Fractured Navajo sandstone near Boulder

Fall colors are usually at their peak during the second week in October. Of the three viewpoints that line up the road to Torrey, Homestead (11 miles north of Boulder) is the most spectacular. From here, your eye embraces hundreds of miles around, including the Waterpocket Fold, the Circle Cliffs, and the Burr Trail. Hwy 12 offers other superb panoramic views of Capitol Reef and the Henry Mountains from the viewpoints at Steep Creek (13 miles north of Boulder) and Larb Hollow (9 miles farther). For photography, the viewpoints on Boulder Mountain are best in the afternoon with a medium to long telephoto. Watch for deer on the road, especially in early morning and evening.

In the immediate vicinity of Boulder, there are some great looking Navajo sandstone petrified dunes. These domes are heavily striated in a manner reminiscent of Checkerboard Mesa and are very photogenic.

Leaving Boulder toward Escalante, you are treated to wonderful slickrock scenery, with soft hues ranging from white to dark pink.

Soon you'll be coming to the unique and spectacular Hogback Ridge, which is so narrow that in one particular tight spot, you can see the landscape on both sides, a thousand feet below. The road then descends through a lovely canyon near Calf Creek (see that section within this chapter) before crossing the Escalante River and climbing again to the viewpoints of Boynton Overlook (14 miles south of Boulder) and Head of Rocks (4 miles further).

West of Escalante, the road becomes more tame and its only landmark is an interesting area of badlands known as the Blues located at the base of the ubiquitous Powell Point.

The Burr Trail

The Burr Trail (BLM Road 100) is an old track used by the Mormon pioneers when moving their livestock from the high-altitude pastures of Boulder Mountain to the warmer grazing areas of the Waterpocket Fold. The trail, graded and oiled in the 1980's up to the boundary of Capitol Reef NP, crosses beautiful country that is still wild and lonely. Just outside of Boulder, the Burr Trail passes through a series of beautifully cross-bedded Navajo sandstone before crossing Deer Creek. Soon after that, you'll cross beautiful Long Canyon. As the Burr Trail becomes a dirt road, the west face of the Waterpocket Fold and Strike Valley come into view very nicely (we'll make a foray into

Long Canyon

Muley Twist to Strike Valley Overlook in the next section). Soon, you'll be crossing the Fold and reaching the steep switchbacks leading down into Strike Valley. If you have a high-clearance vehicle, you can go down the switchbacks and continue south toward Bullfrog Marina or north toward UT 24 via Notom Road.

Photo advice: the road traverses Long Canyon from about Mile 10 through 17 coming from Boulder; its walls are eroded in the form of highly concentrated deep holes dug into the deep-red Wingate sandstone. This phenomenon—known as "Swiss cheese"—makes for great photography, producing highly saturated reds when photographed under reflected light. There is a nice panorama before you drop down into Long Canyon and again as you exit, when the view opens up on the Circle Cliffs, the Waterpocket Fold and the Henry Mountains, with some photogenic badlands in the foreground. Scenery along the Burr Trail is best photographed in the afternoon.

Time required: at least 1-1/2 hour for a short drive from Boulder to the end of Long Canyon and back. Half a day to drive to the boundary of Capitol Reef and do the recommended side trip to Strike Valley Overlook (see later section).

Little Death Hollow

Little Death Hollow is one of the most exciting slot canyons in the Escalante drainage, with just the right amount of technical challenge to spice things up, without being difficult. Although not quite as spectacular as others photographically, this long slot canyon can nonetheless yield some great action shots and its beautiful red walls of Wingate sandstone, often pock-marked with spectacular Swiss cheese, are definitely worth shooting.

For those wanting a quick peek into Little Death Hollow without suffering 8 miles round-trip of nondescript wash-walking from the main trailhead on the Wolverine Loop Road, Horse Canyon road provides an excellent alternative. Get road conditions and weather forecast info from the BLM before embarking on this road, because it's 13 miles one way and very sandy in places. If you get stuck, it will be a long walk back. The road is usually graded once a year. It starts from the Wolverine Loop Road, branching off to the right about 5 miles from the Burr Trail. It is usually graded once a year and is suitable for high-clearance vehicles when conditions are right. Horse Canyon is a wide but beautiful Wingate canyon with some remarkable desert varnish in places. There are very pleasant primitive camping spots at the end of the road, near the mouth of Wolverine canyon and few hundred yards further near the mouth of Little Death Hollow.

From there, Little Death Hollow can be followed for approximately 1.5-miles before encountering the first truly technical obstacle. All the choke stones before that can be easily scaled or skirted and present no real challenge to a fit person.

Time permitting, back at the confluence of Horse Canyon and Little Death Hollow, a 20-minute walk brings you to the Escalante River where you can rest a while before returning to your car.

As you walk back to your car from the mouth of Little Death Hollow, look for a striking Native American profile formed in the distant sandstone to the left, as the wash opens up.

Strike Valley and Upper Muley Twist

Strike Valley Overlook is a remarkable vista point, accessible via a short hike, from where you can photograph the wide expanse of the Waterpocket Fold. It is a must if you are entering or exiting Capitol Reef from the Burr Trail.

From the same trailhead, Upper Muley Twist offers a very rewarding, albeit strenuous, hike and yields more panoramic views of the Waterpocket Fold. The views are a little more open than at Strike Valley Overlook, especially to the north, but are also harder to photograph successfully.

Getting there: via the Burr Trail from Boulder, or via the Notom Bullfrog Road (from UT 24 or from Bullfrog). The junction with the dirt road to Upper Muley Twist Canyon is about 1 mile west from the top of the Burr Trail switchbacks. You can drive the 3 miles to the trailhead only if you have a 4WD or high clearance vehicle. After the first half mile, the road becomes very rough, but it is quite scenic and not dangerous. It's actually a good place to hone your boulder straddling skills if you are not an experienced four-wheeler. Do not attempt this road with a low clearance vehicle. You would become high-centered or would damage your undercarriage. Following the road on foot makes for a very pleasant hike, although you would not want to do this hike in summer.

Strike Valley Overlook is about half a mile east from the trailhead parking and offers a fantastic panoramic view on the Waterpocket Fold. At the edge of the rim, follow it to your right to the very end of the cairns for the best photographic location; you'll find a rock outcrop that makes a good foreground to add depth to this otherwise huge panorama. Use your wide angle in moderation, otherwise you'll end up with an image that doesn't carry enough visual impact. A 35mm will work well, allowing you to include enough of the valley while emphasizing the gentle curve made by the Waterpocket Fold to the south.

If you prefer to explore Upper Muley Twist, just follow the wash at the trailhead until you reach Saddle Arch on your left, at a little under two miles. This arch is not easy to spot at first, but the NPS has recently added a small sign to the right of the wash indicating the Rim trail. It is a very rough climb up but you'll reach the top in less than 30 minutes and the rim of the plateau in another 10 minutes on flat ground. From there, the trail follows the rim north for another two miles, offering spectacular views of the Waterpocket Fold.

You can either retrace your steps or do the full loop coming back through the Upper Muley Twist Narrows, which are not particularly spectacular. Caution: Upper Muley Twist gets awfully hot in summer. Take plenty of water if you want to do the full loop. You'll need minor route finding skills, following widely spaced cairns; some easy scrambling over slickrock is also required.

Time required: for Strike Valley Overlook, about 2 hours from the junction with the Burr Trail if you reach the trailhead by car; a half-day if you reach it by foot; a full day for Upper Muley Twist.

Lower Calf Creek Falls

Lower Calf Creek Falls

This delightful 5.4 mile round-trip walk follows Calf Creek upstream, inside a wide but beautiful red rock canyon, to where the trail ends at the 126-foot high falls. In my opinion, this is one of the most rewarding short hikes in Utah. The self-guided, interpretive nature trail is sandy, but mostly level and easy to follow, making it a perfect family hike. A leaflet with descriptions for the numbered stakes along the trail is available at the start of the hike; it's important to take it so you won't miss the rock art along the way. As you near the falls, the canyon narrows and the trail offers more shade. The desert varnish on the canyon walls becomes more noticeable and offers a pleasing contrast to the tall grasses and cottonwood trees trailside. At the base of the falls is a small pool, which could tempt the summer hiker with a refreshing dip.

Photo advice: a lens in the 28mm-35mm range is necessary to capture the entire falls, while a moderate telephoto will capture some interesting details. The morning will find the falls in shade while full or dappled sunlight may be present in early afternoon. The subtle and varied color of the rock and moss behind the falls is best captured without direct sunlight. In the fall, yellow leaves can grace the rock, adding a nice contrast to the scene. Watch out for wind-blown spray from the falls; protect your gear. While the falls are the main subject, don't neglect the grasses, trees and canyon walls along the way. Beaver dams along Calf Creek can create clear pools reflecting the cliffs and the sky. Avoid weekends, in the high season, when the place is swarming with locals looking for a cool spot.

Getting there: 15 miles east of Escalante and 12 miles west of Boulder on SB 12; turn off at the sign for the Calf Creek Campground. Fee required.

Time required: 3 hours for a comfortable pace and time for photography.

Nearby location: although not as spectacular as the Lower Falls, the Upper Calf Creek Falls are easily reached and provide a nice opportunity to relax in the coolness of the water on a hot day. The 2.2-miles round-trip trail is well marked by cairns and not too steep. There is a spot with very photogenic lava boulders about a third of the way down. The trail splits near the end: the upper trail to the right leads to the top of the falls with some small pools and the lower trail to the left leads to the bottom of the falls with a large pool under a shady alcove. Access to the trailhead is by a short but rough spur road located on the west side of Hwy 12, about 5.5 miles north of the Calf Creek campground, almost halfway between milepost 81 and 82.

Devil's Garden

Don't confuse this site with another of the same name located in the northern part of Arches National Park. Escalante Devil's Garden is a small site consisting of petrified sand dunes, weirdly shaped monoliths, small arches and hoodoos.

Just outside the classic Grand Circle circuit, Devil's Garden is little visited but warrants a detour because of its proximity to Escalante and the considerable photographic potential it offers. If you are spending the night in Escalante, it's possible to make a quick visit at sunrise or sunset, even though more time would definitely be warranted.

There isn't any marked trail and you can wander as you please in the Devil's Garden. However, your natural tendency will be to make a loop around these curiosities following the traces of previous visitors to the top. The spectacular petrified dunes are among the most beautiful on the Colorado Plateau and are to be found at the highest part of the site, about 1,500 feet from the parking lot. The elegant Metate Arch is the most recognizable landmark of the Garden, thanks to its double span.

Photo advice: morning light or early evening is preferred with this type of spectacular formation, but the terrain and the angles vary so it's possible to get some good shots even in the middle of the day. However, the nicest photos are taken in the morning when the Straight Cliffs are well lit in the background. Try some low shots, isolating the formations against the sky to bring out their relief as it's difficult to convey any sense of scale; some have very strange shapes, reminiscent of Easter Island statues. A 20mm works best to frame Metate Arch entirely.

Whimsical figures of the Devil's Garden

Getting there: take Hole-in-the-Rock for about 12 miles from where it branches off Scenic Byway 12; turn right on BLM 225 for another 0.5-mile to the parking lot. Except during or immediately after a violent storm, it should not present any difficulties for the ordinary passenger car until you get to Devil's Garden or the Dry Fork of Coyote Gulch about 15 miles further (see next section).

Time required: 2 hours round-trip from Escalante for a brief visit, but you could easily spend another 2 hours just taking photos. If combining this visit with the Dry Fork of Coyote Gulch, you'll need at least 6 hours.

Metate Arch

Dry Fork of Coyote Gulch & Slot Canyons

Located about 33 miles outside Escalante, the Dry Fork of Coyote Gulch is a unique opportunity to explore a couple of spectacular slot canyons and have a lot of fun, without crowds and commercial trappings. Take advantage of it now, as it is bound to change in the future.

The Dry Fork of Coyote Gulch combines several canyons: the narrows of Dry Fork proper and three slots canyons located in side drainages. These are Peek-a-Boo, Spooky and Brimstone.

When you reach the dry riverbed at the bottom of the trail coming from the car park, the narrows of Dry Fork are located immediately to the left. Though not in the same league as the more famous Buckskin Gulch narrows, they are nonetheless quite spectacular. The walls, a lovely ocher color of Navajo sandstone, are about 10 to 15 feet apart and around 70 feet high. A few minutes walking in the narrows gives those who don't want to venture into the slot canyons a chance to shoot some nice pictures.

Peek-a-Boo is an absolute must for slot canyon devotees. It's an extremely narrow and twisted passage about half a mile long, with beautiful shapes, striations and a unique double bridge. It is blessed with excellent lighting due to the low height of its Navajo sandstone walls. The slot is easy to find, only a couple hundred yards downstream from the narrows of Dry Fork. Follow the dry creek bed of Coyote Gulch to your right until you see the fault in the wall that marks the entrance of Peek-a-boo, to your left. You can only get into it by climbing up the wall, but toeholds cut in the rock will help and no special equipment is needed. Once you've overcome this part, your progress will be easier. You'll have to wriggle through a narrow hole located about 150 feet from the entrance to be able to explore the upper part of the canyon, where you can only advance one step at a time scraping the bottom of your pants. The most spectacular twists and turns are found barely 600 feet from the entrance of the canyon.

Spooky is the next slot canyon, about half a mile downstream, north of a big sand dune. It's incredibly narrow, with interesting textured walls in places and, as its name indicates, spooky. You can easily enter it from the riverbed of Coyote Gulch and a few steps are enough to give you a good idea of its appearance.

Here is a suggested loop including both Peek-a-Boo and Spooky. It requires some scrambling and route finding, and you should not attempt it if you are alone or claustrophobic! Large people should also make sure they won't get stuck at the end of the loop, which is the narrowest section. This section is near the riverbed entrance of Spooky, so it's easy to check before embarking on the loop.

Start with Peek-a-Boo, as it is easier to come back from the top of Spooky. Peek-a-Boo's slot ends up in a shallow wash; locate the cairns to your right and follow them carefully east for about half a mile until you meet Spooky's sandy wash. Follow it to the right, then proceed cautiously into the slot. This exciting little adventure requires a bit of chimneying or potential crawling on the ground, so large photo backpacks are out of the question.

With the arrival of more and more visitors since the creation of the National Monument, this two extraordinary canyons risk becoming a popular destination for lovers of the bizarre.

As for Brimstone, the third slot canyon, it is only for experienced teams of canyoneers and should be avoided by casual photographers. It is located further downstream from Spooky in Coyote Gulch, with a 10-foot drop-off which will be difficult to negotiate on the way back. Once at the mouth of the canyon, you still need to walk another mile in the sand before reaching the narrows. The slot itself is extremely narrow, deep, dark and tortuous. In 1996, a photographer got stuck in Brimstone for eight days, before being miraculously rescued! The story doesn't say whether he got any good images, but it should be enough to discourage anyone who doesn't know exactly what they're doing.

All these slot canyons supposedly harbor a dwarf species of rattlesnake. Fortunately it's not supposed to be aggressive, but you need to be careful where you step and put your hands.

Given the always present risk of flash flood, be sure to check the weather forecast at the BLM headquarters in Escalante before heading for the canyons. June may be the best month to visit, as there are less pools of water and mud and the risk of thunderstorms is statistically much lower.

**Photo advice:** Spooky is best lit around mid-day and it is way too dark at other times. Peek-a-Boo is better photographed in mid-morning or afternoon. A wide

Crawling inside Peek-a-Boo

angle is indispensable in these narrow slot canyons to capture as much as possible of the rock walls on film, as well as to maximize the depth-of-field and avoid blurring the rock walls in the foreground. A tripod is necessary to work with an opening of f/16 or f/22 with slow slide film. With 50 or 100 ISO film, which is typical of slide film, you will find yourself exposing for half a second to several seconds depending on the sunlight. Peek-a-boo's good overall lighting makes it possible to work with a hand-held camera, using ISO 400 or 800 negative film, but you'll pay the price in lack of depth-of-field. It would be ideal to have one camera body for photos taken with slow shutter speeds on a tripod and another for those candid shots of

people that the narrow canyons allow you to shoot. It's useless to carry several lenses, as there's a good chance of scraping them against the walls. If you are taking stock photographs, pay close attention to small details. In the excitement of the moment, it's easy to forget the messy footprints in the foreground, to give but one example.

**Getting there:** to reach the trailhead, follow the Hole-in-the-Rock road 14.5 miles past Devil's Garden (this is 26.5 miles from the intersection with Hwy 12) until you see a sign for Dry Fork Coyote Gulch to your left. Follow the very rough, but nevertheless passable, track (BLM 252) for a mile and a half to the parking area. Be sure to bear left at the spot where the track forks. Leaving the parking area, a trail about half a mile long descends to the dry riverbed of Coyote

Gulch. Although cairns mark the trail, it's not easy to follow. Keep your eyes constantly on the cairns.

Time required: at least 4 hours, round-trip, from Escalante if you don't dawdle and visit Devil's Garden at the same time; 6 to 7 hours, round-trip, for a more leisurely trip to both.

Twisted passage inside Peek-a-Boo

Arch just past the entrance to Peek-a-Boo

Zebra & Tunnel Slots

These two little slot canyons are fast becoming the latest craze among the "been there done that" crowd, now that Peek-a-boo and Spooky have become so popular. On my last visit there, I was stunned to find that a well-defined footpath had developed in many places along the wash. Still, you're bound to meet few souls on the 2.4-mile one-way trip down Halfway Hollow and into Harris Wash. Once at Harris Wash, take your bearings so you can easily locate Halfway Hollow upon your return, then follow the broad wash to the northwest for about 0.6-mile until you catch a glimpse of the Zebra drainage to the right. Follow it as it becomes progressively a narrow canyon and then the slot itself.

The Zebra slot is often filled with deep muddy pools, especially in wet years,

Moki marbles embedded in Zebra Canyon's lovely walls

but it can also be totally dry. Navigating through the slot is easy at first, but gets tricky toward the end when the slot narrows drastically. You'll have to do a bit of easy chimneying in order to get to the best spot, where you can photograph the beautifully-striated narrow walls with *moki marbles* encrusted in the delicate sandstone. The best time to photograph the slot is in early to mid-morning.

Your next destination is the Tunnel slot. The tunnel, which is about 80 feet long and ends as abruptly as it begins, gets its name from the fact that it is almost closed on top. There is plenty of room to move standing up and no obstructions, except for seasonal pools of mud. The normal way to get there calls for retracing your step to the spot where you came in from Halfway Hollow. Continue for another mile in Harris Wash until you find the wide entrance to the Tunnel drainage to your left. From there it is only 0.3-mile to the slot. If you do it this way, you are pretty much guaranteed to find your way to the Tunnel slot, but you are looking at about one hour of walking in the Harris Wash with not much to see. An alternate solution is to go cross-country over what I call the "Sea of slick-rock", turning left as you exit the Zebra slot on the first wide opening and climbing on the gently-sloping slickrock, to reach the Tunnel slot directly at its narrow back entrance. Although this cross-country walk is short, a topo map and some route-finding skills are mandatory. Return to Halfway Hollow via Harris Wash.

Getting there: take Hole In The Rock Road for a little over 7.5 miles until you find a tiny spur road to your right a couple of hundred yards past a cattle guard. This spur road leads to a corral and has plenty of space to park on the side. Cross Hole-in-the-Rock Road, descend into Halfway Hollow and follow it for about an hour until you reach Harris Wash.

Out of Egypt

The Egypt Bench serves as the entry point to some of the most remote and beautiful canyons in the Southwest. The Escalante drainage has dozens of wonderful canyons to explore and photograph, all of them somehow tributaries to the beautiful Escalante River, the last river to be named in the continental U.S.

Walking these canyons is generally easy and is done mostly on sandy ground with occasional wading, making it a relaxing experience. It requires a good topo map, such as _Trails Illustrated's Canyons of the Escalante_ and a good guidebook such as Rudi Lambrechtse's _Hiking the Escalante_, among others (see Selected Bibliography in Appendix). If you wish to bench-walk between two canyons for fun or to save time, you'll need a compass and some route finding skills; if you prefer a GPS, be sure you know how to use it and carry spare batteries. You'll also need a hat, sunscreen and plenty of water. Fresh water can usually be found on the ground in many of the canyons, but it needs to be filtered. Some springs also exist. The Egypt Bench, reached on BLM 240, as well as the Harris Wash (BLM 220) and Early Weed Bench trailhead areas are known for their Carmel formation, while canyons are mostly Navajo and Wingate sandstone. In late spring and through summer, cottonwoods explode with green foliage, creating extraordinary contrast with the red canyon walls and wonderful photographic opportunities. There are endless ways to play with reflections in water holes. Some of the most popular canyons to explore and photograph are Harris Wash, Choprock and Twenty Five Mile Wash, all accessible from side roads off the Hole in the Rock road. Upper Harris Wash is one of the most easily accessible trailheads (at the end of BLM 220, 11 miles from Hwy 12) and makes an excellent first-time experience for a few hours or a day. Choprock is a fantastic destination with many nice narrows to explore but requires at least three days from Egypt (same trailhead as Neon Canyon, explored in the next section). There is an immense and beautiful alcove inside Choprock, a few hundred yards from the confluence with the Escalante, that makes a great base camp for the leisurely exploration of miles and miles of the Escalante river and side canyons. All the canyons on the left bank of the Escalante are located inside Glen Canyon N.R.A. and therefore require a backcountry permit if you stay overnight.

It's fun to shoot reflections in the Escalante Canyons

Neon Canyon

Neon Canyon and the so-called Golden Cathedral are part of the Escalante drainage and are accessible from the Egypt area; however, they merit their own special mention in view of their great beauty and interest to the photographer.

Located inside the lower section of Neon Canyon, the Golden Cathedral is a tall grotto of Wingate sandstone, with two large collapsed potholes on its roof. Wingate is a glorious reddish variety of sandstone often striated with desert varnish, giving it an almost animal fur's-like appearance. The superb light-reflecting properties of the Wingate confer a fantastic red glow to the grotto. Beams of light create whimsical spotlights on the dark-green water at the bottom of the grotto. This is without a doubt one of the most spectacular sights of the Southwest.

However, as with some of the sites located in the Escalante River drainage, it requires considerable effort and preparation to visit. Although, under optimum circumstances, a fit individual can do the trip in one very long day, it is more rewarding to do it as an overnighter or as part of a multi-day backpack into the Escalante canyons.

With time on your side, you'll be able to relax on the soft sand at the edge of the Golden Cathedral and to take pictures at different intervals for best results.

Photo advice: you may want to pare down the amount of photographic equipment you'll take into the canyons, especially if you backpack. The best time to photograph the Golden Cathedral is between 11AM and 2PM depending on the season. You'll want to wait until the entire grotto is in the shade before photographing it. The reflected light from the canyon walls upstream from the grotto is what bestows the glorious orange glow to your images.

Getting there: follow the Hole in the Rock road from Highway 12 about 17 miles. Turn left on BLM 240 toward Egypt Bench and park at the end of the 9-mile dirt road which has steep grades but is usually passable in passenger cars. Walk down the cairned slickrock trail toward Fence Canyon, which you can see in the distance. It takes a bit of easy route finding, but you should nonetheless arm yourself with map and compass. Follow Fence Canyon to the confluence with the Escalante. As you approach Fence Canyon you'll find a trail to the left that bypasses Fence. Fence is generally very muddy. You'll reach the Escalante at the ruins of an old cowboy camp. There are interesting petroglyphs just past the ruins. Wade across the Escalante and follow it downstream, alternating between wading and taking shortcuts on land until you find Neon Canyon. It is impossible to give precise directions as the landscape changes every year depending on water level, but you cannot miss Neon Canyon. At the confluence, turn left and follow the canyon for a little under a mile until you reach the fabulous Golden Cathedral.

Time permitting, you should make it a point to explore the top of Neon Canyon, above and beyond the Golden Cathedral. To do so, backtrack to the confluence with the Escalante. A couple of hundred yards before you reach the confluence, you'll notice to the right a slickrock slope with a forgiving angle.

Climb it and you'll find a good trail on top. Follow it to the right until you get past the potholes of the Golden Cathedral. You'll have a magnificent view of the top of the Cathedral and the verdant streambed of upper Neon Canyon.

Special advisory: one factor likely to determine if and when you'll be able to make the trip is the water level of the Escalante. In a rainy year, you might find it difficult to cross Fence Canyon and wade into the Escalante during springtime

The Golden Cathedral in Neon Canyon

and you may have to wait until early summer to do this trip. Before planning a trip to the Golden Cathedral, inquire about the water level by calling the Escalante Ranger Station or you may find yourself wading into frigid water up to your chest. Any kind of shoes will work for wading. I recommend using a pair of woolen socks to avoid blisters and ward off hypothermia if the water is cold. A pair of polarized sunglasses will help spot treacherous rocks under water, as well as deep pools. Finally, don't forget to get your backcountry permit at the Escalante Ranger station before you go.

Broken Bow Arch

The hike down Willow Gulch to Broken Bow Arch passes through one of the most beautiful and varied canyons in the Escalante. The highlight of the hike is the massive Broken Bow Arch, so named by Escalante schoolteacher Edison Alvey in 1930 when he found a broken Indian bow beneath the arch.

The 4-mile round-trip hike begins on a well-worn path behind the trail register. As you descend, look for a formation shaped like a graduation cap. Upon reaching the wash, head down canyon. The first set of narrows can be bypassed by staying high, on the right (south) side of the canyon. The wash quickly broadens but soon constricts into passable narrows. Shortly, a side canyon appears on the right; consider saving its exploration for the return trip if time permits and continue straight ahead in the main wash. The second canyon encountered is Willow Gulch. As you approach the confluence, you'll notice that the scenery begins to change. Willows and cottonwood appear as the water starts to flow. Bear to the left and follow Willow Gulch down the canyon; it soon widens into a lovely area for camping or picnicking on the large benches, particularly on the left side of the stream.

As you proceed down canyon you may either follow the streambed or the well-worn bypass trails which crisscross it. After a few more twists and turns and a prominent bend in the canyon, Broken Bow Arch comes into view.

Photo advice: depending on the time of day, climb the hills to the east or west of the arch to get the right angle depending on the light. While the arch is the main attraction, the willow, cottonwood and beautifully streaked canyon walls along the way also make good subject matter.

Getting there: to reach the Willow Gulch trailhead, follow Hole in the Rock road about 43 miles from Hwy 12 (1 mile past Sooner Wash in the flat area of Sooner Bench). BLM 276 goes diagonally to the left, leading to the parking area in 1.4 miles. This dirt road could be difficult for a passenger car.

Time required: 1-1/2 to 2 hours to reach the trailhead by car from Escalante. For the hike alone plan on at least 3 hours; more if exploring side canyons and photographing extensively. Including the return trip to Escalante, this hike takes a full day, but can be combined with a visit to the Devil's Garden. For a more leisurely pace consider camping in Willow Gulch. A free permit is available at the

Broken Bow Arch (photo by Scott Walton)

trailhead and many lovely camping spots are located only 30 minutes into the hike, under trees and next to the bubbling stream.

Escalante Petrified Forest

As the name indicates, this Utah State Park was once an ancient forest engulfed millions of years ago by an inland sea. You'll find many multicolored petrified tree trunks as the trail reaches the plateau. Because of its close proximity to the town of Escalante, a quick visit is easy to include in your plans and should not be missed if you've never been to Petrified National Forest Nat'l Park. The moderately difficult Wide Hollow trail winds about a mile through juniper and pinion pines before reaching the petrified trees and a viewpoint overlooking Escalante. The Sleeping Rainbow trail spur adds about 3/4 mile to your visit. It's a bit of an up and down climb and footing can be tricky in places, but it's a worthwhile detour to take for close-ups of the most beautiful and colorful petrified trunks.

Photo advice: to get good color, it's best to photograph the petrified wood away from direct sunlight. If the sun shines brightly, look for pieces of wood shaded by junipers or improvise some kind of reflector. Other than the large quantity of petrified trees, you'll find a forest of pygmy junipers and ancient dwarf pines that make for interesting photos.

Getting there: located next to the lovely Wide Hollow Reservoir, on a side road just west of Escalante.

Time required: you'll need 1-1/2 hour for a comfortable visit. There is not much to see near the parking lot, except for some sample trunks for display, so if you don't have time or don't care to walk, don't bother with this detour.

Hell's Backbone

The Hell's Backbone Road is one of the most scenic and enjoyable drives in the Southwest. Despite a brief hair-raising section near the top, it is easily driven by passenger car when the weather is dry and before snow sets in. It also provides access to one of the most outstanding wilderness areas in the Southwest: the Box-Death Hollow Wilderness. The road—built in the Thirties by the Civilian Conservation Corps—is 44-mile long from Boulder to Escalante and takes about three hours to drive, including short stops. If you are based in Boulder and do not want to do the whole loop, the trip to Hell's Backbone Bridge and back in only 28 miles. The section just before and after the bridge has dramatic views of the Death Hollow Wilderness with its sheer pink Navajo sandstone cliffs contrasting with the green alpine environment (you are at over 9,000 feet elevation). This is an outstanding photo spot during the last hour before sunset. If you do the whole loop, do not miss the short side trip to lovely Posey Lake, which has a nice overlook on the lake. The road widens on the Escalante side and you are treated to an outstanding display of checkerboard sandstone stretching for several miles on the east side of the road as it nears Escalante. The Lower Box Trailhead provides access to The Box, a beautiful canyon tucked in between high sandstone cliffs.

Death Hollow

So you're tired of crowds and want to have a little canyon paradise all to yourself: try Death Hollow. Contrary to its ominous-sounding name, it is one of the most verdant canyons you'll ever see, thanks to its wide-apart white and pink Navajo sandstone walls and pure mountain water. Wildlife and vegetation are remarkably abundant and people are few.

You may find it strange that I'm touting this area, at the risk of attracting the very crowds that would mar the feeling of solitude of Death Hollow. Not a chance, because Death Hollow is so hard to get in and out of—requiring a multi-day backpack and constant wading—that it is one of the least visited narrows in the Colorado plateau and is likely to remain so.

Before planning a trip to the Escalante and Death Hollow, inquire about the water level at the Ranger Station or you may find yourself wading into frigid water up to your chest. Refer to the Neon Canyon section for recommended equipment for wading. When walking on the banks, watch for poison ivy.

Death Hollow

Getting there: Death Hollow is a small tributary of the Escalante, located north of the town of Escalante in the Box-Death Hollow Wilderness. It can be hiked from the top by starting from the Hell's Backbone Road as a multi-day canyoneering adventure or it can be reached more leisurely from the Escalante River trailhead, 13 miles east of Escalante, by walking upstream to the confluence with Death Hollow.

Time required: 3 to 4 days. You'll need a day just to get to the confluence of the Escalante and Death Hollow. You can then wade your way through the canyon for several miles or until you encounter drop-offs that require technical equipment. If you are physically very fit, there is a way to do a short one-day incursion into Death Hollow via a sneak route, requiring that you scramble down, and then up, in excess of 1000 feet of fairly vertical canyon walls. Unless you are very experienced, I recommend that you locate a qualified person to guide you into the canyon because it is dangerous to attempt this difficult route by yourself. Instead, why not take the leisurely route, with or without a local out-fitter, and enjoy a wonderfully relaxing trip. This will allow you to carry more photographic equipment and come back with better images.

Kodachrome Basin State Park

This little Utah State Park has some very interesting formations of Entrada sandstone, but it is the sand pipes—spectacular rock columns forming surreal fingers pointing to the sky—that give esthetic and geologic originality to the place. The columns are cut in a beige colored rock. Large Entrada sandstone monoliths take on a spectacular red at sunset, superbly complementing this panorama. Campsites are available, but the park has become extremely popular in the last few years and you must make reservations for summer or holiday camping. Lots of easy trails ranging from a half mile to 3 miles will take you among the formations. Do not miss the short drive to Chimney Rock—the biggest sand pipe anywhere—and to Shakespeare Arch Nature trail, a short half mile trail leading to a lovely little arch discovered in 1976.

Photo advice: leave the car at the small car park before the campground and follow the trails. The main paved Nature Trail is marked with several informa-tion signs and takes only a quarter of an hour to walk. It's full of interesting views of the finger-like formations mentioned above. For a better view of the park, from the same car park but on the other side of the road, follow the 1.5 mile long

A sand pipe

Angels Palace trail and its side spur on the plateau, offering good bird's eye views of this area. A few hundred yards south, you can also follow the 1.5 mile long Grand Parade trail, which passes by the more spectacular monoliths.

The park is magnificent at sunset when the ocher sandstone walls become blood red. It certainly deserves its name.

Getting there: from Scenic Byway 12, angle south to Cannonville exit (on your right coming from Bryce)

Kodachrome Basin at dusk

and follow Cottonwood Canyon Road for 7 miles; the road is now paved all the way to the campground.

Time required: from Hwy 12, 3 hours round-trip including about 2-1/2 hours to tour the park if you're doing all the described hikes.

Cottonwood Canyon Road

This road, which follows the fantastic Cockscomb fault for the most part, is arguably one of the most interesting Scenic Backways in Utah. It is usually easily traveled by cars, but large recreational vehicles should avoid it. During springtime and the monsoon season, you should stop for information in Kanab or Escalante before embarking, as heavy rains can make the road impassable. It can also be very sandy in summer, before the monsoon. Signs will warn you not to take this route if rain is threatening. This is not an empty warning. After a heavy thunderstorm, the route can become a muddy morass in just a few minutes and trap any vehicle for hours. A few years back, the road remained closed for several months after the Paria River destroyed large chunks of embankment. In its current form, the road has one very narrow section that has been bulldozed on a sandy cliff. Exercise caution there, as people have a tendency to drive a bit too fast on this well-graded road.

If conditions are favorable, which is most of the time, this route is truly enchanting. Don't count on using Cottonwood Road as a shortcut, it is a place where you should take your time. Many interesting spots border Cottonwood Canyon Road and you'll want to stop often to explore and photograph, easily stretching the 2 hours it takes to drive it in a hurry into a much longer time. It's possible to camp anywhere along the road since Grand Staircase-Escalante National Monument is administered by the BLM, and their policy concerning camping in the wild is very liberal.

There's beautiful scenery all along this route: a high plateau to the north, in the center a splendid valley of spectacular formations bordered by cottonwood trees, and colorful badlands in the south. I'll describe the various landmarks and side trips along the road in a north to south direction.

Grosvenor Arch

The first point of interest after Kodachrome Basin is Round Valley Draw, an extremely photogenic slot canyon. It is difficult to access unless you have a 4WD vehicle and a bit of experience in chimneying. You'll need a short rope to lower your camera bag into this slot canyon. The slot begins close to the car park, but most people prefer following the crack for about 300 yards and entering by an easier route at the cairned spot. To reach the draw, make a right on BLM 422 marked Rush Beds, about 7 miles from the Kodachrome Basin turnoff, and follow it for about 1.5-mile near the point where it meets the draw. This road is relatively smooth, but the tracks are very deep and you could become high-centered if driving a passenger car. Exploring this pastel-colored slot canyon takes two to four hours depending on where and when you decide to turn back and whether you want to tackle the big choke stones downstream.

The advice for shooting in slot canyons found in the Introduction chapter applies to Round Valley Draw. When going to Round Valley Draw, do not make the mistake of turning right on the Slickrock Bench Road after the cattle guard. This road leads to the mouth of Hackberry Canyon, visible far below a steep slope-unless, of course, you're planning a foray into Hackberry. From the

Hackberry trailhead, a trail leads down a very steep scree slope to the junction of Hackberry Canyon and Round Valley Draw, but it is much easier to enter and exit Round Valley Draw from the previously mentioned Rush Beds Road. The Hackberry trail continues on for 18 miles until it meets Cottonwood Canyon Road almost opposite BLM Road 430.

Returning to the main road, about 9 miles from the Kodachrome Basin turnoff, you'll soon come to Grosvenor Arch, a spectacular double arch towering high above the ground and well worth the detour. There is a sign marking the well-graded 1-mile BLM 440 on the left. The area around the arch is developed, with restrooms, picnic table and an asphalted trail to the bottom of the arch.

Almost every angle guarantees a good picture of Grosvenor Arch. There is a great angle from the very bottom, shooting straight up with a very wide-angle lens. Late afternoon light is best overall, but early morning works well too, with the roofs of the two spans basked in golden backlight.

About 4 miles past the intersection with the side road to Grosvenor Arch, you'll want to stop at a saddle on a high ridge with extremely colorful badlands on the east side of the road; this is one of the best photographic spots on the Scenic Backway and you could easily spend several hours there.

On the west side of the road, going down, this spot is also the upper entrance to the Cottonwood Wash Narrows. These narrows are only moderately spectac-

Serrated ridge of the Cockscomb fault seen from Cottonwood Canyon Road

ular but they have the advantage of being close to the road. You can also enter from the south, about a mile downstream, from an easily located car park on the right side of the road. From here, follow the footpath crossing the wash and leading to the lower entrance. About 300 yards from the trailhead, to the left, there is an interesting sandstone cliff with many intricate patterns.

Great scenery abounds on Cottonwood Canyon Road

Continuing the road to the south, the serrated ridges of the Cockscomb monocline come into view from a low pass. Park on the side of the road, below the badlands hill to your right, for a great telephoto shot compressing the perspective of the monocline. This is best photographed in the morning.

As you near the southern mouth of Hackberry Canyon, to your right, you'll see an impressive group of white limestone bluffs with shades of purple sticking out at an impossible angle.

The road now levels off inside the fault. One major problem you'll soon notice as you search for photo opportunities, is the almost constant presence of electrical lines that really mar the landscape.

About 25 miles from the Kodachrome Basin turnoff, I suggest that you drive up BLM 430 to the top of the Cockscomb, from where you'll have a fantastic birds-eye view of the fault. This makes a great photo looking north, preferably in the morning, but late afternoon will work too. Looking west across the fault, you'll see the strange cross-bedding of Yellow Rock and, in the distance, will catch a glimpse of Mollie's Nipple and No Man's Mesa. BLM 430 is extremely steep and can be a bit intimidating, but it is not that difficult to drive as far as the crest, which is less than a mile away from Cottonwood Canyon Road. I do not recommend that you continue on BLM 430 unless you have a high-clearance vehicle and have inquired about the road's condition at the BLM office in Kanab or Escalante.

Near the junction between Cottonwood Rd and BLM Road 430, you can climb to little visited Yellow Rock, a vast expanse of colorful slickrock with a large amount of yellow—as the name implies—but also many patches of beautiful reddish rock and some spectacular cross-bedding reminiscent of the Coyote Buttes. The 360° view from the top of Yellow Rock is simply awesome: you can see the colorful formations of the Cockscomb monocline, the badlands above Old Paria, Mollie's Nipple and No Man's Mesa, Hackberry Canyon, Temple Crag, and even Powell Point in the distance. This is an outstanding photographic destination. Late afternoon is recommended to bring out the warm tones of the sandstone on top and the various colors of the formations all around.

To get there, park at the junction with BLM Road 430 and aim west toward the mouth of Hackberry Canyon. You don't necessarily have to find a trail as it is easy to cross the few hundred yards of brush that separate you from the bed of Cottonwood Wash. You'll find the Yellow Rock Trail inside the first drainage approximately 300 yards south of the mouth of Hackberry. The very steep and slippery trail goes straight up on the right side of that drainage. This part of the trail is not for everybody and, if you attempt it, you should be extremely cautious. Once you reach the first saddle after a 15-minute climb, turn left and it becomes fairly level until you reach the bottom of Yellow Rock. Then, ascend cautiously on the slickrock slope to the very top at the southern edge of the rock.

**Getting there:** from SB 12, angle south in Cannonville exit (on the right when coming from Bryce) and follow the signs for Kodachrome Basin SP and Cottonwood Canyon Scenic Backway (BLM 400). After leaving Kodachrome Basin to your left, continue straight ahead on the gravel road.

From US 89, you'll find Cottonwood Canyon Road about halfway between Page and Kanab. It starts near milepost 18, about 4 miles past Churchwells when coming from Page and about 2 miles past the Paria Contact Station turnoff when coming from Kanab.

Time required: between 2 and 5 hours depending on how often you want to stop. Set aside a full day if you want to explore Round Valley Draw and the Cottonwood Narrows and drive up BLM 430 or hike to Yellow Rock.

The Kaiparowits Plateau

The Kaiparowits Plateau forms the central section of the monument. It is a vast, untamed area—perhaps the most remote in the continental U.S. It is crossed longitudinally by Smokey Mountain Road, a 78-mile graded dirt road connecting Escalante to Big Water on US 89. Below the surface lie immense reserves of coal, which, at times, have attracted intense interest from the energy companies. Attempts to mine the coal were initially thwarted by the costly logistics of transporting it from such a remote location and were almost permanently put to rest by the creation of the monument.

One area of particular interest to photographers are the exceptionally colorful badlands at the base of the Kelly Grade. You will be hard-pressed to find more colorful badlands anywhere. The Kelly Grade can be reached with minimum effort from Page in about 1-1/2 hours. Another interesting sight is the Smokey Hollow road, which has colorful formations with a rare variety of red sandstone, greenish Mancos shale such as the one seen at Nipple Bench and streaks of black coal. Unfortunately, this road is seldom graded and is often in such poor condition that it is too risky to take due to deep sandy patches. Each year, several visitors have to be rescued at great cost, so inquire about conditions at the Dam beforehand. Further north, the Burning Coal Beds are a mildly interesting phenomenon: underground coal beds slowly burning, sending up fumes sometimes visible from the road. A trip to these two interesting places can be easily combined with a visit to Alstrom Point/Romana Mesa (described in the Around Page chapter of Volume 2). The rest of the road to Escalante is mostly devoid of interest and the entire trip from Page takes about 5 hours, with several difficult passages. Your time will be much better spent exploring Cottonwood Canyon Road.

Getting there: from Big Water, follow the directions for Alstrom Point in Volume 2. At the sign with the slanted roof, leave BLM 330 to the left and, a half-mile further, continue left on BLM 300 going toward the cliffs and the Kelly Grade. This road is not recommended for passenger cars and is a definite no-no if you go all the way to Escalante. ✿

Wintertime along the Fremont River

Chapter 7

CAPITOL REEF

The Castle

CAPITOL REEF

This extraordinary park is often overlooked by visitors to the Southwest and isn't heavily frequented outside of summer. I see three explanations for this: its geographic location, which makes it less accessible than its better-known neighbors of Bryce and Arches; the limited amount of paved roads inside the park; and the fact that there are no well-known icons that would-be visitors can readily identify.

This trend is gradually being reversed due in part to the added presence of Grand Staircase-Escalante Nat'l Monument to the south and a surge of new motels built just outside the park, in Torrey and Hanksville.

Nevertheless, Capitol Reef is one of the jewels of Utah, thanks to its unmatched geological variety, fantastic scenery, surprisingly rich vegetation and lack of crowds. But be forewarned! This park only reveals a small part of itself to the casual visitor. Sure, you can cross it in the course of a few hours, including a short incursion on the famous Scenic Drive, but there is plenty more great scenery awaiting off the beaten track. Plan on at least two days in the park because you need to hike its many trails and explore remote areas with a 4WD vehicle to fully appreciate it.

One of the principal attractions of Capitol Reef is the great geological diversity of its landscape and sedimentary layers. This translates into an extraordinary palette of hues and textures, great for visitor and photographer alike: cliffs, ridges, domes, canyons, monoliths, badlands come in a huge diversity of colors, which become even more striking during the golden hour. You can better appreciate this exceptional relief with a bit of knowledge of the paleo-environment of

Capitol Reef and the forces of erosion which are constantly at work exposing them. Free brochures are available for travelers at the Visitor Center. Don't miss this opportunity as Capitol Reef, more than any other park, gives you tremendous insight into the geologic history of the Colorado Plateau—the essential ingredient behind these landscapes that we so much admire today.

Torrey, a small town at the west entrance of the park, makes a perfect base for your explorations. Over the course of the last few years, Torrey has seen a great deal of expansion: where in the 1980's there wasn't a single motel, now there are almost a dozen vying for your business. The beautiful oasis of Fruita, inside the park, is especially nice if you are car camping or want to pitch a tent. During autumn and springtime, it is one of the most pleasant campgrounds anywhere.

Panorama Point

Coming from Torrey on UT 24, you discover a superlative road, bordered to the north by impressive cliffs that become even more spectacular during the golden hour, mornings and evenings. Among the formations at the base of the cliffs are Chimney Rock and the Castle. Chimney Rock isn't really awesome in itself, but it photographs nicely in the afternoon from the parking lot, when the dark red Moenkopi formation capped by the white Shinarump sandstone really stands out. As for the Castle, it offers a remarkable collection of sedimentary layers that can be enjoyed right by the side of the road.

One of the best spots to photograph this area is Panorama Point, located about 4 miles past the west entrance of the park and 3 miles before the Visitor Center. From this promontory, you get a splendid panoramic view of the western part of the park with Capitol Dome, the Castle and the Henry Mountains in the distance. A sign claims that this spot is the least polluted in the United States and that, on a clear day, you can see over a hundred and thirty miles! Even though the validity of this claim has become doubtful in this day and age, you'll certainly rejoice in the fact that you can see at least 60 miles on most days.

In the morning, Panorama Point affords an excellent view to the west in the direction of Torrey. Toward the east, a 100 to 200mm telephoto lens works great for capturing Capitol Dome and the Henry Mountains in the afternoon.

Continuing another mile on the dirt road south of Panorama Point, you can take the short 1-mile round-trip foot trail to aptly named Sunset Point, which offers a fantastic view in late afternoon. You can use either a normal lens to photograph the various geological strata of the reef or a medium telephoto to capture the shadows of the formations on the red cliffs. From the same parking lot, a very short trail leads to the Goosenecks of Sulphur Creek, a promontory above a deep canyon that is unfortunately difficult to photograph because of the shadows, although mornings are better. Nothing particularly awe-inspiring or to compare with the "big guys" (Dead Horse Point, Horseshoe Bend, and Goosenecks State Park), but it's interesting to note that these goosenecks are cut through the same layer of sedimentary rock as that of the White Rim of Island in the Sky fame, a formation rarely seen in that section of the plateau.

Fruita Oasis

In all seasons, Fruita is an oasis where it's nice to relax between two rocky landscapes. This old Mormon colony is located on the banks of the Fremont River and has abundant vegetation, contrasting heavily with the surrounding desert. Near the Visitor Center, several cabins containing pioneer-era artifacts are visible from the road and warrant a brief stop.

The historic orchards are opened from June through October for public harvesting. Inside the designated orchards, you can eat as much as you want; however, you pay for the fruits you take outside. The vast grassy area adjoining the pleasant picnic grounds with its peaches, wisteria and jacarandas allows you to get some great shots when they're in flower (March and April). The cottonwoods bordering the Fremont around Fruita are magnificent in spring and fall.

Sulphur Creek, which empties into the Fremont River at Fruita, is a lovely walk. Just behind the Visitor Center, a short footpath quickly brings you to a shallow crossing and a series of lovely pools.

The Fremont Gorge Overlook Trailhead is located near the Blacksmith Shop. This little-known walk provides a great view of the Castle from atop a high mesa. A mid-range telephoto is perfect to frame the castle and surroundings. After a mile or so, the Castle really opens up and, at about a mile and a half, you'll get an optimum view in mid-morning or mid-afternoon.

The Scenic Drive

The Scenic Drive, which begins a bit after you pass Fruita, offers some spectacular views of geological features such as Grand Wash, Fern's Nipple, the Slickrock Divide and the Egyptian Temple, all this along an 8-mile long paved road. Get yourself one of the mini-guides to the Scenic Drive at the entrance and stop at the various landmarks, following the interesting explanations it contains on the sedimentary origins of the park.

After making sure that no flash flood danger is in the forecast, continue your drive on a good dirt road winding down about 2 miles between the tall cliffs of Capitol Gorge. This short but spectacular road is passable to any passenger car in good weather. A 2-mile round-trip foot trail leads toward the end of the canyon, passing by the Pioneer Register and the Waterpocket Tanks (the latter are more interesting when water is present). The 4-mile round-trip hike to the Golden Throne is also worthwhile, but more strenuous.

Although it doesn't give the same impression of isolation as some of the narrower and less visited canyons described in this book, Capitol Gorge is well worth the trip, much as its longer and deeper counterpart: Grand Wash.

The entire Scenic Road is especially photogenic while driving back from Capitol Gorge in late afternoon. That's when you get the best light on the sensuous, multicolored sandstone walls and layers of Capitol Ridge. Less than a mile past the spur to Grand Wash, locate the last little hill before the road starts its descent toward Fruita, park on the right, and enjoy one of the most photogenic

Early morning on the Scenic Drive   *Scenic Drive near Grand Wash*

views in the Southwest. You'll be looking at badlands topped by pillars and cliffs to the right, with the narrow road winding down spectacularly toward the oasis and the Castle in the background. You can use a wide range of lenses to capture either grand scenics or small details of this beautiful landscape.

Hickman Bride & the Navajo Knobs

Following UT 24 from the Visitor Center in the direction of Hanksville, the Fremont presents a festival of colors with a number of orchards. The countless tamarisk trees lining the riverbed are particularly photogenic in autumn.

Shortly before reaching the Hickman Bridge trailhead, stop at the Fremont petroglyphs pullout, as well as at the very moving Mormon schoolhouse. The Park Service has recently constructed a boardwalk that makes it easier to observe and photograph the ancient Fremont glyphs—which are unfortunately badly weather-damaged.

The self-guided nature trail to Hickman Bridge is a short and easy 2 miles round-trip, but don't expect too much photographically, as the bridge is some-

Navajo Dome

what ensconced below a ridge. Press on toward the Rim Overlook Trail, branching from the previous trail after a few hundreds yards, for a series of interesting sights. After about 0.25-mile, Pectol's Pyramid comes into view on the other side of the Fremont; its unique shape makes for an interesting picture. Continue walking another 0.25-mile or so past the sign until you get the best pyramid shape. Pectol's Pyramid can be photographed in the early morning; however, only its left face will be well lit. Mid-to-late afternoon offers better light. Standard focal length to short telephoto will yield the best results. About a 0.5-mile further on the trail, you'll be able to catch excellent views of Navajo Dome to the right with a standard lens to short telephoto.

At the end of the trail, 2.25-miles from the parking lot, the Rim Overlook provides a bird's eye view of Fruita, the Fremont Valley, and the Goosenecks of the Sulphur, but it's a bit too expansive to yield a compelling picture. Continuing toward Navajo Knobs for another strenuous 2.25-miles, you'll be rewarded with a 360° vista of the valley, the domes and the Waterpocket fold.

If you've done this strenuous hike in summer, you may want to stop for a dip in the deep pool located below a small waterfall on the left side of the road, about 4 miles further east on UT 24 past Behunin Cabin. Watch for the strong undertow and, of course, don't venture in the pool in bad weather or during a thunderstorm! A picture of this waterfall was used in the Introduction chapter to illustrate the tremendous power of flash floods in the Southwest.

The Waterpocket Fold

This strange and spectacular geologic formation is unfortunately less spectacular when seen from the ground than in the superb aerial photograph that decorates the National Park Service brochure. But it still warrants a detour if you can afford the pretty full day that it will take to drive the 125-mile loop described below. Note that this tour—one third of it on dirt roads—encompasses the superb Burr Trail as well as Strike Valley Overlook, both described in the Grand Staircase-Escalante chapter.

You can get to the Waterpocket Fold by way of the Notom-Bullfrog road which starts off UT 24, 9 miles east of the Visitor Center. This road is paved along the first 6 miles and well maintained thereafter, so it's suitable to passenger cars in dry weather. However, there is a wash before Sandy Ranch that can present problems after heavy rains or when it's icy in winter.

You get a very good view of the Henry Mountains to the east and the strange nipples of Capitol Dome to the west from the top of the hill, just after you reach the unpaved part of the road. The Waterpocket Fold doesn't really become visible until after you pass the spur leading to the Cedar Mesa campground, about 22 miles from the junction with UT 24. Even there, this extraordinary geological phenomenon remains a bit disappointing when seen from the Notom-Bullfrog road, especially in comparison to aerial photos.

Instead you may want to concentrate on details in the landscape. This area contains amazingly colorful stripes of tuffa, lining up the badlands on the east side of the road. They are best photographed in early morning, when still in the shade, or in late afternoon. However, to really bring out the color, nothing beats an overcast or rainy day; just remember to eliminate the sky from your image.

Badlands along the Notom-Bullfrog Road

About a dozen miles further, you'll come to the well-marked junction leading west to the Burr Trail. As you reach the base of the fold, the dirt road climbs toward the Escalante Plateau in a series of steep and spectacular twists and turns carved in the flank of the hill. These switchbacks may be difficult or even impassable in a passenger car when the road is weather-damaged.

Shortly after the switchbacks, you'll come to the 4WD road leading to Strike

Waterpocket Fold Badlands

Valley Overlook or Upper Muley Twist (refer to the Grand Staircase-Escalante chapter). These are the only points from which you can capture the true expanse of the Waterpocket fold. After another few miles, the Burr Trail becomes paved and leads to Boulder, where it joins UT 12. You can then drive north on UT 12 and west on UT 24 to complete the loop.

Instead of turning on the Burr Trail, you could go on the Waterpocket Fold road all the way to the Bullfrog Marina, where you can cross Lake Powell by ferry to Hall's Crossing and either descend towards Monument Valley or climb back up towards Moab. To go south on the ferry, refer to the Cedar Mesa chapter.

Introduction to Cathedral Valley

Cathedral Valley with its huge monoliths and panoramic vistas is, in my view, one of the most remarkable spots on the planet. An incomparable majesty emanates from the place. Its remoteness and the rare presence of other members of our species make you feel deeply privileged to find yourself in such an untrammeled natural sanctuary. This feeling is even more prevalent if you get a chance to camp at the remote campground in Upper Cathedral Valley. From there you can have the whole valley to yourself during the golden hour. Note that dispersed low-impact backcountry camping is permitted on BLM land just outside the park for even more solitude—although I am yet to encounter another visitor at the remote campground in many trips to this valley.

Happily or unhappily, it is not easy to visit and most visitors to the park abstain from venturing there. Few people choose to drive the 57-mile Cathedral Valley loop crossing many distinctive parts of the valley; the drive requires a minimum of six hours to be thoroughly enjoyed. The Cathedral Valley road is a perfect example of a "feasible" road that's nevertheless risky because of its fragility and isolation. First, the road is only feasible if you have a high clearance vehicle. It is not advised to drive the whole road in a regular car—and even less so in a

Upper Cathedral Valley monoliths

camper. The state of the road can vary a lot, depending on whether you are traveling before or after rains or when the bulldozer resurfaces the road, once a year.

Never set out until you have first inquired of the rangers or one of the local residents as to the condition of the road. The rangers will systematically discourage visitors from adventuring down this and other Cathedral Valley roads in ordinary cars and they do this with good reason: each year visitors get stuck in the mud or a rut that suddenly appeared from nowhere. As a general rule, a 4x4 tow-truck costs $150 an hour from the time it leaves the garage. The cost of the operation can easily reach more than $1,500 to bail you out.

Always check the weather forecast, as some clay-based parts of the road can be impassable to any vehicle when wet. Fill up your fuel tank; take a lot of water and some food, just in case. Don't forget to buy the excellent booklet entitled *Self-guided auto-tour of Cathedral Valley* at the Visitor Center in Fruita. When used in combination with the park map, it is sufficient to do the main loop road. As the mileage of each stop and intersection is precisely recorded, you should encounter no surprises if you stay on the road and check your odometer regularly. However, if you want to drive other roads branching from the main loop road, you'll definitely need to get a topographic map before setting out. This is true of all the roads described below, outside of the main loop road. All these roads include many branching secondary roads that don't show on the large-scale maps and it's easy to set off down the wrong path. Please take this suggestion seriously. You'll often find yourself consulting the topo map. You can get one of these at the Visitor Center.

Once all these precautions are taken, you can start the loop from the River Ford, located 11.7 miles east of the Visitor Center on UT 24 or 7 miles west of Caineville. The reason I suggest starting from River Ford is that it's better to cross the ford at the beginning of the loop rather than having to backtrack if, for some reason, you find out that you can't make it or the gate is locked.

In really good weather, it is also tempting to begin before dawn from Caineville in order to reach Lower Cathedral Valley at sunrise and continue up the valley with the sun behind you. Coming from Torrey, you can stop at the ford first to check it and make sure that you'll be able to cross it later, before beginning the loop counterclockwise at Caineville.

Instead of doing the whole classic loop, it's also possible to reach several parts of the valley from various side roads. Not only will you be able to discover different landscapes, but by combining different approaches, you'll see and photograph the most interesting spots during the golden hour—assuming you can devote a couple of days to the area. The previous recommendations concerning driving apply to all of these side roads, in particular the requirement of a topographic map.

For clarity's sake, the valley's main attractions and their respective access are described separately below.

The South Desert and the Bentonite Hills

The road overhanging the South Desert and the Bentonite Hills, called the Hartnet Road, begins at River Ford and follows a dry riverbed between the extreme northern end of the Waterpocket Fold and the depression of Cathedral Valley. The Bentonite Hills are remarkable for their rounded forms and strange checkerboard appearance colored by the Morrison formation. All the colors of the rainbow can be seen. Many exceptional viewpoints are accessible from the road as you follow it to the northwest from River Ford.

At 14 miles from River Ford, a side road leads to the Lower South Desert Overlook. The South Desert is a large valley running parallel to the Waterpocket Fold. The viewpoint yields a splendid view of Jailhouse Rock, with Temple Rock and the Fishlake Mountains in the background.

Less than 4 miles from the intersection with Lower South Desert Overlook, a 1-mile trail leads cross-country to a saddle with a good view of the great monoliths of Lower Cathedral Valley. If you think this view is beautiful, wait until you're in the valley proper.

About 10 miles further along the road, Upper South Desert Overlook is very impressive and gives a good idea of the depth of the South Desert depression if you include a bit of the plateau in the foreground. From the edge of the knoll, those suffering from fear of heights could get weak in the knees.

During the next mile or so, you'll successively encounter spur roads leading to Upper Cathedral Valley Overlook, Hartnet Junction with Park Creek Road—

The Bentonite Hills

allowing access to UT 72 over Thousand Lakes Mountain—and the Cathedral Valley remote campground. The campground is located just before the switchbacks leading down into Upper Cathedral Valley (all these individual stops are covered in the next section).

Getting there: take the Hartnet road from the so-called River Ford, located a dozen miles from the Visitor Center on UT 24. The biggest problem will be the Fremont River crossing just 3/4 of a mile past the beginning of the road. You ford the river on a rocky bed, which is usually not too deep, but watch out for potential engine flooding in a low clearance car. The ford is passable most of the time; however, the gate is locked during spring runoff and after rains when even a 4WD can get stuck. Check at the Visitor Center where rangers will let you know if it's passable or not. Beyond River Ford, the track is sometimes passable in a passenger car if you pay close attention and drive slowly depending on whether the bulldozer has been through recently.

Time required: 2 to 3 hours to Upper Cathedral Valley.

Upper Cathedral Valley

Located at the far north end of both the park and the Middle Desert, Upper Cathedral Valley is one of the highlights of Utah. The majesty that emanates from the powerful monoliths and the encircling mountains is reinforced by the isolation and the effort it takes to get here.

Upper Cathedral Valley

Once you're in the valley, about 3 miles west of Cathedral Valley Junction you'll see a sign saying "Viewpoint" on the north side of the road. There, you'll find a narrow footpath that takes you up onto the plateau, where you can get a spectacular close-up view of the two main groups of 500 feet high monoliths, with the Walls of Jericho in the background. This easy hike is a 2-mile round-trip and offers different angles for photographing the monoliths. If you came from Caineville, continue up the switchbacks for two miles and you'll reach the primitive campground with only six sites. If you've come equipped, camping here will allow you to catch some fabulous evening shots of the extraordinary walls of Entrada sandstone as they turn bright red against a background of dark gray sky. Canyon country at its very best!

Leaving the campground to your right and continuing up toward the plateau, you'll soon reach the junction with the Thousand Lakes road coming from the mountains and the Hartnet Road coming from River Ford. Follow the latter for a quarter of a mile until you come to the spur road to Upper Cathedral Valley Viewpoint, from where you can admire the whole Upper Cathedral Valley in all its splendor.

On the way to Lower Cathedral Valley (see below) you'll be crossing the Middle Desert with its many different geological features. Just before Cathedral Valley junction, you'll find the Gypsum Sinkhole—a gigantic, sunken artesian well almost 200 feet deep and over 50 feet in diameter—which is well worth the mile-long detour on a good spur road, though it's practically impossible to photograph because of its size.

Getting there: there are four possible ways to reach Upper Cathedral Valley.

The easiest way for passenger cars and small-size campers to get to this distant spot, in good weather conditions, is from the north, by way of a dirt road leaving from the junction of I-70 and UT 10, about 2 miles east of Fremont Junction. This wide dirt road, called Baker Ranch Road, is 27 miles long and crosses the forebodingly-named Last Chance Desert. It is usually well maintained for the use of local miners and ranchers, and doesn't present any major difficulties. The main obstacle is crossing Willow Springs Wash, about a dozen miles down the road. After crossing the usually dry ford, the road quickly rolls along and you rapidly reach Cathedral Valley Junction. It's also possible to reach

The uppermost giant monolith at Cathedral Valley

Cathedral Valley Junction by following the Caineville Wash Road from UT 24 (see below). The other access point to Upper Cathedral Valley is the previously described Hartnet Road from River Ford near UT 24. Perhaps the most scenic access is by way of Thousand Lakes Mountain road (also known as Polk Creek road) coming west from UT 72. About 12 miles north of Loa on UT 72, take the dirt road to the right for about 5 miles in the general direction of Elkhorn Campground. This road is usually in excellent condition until you reach a high altitude pass (at about 10,000 feet) in the Fishlake National Forest. At the fork in the road, do not take the Elkhorn Campground spur to the right; instead, continue straight ahead for 7 miles, following the signpost indicating Cathedral Valley. Here the descent becomes quite tricky and it is out of the question to take an ordinary passenger car over this portion of the road. A high-clearance 2WD vehicle can make it easily, except in winter or during spring runoff. This route is especially remarkable as it makes a spectacular transition between two radically different ecosystems, one a high-altitude alpine environment and the other the exceptional desert of Cathedral Valley. There are exceptional photographic opportunities, especially in autumn, when you'll pass through strands of yellow aspen mingling with green conifers before reaching the ocher color of the desert. These mountains are the habitat of a great variety of wild animals—in the course of one trip, I counted almost a hundred mule deer coming down the side of the mountain in great leaps and bounds.

Time required: you can reach Cathedral Valley Junction in approximately 1 hour from the I-70 off-ramp, provided you don't stray off the path. A topo map will help you sort out the many side roads. You should also be able to reach Hartnet Junction from UT 72 in about an hour. Count on 2 to 3 hours for the other routes. Getting there is one thing, but it's a shame if you can't devote at least a couple of hours to exploring this exceptional spot.

Lower Cathedral Valley

Lower Cathedral Valley is better known by the name of the two fantastic monoliths that it harbors. The Temple of the Sun and the Temple of the Moon illustrate many coffee-table books and well-deserve their names. Reaching up 400 feet from the desert ground as if trying to grasp the heavens, these two solitary temples cut an imposing profile against a rich blue sky of unmatched purity. At sunrise, these "high priests" of the mineral universe don their incandescent garments for a brief, fleeting moment, to celebrate the miracle of nature.

Both monoliths can be photographed individually at close range or you can shoot them together from nearby Glass Mountain, using a short telephoto to collapse the perspective of the two Temples and the cliff behind them. The hoodoos at the foot of the cliff are also quite nice. Glass Mountain itself—a small mound consisting of selenite crystals—is an interesting geological curiosity, but doesn't make for an interesting photograph.

Getting there: to get to Lower Cathedral Valley and the famous Temples of the Sun and the Moon, it's best to come from the Caineville Wash road described below. It is the easiest and fastest way to get there for sunrise and, under good conditions, you can make it in a passenger car, although it's going to be a bit bumpy. Coming from I-70 via Cathedral Valley Junction, you'll pass numerous washes between the two valleys about a dozen miles apart and the state of the road can be extremely variable.

The Temples are located 17 miles from Caineville. A spur road about a mile long leads from the main loop road to the foot of the temples and to Glass Mountain.

Time required: 3 hours round trip from Caineville; 2 hours one–way from either I-70 or UT 72.

Temple of the Moon in Lower Cathedral Valley

The Caineville Badlands

The Caineville Badlands are a vast isolated expanse of dark gray hills of Mancos shale striped with interesting colors. Traveling through the heart of these badlands on the Caineville Wash road, you'll encounter from time to time round blocks of basalt tossed out by the explosion of Boulder Mountain about 50 million years ago and then later deposited here by glacial action. These badlands are actually very deep, forming a bed of sedimentary rock between 2,000 to almost

3,000 feet thick. While contemplating this extreme desert universe, it's easy to imagine the Inland Sea that once covered this part of the valley.

Taking in the view to the northeast, you'll see the imposing presence of a mesa called Factory Butte rising on the horizon like a tall ship. There are a couple of spots on the north side of the road near Caineville where you can actually drive on BLM land and get close to the badlands for further exploration.

The badlands along UT 24 and Caineville Wash road are best photographed in late afternoon.

Getting there: you'll find the Caineville Wash road about 19 miles east of the Visitor Center on UT 24. A sign by the side of the road indicates the distance to Lower and Upper Cathedral Valley. This road will take you right into a fantastic universe of badlands in just 2 or 3 miles, passing the northern edge of the Bentonite Hills. If you want to continue on to Lower Cathedral Valley, this road can usually be negotiated with a passenger car by driving carefully, if the weather conditions are right, but it's a long drive (about 35 miles round-trip) and you'll be bounced and jolted the whole way.

Time required: less than an hour for a quick excursion into the heart of the badlands; 3 hours round-trip for the drive alone if you continue on until Lower Cathedral Valley. ✿

Goblin generals surveying the land

Chapter 8

THE SAN RAFAEL SWELL

Buckhorn Wash Pictographs

THE SAN RAFAEL SWELL

The San Rafael Swell is one of the last great wilderness areas of the Southwest without National Park or Monument status. Although this area has been under consideration for more robust federal protection at various times in the past, it is unlikely that the current status quo will change. If this were to happen, it would undoubtedly attract a much larger number of visitors. For now, few people are aware of its expansive panoramas, monoclines, buttes, deep canyons, and rock art and even fewer are venturing on its confusing network of dirt roads. And indeed many people representing different political sensibilities would rather keep it that way. The most prominent feature of this area is the San Rafael Reef, an imposing circular plateau located west of the Green River on either side of I-70. The Reef takes its name from its shape, that of a serrated reef, dominating this wild desert region. This reef consists of several sedimentary layers pushed almost vertically into position by the shifting of tectonic plates.

Factory Butte

I have to admit that I am particularly fond of Factory Butte, despite the fact that it generally elicits a big yawn from other photographers. I don't exactly know why I'm so fond of it, but I suppose it's simply because of its awesome shape and sheer volume—a cross between a gigantic nuclear power plant and the Titanic. Every time I drive along the Fremont River, on my way in or out of Capitol Reef, I feel a pinch of excitement when the majestic butte comes into view. It took me several tries to capture a satisfactory photograph of Factory Butte, however. Once, for lack of adequate scouting and preparation, I missed the sunrise by a few minutes despite getting up at the crack of dawn. Finally, I decided on a more systematic approach. I scouted various locations in the evening, alongside Muddy Creek road, photographing until nighttime before returning to Hanksville. The next morning, I made sure I arrived at the chosen location with a few minutes to spare; I firmly planted my tripod, waited and was finally rewarded with a fantastic sunrise shot—the warm light illuminating the Martian foreground and bringing up extraordinary shadows on the lovely badlands at the base of the butte.

Photo advice: excellent views of the butte start opening up on the eastern side at about 4 miles from UT 24 on Muddy Creek Road. Factory Butte is best photographed at sunrise and in the early morning. There are lovely badlands on the southern end of the butte that can also be photographed in late afternoon.

Getting there: drive 11 miles out of Hanksville toward Capitol Reef and turn right before Cainville on a dirt road leading toward the butte. Warning: do not try to cross Muddy creek as a shortcut to Goblin Valley, unless you have talked to a BLM ranger in Hanksville and confirmed the creek is passable. The creek often has quicksand and it is very easy to get stuck there. A tow from Hanksville will cost you at least $800 and your engine may become silted beyond repair.

Factory Butte at sunrise

Dirty Devil Overlook

While traveling from Hanksville to Hite or vice versa, you may want to take a quick side trip across the Burr Desert to the Dirty Devil River Overlook, also known as Burr Point. It offers a remarkably expansive panorama of the canyon area formed by the Dirty Devil River, which is fed by the waters of Muddy Creek and the Fremont River.

Photo advice: the view is spectacular and would lend itself well to photography with a panoramic camera. This is an excellent late afternoon location.

Getting there: travel 15 miles south of Hanksville on UT 95 and turn left at the Burr Point sign. The 10-mile dirt road is well graded and suitable for passenger cars, except during and after a rain.

Goblin Valley from the main viewpoint

Goblin Valley State Park

In Goblin Valley, erosion has carved an extremely pliable variety of Entrada sandstone into extravagant shapes offering your astonished eyes a spectacle of goblins, ghosts and other fantastic creatures seemingly awaiting a magic wand to awaken them and start them walking as if in an animated motion picture. If you are on a family vacation, it's almost guaranteed that your imagination will be as stimulated as that of your children.

A formation called the Three Judges greets you on the left as you enter the park; it deserves a photo if the light is right. But it's at the covered viewpoint at road's end that the most compelling sight awaits you—a vast army of goblins, camped in the depression below the parking lot, mineral creatures looking like something out of a Tolkien story.

Start your visit by enjoying and photographing this panorama right from the observation point, as it is truly superb. In summer, you risk catching in your viewfinder lots of Lilliputian-sized humans photographing these ferocious goblins. This formerly little-known park now receives about 85,000 visitors a year. Out of season, you'll have it all to yourself.

Goblin Valley has two official foot trails: the mile-long Carmel Canyon loop with its landmark Three Judges and the 3-mile long Curtis Bench trail, offering a superb view of the Henry Mountains from its highest point.

A strangely phallic mushroom rock

However, the most interesting walks simply consist of descending into the depression from the covered viewpoint and walking among the goblins where you can let your imagination run wild.

Photo advice: avoid visiting Goblin Valley when the sun is high in the sky as your pictures will have too much contrast and will look flat under a uniform sky. Ideally, early morning or evening is best, as the main view of the depression is oriented to the south. You can take excellent shots from the covered vista point using a variety of lenses. A telephoto will work well to compress the perspective and make the goblins very dense on your picture. If you are in a hurry or have little time left before the good light vanishes, the goblins located on the left side of the basin generally offer the best photographic opportunities. There is a particularly remarkable spot that you should photograph: crossing the basin at 1 o'clock in the direction of the cliffs, look for a large copper green dome. It may look quite far from the observation point, but it's really only a short 10-minute walk. Climbing up, you'll find a passage leading behind a group of very high formations. You'll come out into a veritable fantasyland of spires and chimneys. It's a spot you shouldn't miss.

Getting there: you can reach this Utah State Park by UT 24 from Green River to the north or from Capitol Reef to the south.

The turnoff from UT 24 is located 24 miles south of I-70 and about 20 miles north of Hanksville, at milepost 137. Drive west for 5 miles then turn left toward the south and drive 6 miles on a newly paved road to reach the entrance of the

Mollie's Castle

park. Herds of antelope are sometimes visible along the road.

Time required: at least 1-1/2 hour if you want to photograph extensively and wander around among the goblins. If you are there during the full moon, a night walk can be a magical experience.

Nearby Location: Mollie's Castle is a beautiful group of goblin formations and mushroom rocks located about 8 miles north of the Hanksville airfield. In fact, you'll pass right though it on UT 24. The main group is located on the west side of the road, but a lovely "detached mansion" is also on the east side and is easier to photograph. Both are extremely photogenic in the early morning sun when coming from Hanksville.

Little Wild Horse Slot Canyon

Narrow passage in Little Wild Horse Canyon

This highly rewarding mini-adventure, both very visual and tactile, lets you penetrate right into the heart of the San Rafael Reef. You're guaranteed to bring back some amazing memories and shots from a trip inside Little Wild Horse Canyon. Access is very easy and the walk through the canyon is not particularly difficult. This explains why Little Wild Horse Canyon has become a classic hike and one of the most visited locations in San Rafael Reef, especially in season and during legal holidays.

After parking your car, find the trail leading to the dry wash bed and follow it for a few hundred yards. As the riverbed narrows, about 10 minutes after leaving the trailhead, you'll come to a sort of dry waterfall about 8 feet high. The best way to get around this obstacle is to ascend the inclined plane on the left and return to the wash just after the dry fall.

Follow along for about 200 yards past the dry fall and turn right at the easily missed fork into Little Wild Horse Canyon. The other fork leads to Bell Canyon.

A popular loop hike, not explored in this guide, is to follow Little Wild Horse Canyon for about 2 miles to its end, then follow a jeep trail west, then south, to the entrance of Bell Canyon. You can then descend this shorter slot canyon until it meets with Little Wild Horse. It takes about four hours to do this loop, but the best photographic opportunities are in Little Wild Horse Canyon, so we'll concentrate on a round-trip inside this canyon.

Little Wild Horse Canyon starts revealing its strange splendor a few hundred feet further on. It begins with a series of very interesting niches as well as ground and polished protrusions carved out by water action on the walls. At a height of about 200 feet, the latter are tightly constricted in some places, no more than a couple of feet wide at shoulder height. In some places, you'll need to place both hands on the rock wall and perform a series of push-up motions so you can move forward inside the highly slanted, shallow corridor. But, generally speaking, the walk is never difficult. However, be careful you don't get stuck and twist an ankle when the fault contracts down to a few inches under your feet.

Follow your exploration up-canyon for as long as your heart desires but go at least a half-mile to really take in the atmosphere of the place. After the first hundred yards or so, the slot canyon widens, but a

Exploring Little Wild Horse Canyon

second section, even narrower than the first, and also much more interesting, awaits you a bit further on. Keep walking until you reach a sort of wide section, with some trees, about 50 minutes from the fork with Bell Canyon. The canyon continues on even higher, but by now you have done the most interesting part.

Photo advice: read the general recommendations on photography in the Introduction, as well as that specific to the Dry Fork of Coyote Gulch in the

Polished sandstone in Little Wild Horse Canyon

Grand Staircase/Escalante chapter. Little Wild Horse Canyon consists of a very brown type of Wingate and Kayenta sandstone near the ground with light colored Navajo sandstone on the very high walls. All this combines to make it quite dark, unless you visit the canyon around mid-day.

Getting there: leaving Goblin Valley State Park, turn left soon after the park exit on a road marked by a sign saying Little Wild Horse Canyon. This road is generally well maintained and easily traveled in an ordinary passenger car or camper. It's a good idea to get the latest information from the Goblin Valley rangers since you'll be crossing a sandy wash about 2 miles from the intersection with the Goblin Valley road. In case of recent rains, the road may be washed out. You'll come to a car park in about 5 miles. In case of flash flooding, your car will be protected here as it is above the riverbed. A sign tells about such a flash flood experienced by a visiting couple, with a photo showing their Landcruiser washed away by the high water. Take this very seriously, particularly on a summer's afternoon. Flash floods are generated by rain falling on the Reef far above the entrance of the canyon and you won't necessarily see it. If you are caught by a flash flood while you are in the canyon, you'll be in great danger. Never forget that it's storms such as these that are responsible for the creation of the magnificent walls of this slot canyon.

Time required: 3 hours round-trip, including the hike, from Goblin Valley.

Nearby locations: Crack and Chute are two other famous slot canyons in the vicinity. To reach them, take the Goblin Valley turnoff on UT 24 but, instead of turning left to Goblin Valley SP, continue straight on Temple Mountain Road for about 2.5 miles, then turn left on the Behind the Reef dirt road; continue for about 4 miles until you reach Crack canyon. Chute is about 2 miles further.

On the way to Crack and Chute, about a mile past the turnoff for Goblin Valley SP, look for some beautiful rock paintings on the right side of the road. There is a wide parking area you can't miss. Unfortunately, these beautiful pictographs have been defaced with a chalk outline in recent years.

If you follow Temple Mountain Road further north, you'll enter Sinbad Country, an attractive combination of vast desert expanse, small hills, buttes and grassland, with lots of interesting canyons and rock art waiting to be explored away from crowds. Temple Mountain Road is a well maintained dirt road usually passable by passenger car all the way to I-70 and it can be a good shortcut to Little Wild Horse Canyon or Goblin Valley SP from the Interstate (taking the South Ranch Exit 129).

Along Interstate 70

As it crosses the San Rafael Swell between Fremont Junction and Green River, I-70 is without contest one of the most scenic highways in the Southwest. This freeway was the last portion of the east-west interstate system to be finished, opening up an extremely remote part of rural Utah to visitor traffic. A series of rest areas line the freeway, allowing you to photograph spectacular views of the San Rafael area. All merit a stop, but with a bit more time you'll find a lot to explore and photograph on short road trips from the freeway.

Technically, the vast anticline called the San Rafael Swell doesn't begin before Fremont Junction on its western slope; however, the section of the freeway between Salina and Fremont Junction is just as spectacular.

Coming from Green River, the sudden presence of the swell is felt sharply as you penetrate the impressive barrier of the San Rafael Reef through Spotted Wolf Canyon. The first viewpoint is located just before the Reef. There are great, unobstructed views to the north from a little hill above the rest stop. For more intimate views of the reef you should visit Black Dragon Wash, which penetrates deep into the reef and offers an interesting rock art panel (see section below).

The second rest stop on the eastern side, at milepost 144, has a fantastic view on the reef from above, looking down into Spotted Wolf Canyon and the Book Cliffs on the horizon. It's a great wide-angle shot if you don't mind including the gently curving freeway in the foreground.

Other rest stops along the freeway in the center of the swell are also worth stopping. Exit 129 provides access to Buckhorn Draw and the Wedge Overlook via BLM road 302 (see section below). Time permitting, the gravel road at Exit 114 brings you in about 18 miles to the town of Moore, which is 7 Miles from the Rochester Rock Art Panel (see section below).

Exit 89 near Fremont Junction is the northern entry point for Cathedral

I-70 crosses the San Rafael Reef near Green River

Valley, as described in the Capitol Reef chapter. From Fremont Junction, UT 72 heading south to Loa is an enchanting highway with almost no traffic. It meanders through soft valleys before climbing to almost ten thousand feet to where you can find a few groves of early-turning aspen just past the Desert View rest stop. The rest stop has a distant but interesting view of Upper Cathedral Valley.

Nearby location: much further on I-70, 21 miles southwest of Richfield, the Fremont Indian State Park is a worthwhile stop to stretch your legs on the interstate. The museum has excellent exhibits of the Fremont culture, including a reproduction of a pit house. There is also a reconstructed pit house outside. Although there is a large quantity of pictographs, accessible from numerous interpretive trails, they are generally hard to locate. Be sure to ask for the various trail fliers to make your visit more instructive and enjoyable.

Black Dragon Wash

The highlight of this popular rock art panel, located off I-70, is an interesting panel representing a strange bird-like figure resembling a pterodactyl.

To visit Black Dragon Wash, you must be coming from Green River, as there is no exit from the south side of the freeway. You could use one of the occasional median crossings, but these are normally for emergency use and the highway patrol frowns on it. Technically, there is no exit either on the north side, just an unmarked pull off area past milepost 146, which you'll find approximately 3/4 mile beyond the bridge over the San Rafael river or about 14 miles west of Green River. There is a marked BLM dirt road and a cattle gate, which you have to open and close behind you. Follow the road north for about a mile in open country, then another quarter mile inside the reef; it is in decent shape and passable to a passenger car. With high clearance, you'll be able to drive the last 0.6 miles to a parking area located right below the panel. Passenger cars should stop before that, when things become rough.

The panel is on the north side of the canyon. It is at least 30 feet up on the cliff and appears rather small to the naked eye. Someone apparently decided one day that the red pigment had become too faint and drew a white outline with chalk around the dragon to make it easier to see. This exemplifies too well the risk of leaving prominent rock art unprotected. Outlining Indian rock art with chalk or drawing over it or around it is no different from painting over Michaelangelo's work in the Sistine chapel.

Once you have located the dragon, make your way up the rocky path that leads to the base of the ledge where it's drawn. Be extremely cautious as the path is slippery and the ledge is extremely narrow; one misstep could lead to a serious fall. You'll need a 24mm to fit the dragon into your frame; it's about 7 feet wide from wing tip to wing tip. It's a good idea to take several shots, underexposing a bit on at least one. About 60 feet to the left of the dragon, and a bit higher, is a small panel of human figures.

Time required: 1 hour round-trip from I-70.

Nearby location: about half way back from the Black Dragon parking area to I-70, you can turn west on a short 0.25-mile spur leading to the Petroglyph Canyon trailhead. Walk southwest along the reef for about ten minutes until you reach the mouth of Arch Canyon. Head inside the canyon and soon after its entrance take a short spur southwest and look for a small but undamaged panel on the north wall.

The amazing Black Dragon

The Wedge Overlook and Buckhorn Draw

To the north of Fremont Junction on I-70, Highway 10 to Price offers the easiest access to the heart of the Swell, although it's possible to come from Exit 129 off I-70. About 1.5 mile north of Castle Dale, take the marked and well-graded gravel road, suitable to passenger cars in dry weather. Follow it east for 13 miles and, at the fork, turn south for another 7 miles on an equally good road leading to a breathtaking view of the San Rafael River at the Wedge Overlook. The viewpoint is 600 feet above the gorge—a great destination to photograph "Utah's Little Grand Canyon". Driving back 7 miles, turn right on BLM Road 406 for about 2 miles and right again on BLM 332 to visit the Buckhorn Draw Area and photograph the recently restored Buckhorn Wash Pictograph Panel. The panel, in the Barrier Canyon style, is right by the side of the road; it is fenced off but easily photographed with a normal lens to mild telephoto. These are, in my opinion, some of the finest pictographs in the Southwest. Road 332 continues toward I-70, which it meets at Exit 129. It traverses the superb Buckhorn canyon followed by grassy open areas, allowing you to make a loop around the heart of the Swell. This is a remote area of magnificent scenery, although easily accessible, yet few people know about it. A great place for camping and relaxing.

The Wedge Overlook

The Head of Sinbad

The Head of Sinbad is renowned among photographers and rock art afficionados for its two beautiful pictographs, which until now have been spared by vandals. This site is very close to I-70 and easy to visit when traveling on I-70.

With the former access near milepost 122 now blocked by boulders, the only access as of this writing is from Exit 129 on I-70. Take the good dirt road and follow it southwest for about 10 miles toward Swasey's Cabin. Then, make a sharp right (north) toward I-70, take the narrow tunnel under the Interstate and, at the fork, go right for 0.25-mile, then right again at the next fork until you reach the car park. One of the panels is exquisite in its simplicity: a single shamanistic antropomorph with interesting hairdo, surrounded by two elegant and simply ornamented stick-like motifs and a curiously waving buck, revealing the artist's sense of humor. On the way back, cut right at the first fork and drive 0.5 miles to pay a visit to Dutchman Arch.

Time required: about an hour from I-70 including photography.

Rochester Rock Art Panel

The Rochester is a large petroglyph panel consisting of numerous animal figures carved on smooth rock. It's easily accessible, via a good dirt road and an easy trail, and makes a good picture if you are looking for rock art. The location, on a rocky promontory overlooking the Muddy River 200 feet below is also quite nice. If you are going toward Price or Nine Mile Canyon from I-70, you should consider this short but interesting detour.

From Exit 89 on I-70, take UT 10 north and drive 3.5 miles past the town of Emery. Near Milepost 18, turn right in the direction of Moore, then south at the first gravel road to your right; this road has a small sign indicating the panel. Follow it for about 3 miles to the parking area. The easy 0.5-mile foot trail leads to several scattered groups of glyphs but the main panel, facing east, steals the show.

Time required: about 2 hours round-trip from I-70.

Nine Mile Canyon

Don't let the name fool you. Nine Mile Canyon is 40-miles long and takes at least half a day to thoroughly enjoy. The canyon got its name from a nine-mile triangulation done by one of J.W. Powell's topographers during the mapping of the area. Nevertheless, the 100-mile round-trip from Wellington to the gate which ends public access provides an exquisite foray deep into the Book Cliffs wilderness. The road leaves from Wellington, just south of Price, and takes you through one of the largest concentrations of rock art in North America. The road goes through a remote area offering an interesting variety of landscapes, from semi-alpine to fertile cultivated land to dry canyons. Due to the rarity of human presence, an abundance of wildlife can be seen on the road at dawn or dusk.

Although just driving this scenic byway is sheer pleasure if you have time on your hands, most photographers will want to visit the canyon to photograph rock art, and in particular the famous Hunting Scene panel, located near the end of the canyon.

Photo advice: petroglyphs and pictographs, mostly of the Fremont era, can be

The Hunting Scene in Nine Mile Canyon

found by the hundreds on the canyon cliffs, but unless you use the BLM book-let and drive very slowly, you will miss most of them. So take your time, bring detailed written information such as the flier published by Utah's Castle Country Travel Service, and, if possible, binoculars to spot items high on the canyon walls. You will need a telephoto to photograph many of the rock art panels; others are at eye level or slightly above and call for a normal lens.

Getting there: the well-marked road leaves US 191 at the southern end of the town of Wellington, about 8 miles south of Price. The road is called Soldier Creek Road after the Buffalo Soldiers, the famed troop of black cavalrymen who actually built it in 1882. A marker at the truck stop retraces the history of the road and points out the location of some of the more prominent panels. The road is paved for the first 12 miles, then becomes a well-graded dirt road suitable for passenger cars, even though it's not advisable in wet weather. Less than 9 miles after the end of the pavement, you reach the bridge over Minnie Maude Creek which marks the official entry into Nine Mile Canyon. The Hunting Scene Panel is located on Cottonwood Canyon Road, 1.2 mile from the fork with Nine Mile Canyon road and about 24 miles from Minnie Maude Creek.

Time required: at least half a day from Wellington.

The Crystal Geyser

Near Green River is a little-known but quite interesting natural phenomenon: a geyser! The trouble is: it isn't Old Faithful! And the main reason for that is that the geyser erupts only once or twice every 24 hours. So you'll need either luck, to be there at the right time, or patience. I was fortunate enough to see the geyser erupt on my very first trip there, so don't despair.

Photo advice: anytime in the day is fine to photograph the geyser if it's erupting. Be sure to protect your equipment if you're shooting at close range or some nasty whitish paste will blanket it and it will be hard to remove. The geyser is not hot so there doesn't seem to be a danger of getting burns, but you should be cautious of where you step as there are a couple of hot bubbling mud holes next to it. Overexpose half a stop to accurately convey the color of the column of water.

Getting there: from the east exit of Green River, take the frontage road for approximately 3 miles going east. There are actually two frontage roads, one north of I-70 and one south. The north frontage road eventually goes under the freeway and merges with the south one. Continue due south for another 3 miles in a desolate landscape until you reach the geyser near the riverbank.

The Crystal Geyser

Sego Canyon

Sego Canyon is as good as it gets for motorists intent on Fremont rock art without sweating it out. If you are traveling on I-70 between Green River and Grand Junction, all you need to do is take Exit 185, 25 miles east of Green River, drive north past Thompson Springs and continue 3.5 miles further on a paved road! Just follow the sign over the tracks and up canyon to a beautiful Barrier style panel. The exhibit is well worth the short detour if only for its interpretive markers, which provide a very nice overview of the various periods and styles of rock art.

After photographing the rock art, drive 0.5-mile further up canyon on a well-maintained gravel road and turn right for about another mile until you reach the little ghost town of Sego.

Nearby location: the Copper Ridge Sauropod Track site displays beautiful fossil tracks of a brontosaur and carnivores from the Jurassic period. To get there from I-70, take exit 180 at Crescent Junction and drive south on US 191 toward Moab for 8.5 miles. The turnoff is 0.25-mile past milepost 149. Cross the railroad tracks on the east side of US 191 and follow the dirt road—suitable for passenger cars in dry weather—for 2 miles to a parking area. The tracks are 100 yards up the hill to the east. ✿

House on fire in Mule Canyon

Chapter 9
AROUND CEDAR MESA

Kachina Bridge

AROUND CEDAR MESA

This chapter encompasses, in a very general way, the Blanding/Hanksville axis that allows you to get quickly from Monument Valley to Capitol Reef, leaving Moab for later.

If you have a choice when creating your itinerary, note that it's better to travel from Blanding to Hite in an east–west direction, which allows you to follow along with the sun at your back instead of in your face.

Edge of the Cedars State Park

The little town of Blanding, located at the foot of the magnificent Abajo Mountains, would be unremarkable if not for the Edge of the Cedars State Park and its wonderful museum. The park definitely merits a stop for its exhibits of Ancestral Puebloan culture as well as modern Navajo (Dineh) and Utes (Ncuc) artifacts. Behind the museum, there are some Pueblo-type ruins which were inhabited until about 1220 AD. They are moderately interesting but pale in comparison with others—although you get a chance to descend into a reconstructed kiva. So stow away your gear and devote an hour of your time to visiting the museum. You won't be sorry you did.

__Getting there:__ the park is in the town of Blanding on US 191 and to get there is a bit like following the yellow brick road as you are guided to the museum by a series of Puebloan icons painted on the surface of the paved road.

Time required: 1 hour.

Butler Wash

The road from Blanding to Hite, which partly follows the Trail of the Ancients, is absolutely spectacular and little used except in the summer months. At that time, you'll encounter a lot of motorhomes hauling boats in the direction of the Hite marina, the northernmost of the four marinas on Lake Powell. An easy 1-mile round-trip trail takes you to a nice balcony-shaped ruin hanging over a grotto in the canyon below. Butler Wash is best in mid-morning. The dwelling is then evenly illuminated and the light is not yet too harsh. Earlier than that, you'll need to warm up the scene and later in the afternoon you'll be shooting against the light.

Getting there: about 10 miles west from US 191 on UT 95.

The Comb Ridge

Passing the great rectilinear wall of Comb Ridge, which spreads over dozens of miles from north to south, the road gains elevation and crosses a vast juniper forest. The views of the Abajo Mountains to the north and the Henry Mountains to the northwest are spectacular. Along with the Cockscomb and the Waterpocket Fold, the Comb Ridge is one of the big three faults that traverse the Colorado plateau. One of the best vantage points to observe the fault is right by the side of UT 95, between Blanding and Natural Bridges Nat'l Monument. You can get a fantastic view of miles of the ridge toward the south from right before the fence, as you come into Comb Wash valley from Natural Bridges. There is a pullout just big enough to fit one car. If you're coming from Blanding, you'll first pass through an enormous man-made cut in the ridge before the road opens up into the valley. Stopping here is prohibited and you should park somewhere in the valley and walk a couple of hundred yards to the previously described vantage point on the other side of the road. The ridge consists mostly of Kayenta sandstone, with a bit of Navajo sandstone on top. It glows a rich red in the late afternoon sun and that's the best time to photograph it.

Mule Canyon

Mule Canyon is an outstanding location both for leisurely hiking and photography of small Puebloan dwellings and granaries.

The Mule Canyon system consists of two different arms, separated by less than 0.5-mile at their entrance. Both the northern and southern arm extend for roughly 5 to 6 miles. They are both easy level walks, with few obstructions, a shallow stream, often dry or reduced to a trickle. They offer outstanding walks in solitude, inside sunny canyons with shallow walls. They both have nice, if small, ruins of dwellings and granaries, easy to spot and get to and fun to photograph. In my opinion, South Mule Canyon is more accessible and contains more interesting ruins, but offers less solitude than its northern neighbor.

Photo advice: consider a short foray into the southern arm of Mule Canyon. At just a bit over a mile, just after a bend, you'll come to an interesting set of ruins and granaries to the right. The ruins are located under a cliff overhang, which looks like flames under the right light. Best lighting is in mid to late morning to take advantage of reflected light. You'll need to hike another mile to come to the next set of ruins. The largest ruins are reached after three miles.

Getting there: the two canyon trailheads are on an unmarked BLM road located on the north side of UT 95, 0.25-mile east of the marked Mule Canyon Ruin exhibit. The above-mentioned ruin is a reconstructed kiva and is not particularly interesting. I have always perceived it as a decoy, built to steer people away from the canyons, while at the same time satisfying the curiosity of passersby who are in a rush. Like all noteworthy canyons on Cedar Mesa, there is a small fee for self-registration. Be sure you take some change to the trailhead.

Road Canyon

There is an abundance of canyons on the Cedar Mesa and almost all of them contain Indian ruins. One such canyon with outstanding ruins is Road Canyon. This trip requires some navigation skills and is best done with a partner, but it is well worth it. Not only is it a very pleasant canyon, quite verdant and open, but it contains some of the most photogenic dwellings on the Cedar Mesa plateau.

The ruins are not hard to find, but they do not jump at you either. You must be on the lookout or you might miss some, as they are mostly located high up on the cliff. Access to most of the ruins is not difficult, but, in some cases, requires a bit of climbing on slanted slickrock.

Tread lightly near the ruins. Do not get too close, touch the walls with your hands or remove any artifacts. It is a privilege to visit such a lovely canyon and you should leave no trace of your passage.

Photo advice: any time of the day is fine. You'll have good reflected light in the morning, when the ruins at the beginning of the canyon are in shadow. Some of the ruins will be in full light from midday to mid afternoon.

Getting there: 3 miles east of UT 261 on Cigarette Spring road (CR 239), just opposite Government Trail road (about 13 Miles south of UT 95, almost a mile past milepost 20). Pay your fee at the station, located about 1 mile from the turn off, then drive straight ahead for another 2 miles, until you reach a fence. This is where you park. Getting into the canyon is the hard part. You can find a lengthy description of its access in Rod Adkinson's excellent book *Hiking Grand*

One of the many spectacular ruins on the Cedar Mesa

Staircase-Escalante & the Glen Canyon Region. A GPS is helpful, but not necessary, as long as you take mental notes of various way points—forwards and backwards—along the way to the main canyon. Otherwise, getting out could be a problem, especially late in the evening after several hours of exploration.

Time required: 2 hours to photograph the first few ruins. A half day to enjoy the canyon at a relaxed pace.

Grand Gulch

Grand Gulch has become the Mecca of Indian ruins and rock art on the Cedar Mesa plateau. During springtime and autumn, it attracts many visitors, particularly small groups, eager to explore easily accessible ancient Puebloan ruins while enjoying a laid-back backpacking experience in a pleasant canyon. The combination of moderately difficult terrain and a high concentration of well-preserved dwellings, granaries and rock art makes it a very rewarding trip.

Walking the entire length of the canyon from the main entry at Kane Gulch to the San Juan River is 53 miles and few people tackle such a daunting trip. Most people concentrate on the upper part of the canyon, which has the easiest terrain and the highest concentration of ruins; it also offers several exit points making it more flexible to plan two to five day trips inside the Gulch. For those who would like to enjoy the wilderness experience without roughing it too much, there are a couple of accredited tour operators offering increasingly popular llama trips. I recommend these llama trips strongly to photographers, for they remove the burden of dealing with the complex logistics of a private backpacking trip in such a deserty environment. You are fed and pampered, led by experienced guides to the best places that could otherwise be missed, and your llama companions do all the carrying, freeing you to hike only with your day pack. If you are a large format photographer, this may well be your only option. A llama trip will usually allow you to visit all the major sites between Kane Gulch and Bullet Canyon.

If you want to see parts of Grand Gulch, but you have neither the time nor inclination to backpack or join a 4 to 5 day commercial trip, it can be done with moderate effort on consecutive day-hikes.

Todie Canyon and Bullet Canyon are the most rewarding entry points for short incursions into the Gulch. Todie Canyon is not as visited as Kane Gulch, but has interesting structures, including some photogenic little granaries. From the Bullet Canyon trailhead, Jailhouse Ruin and Perfect Kiva make a moderate under 10-mile round-trip. These sites, although popular, are only mildly photogenic. In Kane Gulch, a 10-mile round-trip hike from the ranger station brings you to the confluence with Grand Gulch and good ruins at Junction Ruin and Turkey Pen. For an excellent two to three-day backpack trip, requiring a car or bike shuttle, you could enter at Todie and exit at Kane Gulch or vice-versa. An easier half-day hike in the central section of Grand Gulch is to the Big Man pictograph panel, reached by the well-maintained Government Trail and an easy up-canyon hike.

**Photo advice:** arguably the best ruin complex in Grand Gulch, Split Level House is named for two connected dwellings located at different levels under an alcove, also sheltering a small kiva, granaries and pictographs; it is located 13 miles from the Bullet Canyon trailhead. A couple of hundred yards inside Sheiks Canyon, the Green Mask site has excellent pictograph panels; it is located 1.4 miles upstream from Bullet inside Grand Gulch. Considering the distances involved, you're not going to have much control over light at the various sites. Most ruins are under ledges and therefore in shadow. Bright daylight helps create a warm glow that is very pleasant on film.

Getting there: the Kane Gulch Ranger Station is on the east side UT 261, 4.5 miles south of its junction with UT 95. This is where you'll get your backcountry permit if you stay overnight; during the high season, permits should be reserved in advanced from the BLM office in Monticello. Day hikers just pay the $5 entry fee common to all hikes on the Cedar Mesa plateau. The Kane Gulch trailhead is just across the road from the Ranger Station. The Todie trailhead is located further south near milepost 25, at the end of a good unmarked 1.5 mile dirt road; there is no sign. The Bullet Canyon trailhead is just past mile marker 22 on CR 251. The Government Trail road (CR 245) is well marked, almost a mile past milepost 20 or 13 Miles south of UT 95.

Natural Bridges Nat'l Monument

This National Monument is often passed by, not only because of the additional mileage it requires—and thus the delay this imposes—but also because many visitors incorrectly assume that it's some sort of second-rate Arches, which is not the case at all. This beautiful little park has a personality all its own, but it only reveals its beauty and interest to those with plenty of time and willing to do some walking. Natural bridges are eroded by the action of water flowing from rivers, as opposed to arches, which are eroded by wind and sand.

The three gigantic natural bridges here—Sipapu, Kachina and Owachomo—are spectacular. Because of their particular geological origin, they are set deeply inside canyons, instead of being in the open like arches. This makes the bridges difficult to photograph from the top of the canyon, but if you take the time to go to the bottom you'll be rewarded by superb views of these huge bridges.

The three bridges are located on a 7-mile one-way loop road.

Owachomo Bridge with frozen creek

Sipapu Bridge only reveals its splendor from the bottom

Sipapu Bridge is the longest, with a span of 286 feet, and is arguably the most elegant of the three. Forget the viewpoint, however, because the bridge appears totally lost among its whitish Cedar Mesa surroundings. Instead, take the 1.2-mile round-trip hike down into the canyon and you'll reach the bridge in less than a half-hour. It's a 500 feet elevation drop, so it's fairly steep in places and you'll be using ladders. Sipapu is a nice mid-morning view and there are some spectacular angles looking up to the bridge from the bottom of the canyon, with some nice reflected light from the different walls.

Kachina Bridge, being just a bit shorter than Sipapu, is most notable for the thickness of its span. Just under 100 feet thick, it resembles a gigantic rock muscle stretched 130 feet above your head.

The trail leading to Kachina Bridge from its overlook is a tad longer than Sipapu's; however, elevation gain is only 400 feet and the hike feels markedly easier. If you're not in great shape, but still want to see a large bridge, Kachina is for you. An added benefit is the presence of a kiva and pictographs behind a small talus to the left of the bridge.

If you have time, I strongly recommend hiking the section at the bottom of White Canyon between Kachina and Sipapu. It's an easy level walk alternating between a sandy path and the dry bed of the canyon. It's a unique opportunity to do a day hike inside a wild Cedar Mesa sandstone canyon in a relatively safe environment. At Sipapu, you should not have too much trouble hitching a ride back to your car, which is at the next stop on the one-way road.

Owachomo is very easy to reach, which is a good reason for not missing it, though it is dwarfed in comparison with the other two.

Photo advice: the Canyon consists of a very ancient, light-colored Cedar Mesa sandstone, which is difficult to expose on a sunny day. It isn't easy to photograph the bridges from the road as they have a tendency to blend into the canyon. You'll have to find a way to isolate them, preferably against the sky, to convey the true measure of their size and the feeling of power, which they project when close. There is only one way to do this, and that's by descending into the canyon. If you decide to do this, you're most likely to do so at Owachomo, where the

Sipapu Bridge makes for an interesting shot from below

bridge is located only a few minutes from the road. In that case, don't stop when you arrive at the bridge, but follow the trail going under it and to the left, descending towards the creek flowing below. The creek makes a nice foreground and the angle you'll get from below provides an easy exposure of the bridge throughout the day.

Getting there: from Monument Valley by way of UT 261, with the added bonus of the beautiful viewpoints of Mokey Dugway and Muley Point, or by the superb UT 95 leaving from either Blanding or Hanksville. These two roads between Blanding and the San Juan River form the Trail of the Ancients.

Time required: 2 to 4 hours in the park; add a half-day if you decide to make this trip while traveling on US 163 between Monument Valley and Bluff.

Quiet morning at Hall's Crossing (Photo by Gene Mezereny)

Crossing Lake Powell

You can cross Lake Powell in two ways. The main, most frequented route is UT 95 going straight towards Hite, passing Natural Bridges National Monument. You can also take UT 276—the old Hole-in-the-Rock Trail of the Mormon pioneers (see the Grand Staircase-Escalante chapter)—slanting due west to catch the ferry at Hall's Crossing and rejoin the Notom-Bullfrog Road leading to Capitol Reef.

In the first instance, beyond Natural Bridges National Park, UT 95 follows spectacular White Canyon, dominated by the monoliths of Cheese Butte and Jacob's Chair. It's possible to descend into the canyon by a road on the left, about 2 miles after the sign for Jacob's Chair.

Arriving at Hite Crossing, you'll leave the marina to the west and cross in succession the Colorado and the Dirty Devil rivers in the middle of an amazing landscape of petrified dunes.

After 2 miles on the north shore, you arrive at a viewpoint overlooking Lake Powell and affording an exceptional vista. Past the viewpoint, the road begins its climb to the north, crossing a superb canyon of Entrada sandstone in the vicinity of Hog Springs, where it changes to Navajo sandstone. It would be difficult to find a prettier spot. This area has a number of little side canyons waiting to be explored.

In the second scenario, catch the John Atlantic Burr Ferry, which leaves Hall's Crossing every two hours between 8 AM and 6 PM in summer, between 8 AM and 4 PM in fall, and 8 AM and 2 PM in winter. It leaves on the odd hours from Bullfrog between 9 AM and 7 PM in summer, 9 AM and 5 PM in fall and 9 AM and 3:30 PM in winter. The service is generally interrupted for maintenance in February. Always verify the schedule when you are near the Hall's Crossing marina by calling (435) 684-3087.

Time required: 1/2-day just for the drive.

Mokey Dugway and Muley Point

If you go up to Natural Bridges National Monument by way of the Trail of the Ancients (UT 261), beginning 4 miles north of Mexican Hat, you'll be driving on an amazing route carved into the flanks of the cliff during the 1950's for the use of local uranium mines. It's all gravel road with 3 miles of hairpin turns climbing to the top, but it's wide and doesn't present any problems. You reach the top about 1,000 feet further up, at an altitude close to 6,000 feet, at a place called Mokey Dugway. Here you'll have a spectacular view of the Valley of the Gods. Monument Valley is also visible in the distance to the southwest.

A bit higher up on the plateau, a road heading west takes you to the viewpoints of Muley Point. There are two viewpoints: the first one, at about 3.7 miles, yields wonderful views of the goosenecks of the San Juan River. The second one, at Mile 5, marks the end of the road and affords a closer and more open view of Monument Valley, as well as an almost 360° panorama, including Navajo Mountain, the Henrys, the Abajos and Sleeping Ute Mountain.

Photo advice: these landscapes are so incredibly vast that it is easier and probably more interesting to simply admire them than to photograph them. If you want to photograph Monument Valley in the distance, you'll need a telephoto in the 200-300mm range. The view is often too hazy, but you could get a good shot after a rain, with some nice clouds or dramatic sky.

Goosenecks of the San Juan

Only about 30 miles north of Monument Valley, there is a little Utah State Park largely ignored by travelers, who are still in a euphoric state from their visit to Monument Valley and in a great hurry to get to Arches and Canyonlands. I have sent a good number of travelers to Goosenecks State Park and all of them, without exception, have come back raving about it.

It's only at the edge of the canyon that these goosenecks can be seen and they won't fail to surprise you. Here, the San Juan River has cut out four successive bends over 1,500 feet in depth in a shale core, twisting and turning for more

Gooseneck of the San Juan

than 5 miles in a space of less than a mile. This view is more remarkable for being odd than for sheer beauty. You are presented with a geological phenomenon that defies the imagination. It's the kind of view of which we say, "you have to see it to believe it". Go there and you won't regret it.

Photo advice: the goosenecks make for eye-catching pictures no matter what size of wide-angle lens you have. There's no way you can get them all into one single shot, unless you shoot from a small airplane.

Getting there: 4 miles north of Mexican Hat on US 163, turn at the sign for the park. Follow the narrow paved road for another 4 miles as it winds through the middle of the plateau.

Time required: 1-hour round-trip from US 163.

Valley of the Gods

Just a few minutes away from Goosenecks State Park, you'll encounter an interesting track forming a loop around the place known as the Valley of the Gods. Strewn about the valley are imposing monoliths, quite different from those found at Monument Valley. Though quite beautiful, this valley doesn't offer the same photographic variety of the latter. The main advantage of the Valley of the Gods is that it is much less visited and an impression of solitude reigns here. You'll truly have the impression that you are embarking on an adventure, which is not the case in the highly controlled world of the Monument Valley Tribal Park. I particularly like the northeastern side of the valley, where the road abruptly forks to the west behind one of the tallest monoliths. I call this particular spot the Rincon and I like to park there and explore on foot. This area has by far the best views in the entire valley. The western part of the valley, near the Bed and Breakfast, is a bit of a letdown.

Photo advice: these Gods, immense monoliths rising high into the sky, won't disappoint you. It's better to start the circuit from the east side to get the better views, so the light will be good in early morning. But if you drive the road after the middle of the afternoon, when the rocks take very warm colors, take it from the opposite direction in order not to have the sun against you. The prettiest part is around the middle of the track.

Getting there: from US 163, 8 miles northwest of Mexican Hat (4 miles from where it branches off UT 261 climbing to Natural Bridges). The track begins on the left side of the road and is marked by a sign. You can also take the track in the opposite direction, from UT 261, just before it ascends the mesa. The track is 17-mile long and is generally passable by passenger cars and small-sized campers except in wet weather.

Time required: 1 hour just to drive the loop, but 2 hours if you want to do it without rushing to take your photos.

Valley of the Gods

Mexican Hat, Indian Blanket & Lime Ridge

All right, I'll be the first to admit that photographing Mexican Hat is a bit cheesy, but it's so tempting to stop and gawk. Judging by the number of cars that pull off for a close-up view and a quick snapshot, the temptation is universal. In fact, it's got to be one of the most photographed formations on US 163.

A well-graded dirt road makes a circle around the southern side of the Hat, allowing you to pick up the view you prefer.

Mexican Hat rock

Nearby, as you drive on your way to the Mokey Dugway or Bluff, do not miss the colorful "Indian blanket" patchwork on the cliffs overlooking the San Juan river, on the east side of the road. Farther up, as you approach the junction of US 163 and 191, you'll be passing by the spectacular Lime Ridge before once again crossing our old friend the Comb Ridge, previously discussed in the Cedar Mesa chapter. All these exceptionally scenic geologic features would be best observed and photographed from an airplane. ✿

Fisher Towers reflection

Chapter 10

AROUND MOAB

Wilson Arch

AROUND MOAB

If there's one town in the West that has changed drastically in the last twenty years, it's Moab. I knew Moab in 1975 when it was still a small hamlet with a couple of stray motels, a few odd restaurants and certainly no liquor. Today, with dozens of motels, Moab has become a cosmopolitan Mecca for tourists where they can buy cool bumper stickers saying "Paris, London...Moab" and relax after a long day of hiking, rafting, four-wheeling or mountain biking in one of the two microbreweries in town.

Moab is certainly the jumping-off spot par excellence for those two scenic giants of the Colorado Plateau, Arches and Canyonlands. However, the area around Moab contains quite a few remarkable sites that would be a shame to miss. This chapter deals with those sites that don't quite have the stature of National Parks and Monuments, but can be just as fascinating and full of photographic opportunities.

While in Moab, be sure to look up Tom Till's exquisite photography in his gallery on Main Street.

Potash Road

Scenic Byway 279 (a.k.a. Potash Road) begins off US 191, about 1.5-mile past the Colorado River Bridge north of Moab.

This highly scenic road follows the right bank of the Colorado River below steep Entrada sandstone cliffs adorned with desert varnish. Indian pictographs cover the canyon walls at some signed points and rock climbers from all over the world show off their skills—and colorful equipment—on the slickrock. This road provides access to landmarks such as Poison Spider Mesa and Corona Arch (see the next sections) and farther away, to Thelma & Louise Point (remember the last scene…), the Shafer Trail and the White Rim Road.

The road gets its name from the vast potash extraction site it serves; the site is located at the end of 17 miles of paved road, followed by a few miles of rough dirt road, passable by passenger car. At the Potash site, water from the Colorado River is pumped into underground galleries where it dissolves potash salts, which are then aspirated back to the surface and into large evaporation tanks. On the paper, it doesn't sound really exciting for the landscape photographer. However the colorful tanks display a spectacular palette, ranging from turquoise to deep dark blue and offering a shocking contrast with the red Entrada of the surrounding cliffs. To photograph this surreal sight, drive toward the farthest tanks and climb on a slickrock ridge below the cliff to the right to get a better view. The best light is in late afternoon when the light is evenly distributed on the whole scene. Another good view of the tanks is from Hurrah Pass, accessible by high clearance vehicle from a side road off Kane Creek Road. Kane Creek Road starts in downtown Moab and follows the south bank of the Colorado River (opposite SB 279) before ascending Kane Spring canyon. The evaporation tanks can also been seen, albeit more distantly, from Dead Horse Point SP (see Canyonlands-Island in the Sky chapter) and Anticline Overlook (see Canyonlands-Needles chapter).

The Potash Road also leads to the main put off and staging area for Colorado River trips in Canyonlands Nat'l Park and Cataract Canyon.

Poison Spider Mesa

I highly recommend the drive/bike/hike trip to Poison Spider Mesa, less for the location itself than for the extraordinary view it provides over the jumble of rocks and fins known as "Behind the Rocks" spread beyond the Colorado River.

Photo advice: great views open up after about 3 or 4 miles from the beginning of the 4WD road, but you can also get good shots of the Behind the Rocks fins and coneheads by climbing up one of the steep slickrock hills at the end of the initial switchbacks. Exercise much caution in doing so. A 200mm to 500mm telephoto will yield spectacular results shortly before sunset, with the extraordinary rocks lit up by the sun and the Manti-La Sals as a backdrop. This shot is a favorite of mine.

Getting there: follow SB 279 for about 6 miles from the beginning of the road and exit at the Dinosaur Tracks sign. Passenger cars and RVs should stop at the car park located at the beginning of the road. High-clearance vehicles can drive

Behind the Rocks, seen from Poison Spider Mesa

the first half-mile of the track and park under the electrical line. After that, the track is strictly 4WD territory and requires very good driving skills.

Bowtie & Corona Arch

Graceful Corona Arch (photo by Philippe Schuler)

This is an easy, uncrowded and very rewarding 3-mile round-trip hike to two spectacular arches: lovely Bowtie Pothole Arch and massive Corona Arch.

Corona Arch is one of the prettiest arches in the Moab area, thanks to its graceful span and an unobstructed view from both sides. Some people like to call it "Little Rainbow Bridge" and its shape is indeed reminiscent of the well-known landmark near Lake Powell (see Around Page chapter in Vol. 2).

Photo advice: afternoon is best to photograph Corona arch from the slickrock bench. You can also walk under it and photograph it from the other side if you come around mid-morning.

Bowtie Pothole Arch

Getting there: drive 10 miles out of Moab on Scenic Byway 279 until you reach the marked car park for Corona Arch. The well-maintained trail climbs gently at first and makes use of safety cables and small ladders toward the end to reach the slickrock bench where the arches are located.

You can also park near a small canyon located 0.5-mile before the Corona Arch car park and hike through a thickly forested canyon and up to a plateau that yields a nice, but distant, view directly facing Corona Arch.

Time required: 1-1/2 to 2 hours for the hike under the arches.

Tukuhnikivats Arch

Tukuhnikivats Arch is an outstanding little arch, located at the southern tip of the area called Behind the Rocks, southeast of Moab. It has a very unusual square shape on one side and a rather rough texture. It makes a great photo, framing the Manti-La Sal Mountains in the background—when they are not hidden by clouds. On your way to the arch, you'll pass outstanding fins and beehives of Entrada sandstone, in the shape of conical skulls, to the left of the dirt road.

Photo advice: a 28mm or lower is required to frame the arch completely, as there is very little room to walk around it. Don't go much lower than 28mm or the Manti-La Sal Mountains will appear very small in the background. This is an excellent afternoon location, but on a recent occasion I've been there in the early morning and have enjoyed great light on the coneheads from a couple miles down the Behind the Rocks road.

Getting there: follow US 191 south for a little over 12 miles from the Kane Creek Blvd crossing in downtown Moab. You'll come across a track leading off to the right. Watch out as this dirt road is not posted on US 191 and is easy to miss; however, there is a small sign on the road itself indicating Pritchett Arch

Lovely Tukuhnikivats Arch

and a large signpost with a topo map of the area can be found a bit further. The road soon branches at 0.4-mile, with the left fork going toward Pritchett Arch as well as the northern section of Behind the Rocks. Take the right fork, then turn left at 0.8-mile. This road can be driven with a passenger car for the first 0.5-mile or so and will let you get near the coneheads. Park alongside the road where it begins to get worse and continue on foot for another 2 miles, staying north each time you encounter a spur road. With a 4x4 vehicle, you can get within a mile from the arch. The arch becomes visible as a small opening high on the left side of the trail. It looks very small from the bottom. Don't let this discourage you; it's not that small once you're there. The trail becomes very steep in the last 300 yards and could be dangerous if you hike alone.

Time required: 2-1/2 hours round-trip from the intersection with the 191 to get to the arch and back; 3 to 4 hours round-trip to drive the Behind the Rocks road up to Pritchett Arch.

Wilson Arch

See an arch without leaving your car? Easy enough. Twenty-four miles south of Moab, you'll find Wilson Arch right next to US 191. But if you want to climb to the arch to admire the beautiful view of the Abajo Mountains, prepare yourself for a rough ascent (about 150 feet of elevation gain in just 600 feet of trail). The descent on the slippery slickrock is even more difficult. Be extremely cautious. Afternoon is the best time to photograph the arch.

The La Sal Mountains Loop

This magnificent 62-mile loop passing by the base of the La Sal Mountains offers a remarkable variety of landscapes, from alpine lake to canyons. A number of viewpoints along the roadside will let you photograph the summits, the pine forests, the canyons above Moab, and the Moab fault in the background. It's hard to beat that. The loop rejoins UT 128 just after the lovely little community of Castle Valley, at the foot of the towering monoliths of Castle Rock and the Priest and the Nuns.

Photo advice: the preferred route is from the south, as the descent into Castle Valley is spectacular. The view from Castle Valley Overlook is best in the afternoon, when the Priest & the Nuns are getting very good light. This trip can be combined with a late afternoon arrival at the Fisher Towers (refer to that section in this chapter).

Getting there: from the south, drive about 7 miles south of downtown Moab on US 191 to catch the clearly marked loop, on the left. From the north, take UT 128 just before the bridge over the Colorado River and drive about 16 miles to the Castle Valley sign, where you turn right. The road is paved except a very short graded gravel section, which is suitable for passenger cars. The upper part of the loop is closed or impassable in winter.

Time required: 2-1/2 hours to 3 hours.

The Priest & the Nuns, near Castle Valley

The Colorado Riverway (SB 128)

You'll drive this outstanding Scenic Byway if you come from the east on I-70, on your way to Moab. If you come from the south and Moab is your northern-most destination, you will miss it, so I strongly recommend that you take an afternoon or even a day to drive it. It's a 30 miles one way drive from the turnoff with US 191 north of Moab to the historic Dewey Bridge. This road provides superlative views as it follows the twists and turns of the Colorado River through Professor Valley, winding its way at the foot of red canyon walls alternating with wide-open areas offering tantalizing glimpses of the La Sal Mountains. You can include side trips to Negro Bill Canyon (well-known for its hiking opportuni-ties), Castle Valley and its impressive mesas reminiscent of Monument Valley, and the magnificent Fisher Towers (see next section), all extremely photogenic locations. All the beautiful scenery along this stretch of road is better lit after the middle of the afternoon and through sunset.

For those with time on their hands, a 4WD vehicle and adequate driving skills, a long and very rough road begins just before the Dewey bridge and leads south to Top of The World. As its name suggests, this location provides fantastic scenery overlooking Professor Valley and Onion Creek Canyon; it is one of the best panoramas in the entire Moab area.

In spring and summer you'll see commercial raft trips floating down the Colorado River. There are no rapids there, just a quiet float suitable for families

Scenic Byway 128 is a lovely stretch of road north of Moab

with kids. These half-day trips are more rewarding for the beautiful scenery than for their thrills; but they do provide a taste of the longer and better trips down river from Potash to Cataract Canyon.

The Fisher Towers

Driving from Moab on Scenic Byway 128 through Professor Valley, you'll reach the amazing Fisher Towers, rising almost a thousand feet high on your right, at the far end of Richardson Amphitheater. These monoliths are extreme-

The Fisher Towers from trail's end (photo by Philippe Schuler)

ly photogenic, especially at sunset, when the dark brown walls become almost completely red for just a few minutes. In the entire Colorado plateau, you'd be hard put to find a spot more red than this one. You'll find an interesting little group of goblins and chimneys to the right of SB 128, just after you pass the track leading to the Towers.

From the trailhead close to their base, follow the trail down and around the Towers. There are plenty of great views along the way. After a mile or so, you reach the base of the Titan, which is the tallest tower. You can backtrack at this point, but I recommend that you follow the trail to its very end, where you'll eventually reach a ridge with a fantastic 360° panoramic view. From there, you can see and photograph the Towers with the shiny ribbon of the Colorado winding in the background, the very colorful badlands of Onion Creek Canyon on the other side and Castle Rock. The 4.5-mile round-trip trail goes up and down; sometimes, following the cairns is not so obvious and you'll have to exercise caution near drop-offs if the trail is slippery after a rain. In summer, take lots of water and use hiking boots on this trail.

Photo advice: the Fisher Towers are definitely an afternoon location. If you hike the entire trail, you should start in mid-afternoon in summer or shortly after mid-day in the wintertime, so you can be back before sunset to shoot the red monoliths from one of the pullouts on SB 128.

It's also possible to get stunning vertical shots of the Towers from the edge of the river with a medium to long telephoto lens, using their reflection in the water as a foreground. A polarizing filter is a must to control the amount of reflection. To get this shot, continue north on SB 128 for about 3.75 miles after the turnoff to the Fisher Towers and park about 150 yards past a cattle guard, at the second pullout on the left. Near a big flat rock along the road, you'll notice a small path-way descending to the edge of the river through the undergrowth. The path leads to a flat rock miraculously placed in the river close to the bank; depending on the water level you may have to stretch your legs to get to it. The slope may be muddy after a rain, so exercise caution. From this precarious vantage point, you get an awesome view of the Towers. Be there about one hour before sunset to avoid the shade at the bottom of the Towers and on the Colorado River. The towers glow an astonishing bright red just before sunset. This shot is even better in winter and spring, when the La Sals are capped with snow.

Some local photographers have also produced beautiful shots of the Fisher Towers with a full moon in the background. If you shoot the Towers just before they are in shadow, you can keep the exposure within a one-stop range over the entire picture and get a perfectly exposed moon in the deep blue sky.

Getting there: at the north end of Moab, take SB 128 heading for the Colorado River and drive 21 miles northeast from US 191 (or 5.5 miles past the Castle Valley turnoff). The 2.2-mile track leading towards the Fisher Towers trailhead is marked and generally in good condition for passenger cars.

Time required: 1-1/2 hour for a short hike; 4 hours including the described hike and pre-sunset shot by the river. ❀

The Courthouse Towers (photo by Tom Till)

Chapter 11
ARCHES NAT'L PARK

The "classic" view of Delicate Arch

ARCHES NAT'L PARK

Almost everything has been written about Arches National Park in traditional guidebooks. What more can be said? That it's only been thirty years since it was an isolated and little visited spot? That there was only a simple dirt track when Edward Abbey was a ranger there and wrote Desert Solitaire? Today, you're practically assured of finding a crowd rivaling that of the Grand Canyon, especially during the summer and on weekends.

Located 5 miles north of Moab, this relatively small National Park is incredibly spectacular and exercises a particular attraction for visitors from all over the world, not only for its extraordinary concentration of arches, but also for its fantastic monoliths and fins with the Manti-La Sal Mountains in the background. The park can be visited year-round, but spring and fall are the best seasons. Summer is very hot and the long hours of bright sunshine make it difficult to photograph the park. Winter can be magical after a fresh dusting of snow.

It's possible to see the main sights in one day, as the very scenic paved road is only a 45-mile round-trip, including short side attractions. However, you should spend at least two days in the park if you want to do most of the rewarding hikes and photograph the highlights at the best time of day. The park is open 24 hours a day, so you'll have no problem being in the field before sunrise or for a moonlight walk, even if you stay in Moab instead of the park's campground.

Park Avenue & the Courthouse Towers

This is your first contact with the unique landscape of Arches National Park and an interesting stop. The best light is in mid-morning or from mid-afternoon on. It is fun to shoot Nefertiti's Head and its beacon-like neighbor on top of the west cliff with a 200 to 300mm telephoto. At the end of the 1-mile trail between the high walls of Park Avenue, you'll find the very photogenic Three Gossips. Nearby, the Courthouse Towers have some shadow from early spring to early summer. However, that's also the season when wildflowers appear in front of the butte for a glorious photo made famous by Tom Till and many times imitated.

The Petrified Dunes

The Petrified Dunes are interesting Navajo sandstone formations, located close to the road and offering many photogenic compositions, provided you're there at the right time.

Park at the Petrified Dunes pullout before sunrise and walk in the direction of the dunes. Once there, walk for about 50 to 100 yards more into the heart of the dunes or until you come to a spot that seems picturesque and where you can't see your car. The sun rises behind the Manti-La Sal Mountains and directly lights the Great Wall, a series of rock faces several miles long that glow bright red with the appearance of the first sun rays. You can photograph these red walls with the petrified dunes in the foreground. A graduated neutral density filter is a must to preserve the detail of the dunes and still correctly expose the walls.

Balanced Rock

Often photographed, always beautiful, Balanced Rock is a geological rebel, defying the unstoppable forces of erosion. Unfortunately, it is bound to lose its fight at some point and be toppled over like the rest. This will undoubtedly happen very soon in geological time and could even happen soon in our own narrow human scale of time. So, don't wait; record its beauty for the sake of your children, before it disappears forever. You can see it close up by doing the 0.25-mile loop, but it also can be viewed from numerous vantage points farther away.

Photo advice: you can photograph it from close-up with a wide-angle lens or from the other side of the road with a 135 to 200 mm lens, to isolate it against the backdrop of the Manti-La Sal Mountains and get rid of the cars and tourists. The end of the afternoon is best to do this. Night photos under a full moon give great results and are fun to shoot. From this spot, I also like to shoot the tall pillars located near the Windows, using a 500 mm telephoto (see front cover photo). There is also a good shot of Balanced Rock at sunset from the intersection of the Windows and Garden of Eden roads, also with a powerful telephoto.

The Windows

This section of the park has a series of impressive arches that are easy to reach. From the parking lot, start your walk in the direction of Turret Arch and the North and South Windows. Near the South Windows, a spur trail lets you make a loop around the backside of the Windows; very few people use it and it's a real place for photography. Continuing past Turret Arch and South Windows, you'll

Balanced Rock

Fantastic rocks behind the Windows

come to a group of very interesting monoliths. Exercising caution, you can climb behind North Window to shoot the classic photo of Turret Arch framed within the arch's opening. This is an excellent mid- to late-morning shot.

Back at the parking lot, cross the road to go to Double Arch where you can walk right under the double spans of this gigantic arch.

If you are lucky enough to be at Arches during the full moon, a night walk in this part of the park can be very rewarding. In summer, around midnight and under a full moon, the heat radiating from the ground and currents of cool air mix in a delicious swirl around you and the rock formations of the Windows take on a fantastic quality.

Turret Arch seen through the North Window

Double Arch

Panorama Point

This spot provides a bird's-eye view of a good deal of the park, very lovely at the end of day, but too vast to be photographed with much success. You can, however, get a good morning view of Balanced Rock and also of the Devil's Garden with a 200 to 300 mm telephoto.

Wolfe Ranch Petroglyphs

Most visitors stopping at the Wolfe Ranch car park are anxious to be on their way to Utah's most prominent of icons: Delicate Arch. Few visitors go out of their way to look at these almost modern petroglyphs. This is sad, because it is such a beautiful panel. Hopefully, this entry in the book will pique your curiosity and entice you to take the short detour to see and photograph the Wolfe Ranch rock art.

The small but well-preserved panel illustrates the way of life of local Ute tribes. Bighorn sheep, horses and riders are featured prominently on the panel. It is easy to assume that tribal artists endeavored to represent scenes of hunting.

The panel is well lit and surrounded by vegetation. I find it beautiful, because of its simplicity, and a perfect subject for imaginative photography. The immediate area surrounding the mural is cordoned off, but the panel is close enough for standard lens or short telephoto photography.

Photo advice: as with most rock art, well-exposed panels have a tendency to absorb more light and thus to turn gray on film on heavily overcast days. Be sure to have a warming filter handy for such occasions.

Getting there: at the Delicate Arch parking lot, follow the main trail past Wolfe Ranch. After a hundred yards or so, you'll come to a small wooden bridge. Immediately after the bridge, you'll find a small trail to the left. Follow it for another 200 yards until the panel comes to view. You can continue on this trail to meet the Delicate Arch trail.

Delicate Arch

Arches National Park, and the State of Utah, wouldn't be the same without the extraordinary symbol of Delicate Arch. What sets this arch apart is not its size, but its incredibly graceful shape and stunning location above a curving slickrock basin with the Manti-La Sal Mountains in the background.

Delicate Arch is not easy to get to and that's just as well because it somewhat limits foot traffic, which is already very high. You can reach it by taking a trail that's about a 3 mile round-trip, half of which is marked by the footprints of previous visitors on the slickrock as well as by strategically-placed cairns. Though it may be easy to climb to Delicate Arch during the day—count on about 45 minutes one way—it's another matter to try and do this at night. Take a flashlight and exercise extreme caution when descending after sundown. It's easy to take a bad fall if you tend to shuffle along and not lift your feet sufficiently.

Visiting Delicate Arch in the middle of the day is not recommended. This is partly because the climb is hard and can be exhausting if the temperature is high, but also because the arch doesn't reveal all its splendor until late afternoon. You can get information at the Visitor Center or in town as to when the sun will set and figure the best time to climb to it. In any case, Delicate Arch is the perfect hike to end your day in the park.

Photo advice: the best season for photographing Delicate Arch is winter, when the arch is entirely basked in sunset. In late spring, a small amount of shadow becomes visible at the bottom and by July, half of the arch is in shadow at sunset. Keep this in mind and don't arrive too late so you can avoid that nasty black shadow, even if you have to settle for less red on the arch. In summer, you'll be better off leaving the trailhead at least 1-1/2 hour before sunset. There aren't many angles to use at sunset. Backlit shots taken from the extreme left of the arch aren't very satisfactory and the view directly down the axis of the arch is only suitable for family photos. The best vantage point by far is from the edge of the rock ledge encircling the arch, where the trail comes out. Try to position yourself so that the highest peaks of the La Sal Mountains are profiled on the horizon between the base and the summit of the arch, a height of about forty feet. The peaks are frequently adorned with a rosy veil during the last moments of sunset when the arch is lit up in red. If you can, stay for twenty minutes after

Delicate Arch seen from the Viewpoint

sunset to capture the residual lighting in the clouds and just to appreciate this sublime spectacle while the rest of the crowd hurries toward the parking lot.

Delicate Arch Viewpoint

The road continues for one mile past the Delicate Arch trailhead to a distant viewpoint of Delicate Arch. It's quite interesting to go there to see how precariously the arch rests on the plateau. You reach the upper viewpoint at the end of a moderately difficult 1.3-mile round-trip trail. The view of the arch and the cirque from the ridge, with a 200-foot drop-off below you, is startling. Photographing the arch requires a long focal length: a 200mm telephoto lens will isolate the arch perfectly, but anything above 100mm will do. A 24mm lens is necessary for a panoramic view of the cirque and to include the butte to the right. This trip should preferably be made before the end of the afternoon, otherwise the arch will be in the shade.

The Fiery Furnace

The huge sandstone fins of the Fiery Furnace form an excellent foreground with the La Sal Mountains behind them. Ironically, the Fiery Furnace is the coolest place to be in Arches when it's hot, because you're constantly walking in the shade and there is always a light draft running through it. You are encouraged to visit the Furnace with a group, for good reason: many people have gotten lost in this maze of confusing narrow canyons and dead-ending passageways. Nevertheless, it's possible to venture alone into this area off-season, after following a 20-minute video orientation and paying an extra fee. Although there is nothing wrong with a solo visit inside the Furnace, you won't feel comfortable doing so on you own the first time, because it's so easy to loose orientation—even with a compass.

For a first time visit, it's a good idea to join the guided walk. A Park Ranger shows you hidden arches, such as Surprise Arch and Skull Arch, and explains basic facts concerning the geology and ecology of the park, such as the difference between an arch and a bridge, Entrada and Navajo sandstone, and the usefulness of cryptobiotic crust. The guided tour is given twice daily during the high season. Hiking time is about 3 hours, at a relaxed pace, and you'll cover a distance of approximately 2 miles. You can reserve at the Visitor Center up to seven days

The fins of the Fiery Furnace

in advance by paying an extra fee. Be careful, this tour fills up quickly. As your group may have as many as 25 bodies who must move together, it is not an ideal situation for photography. However, nothing prevents you from returning on your own the next day and retracing your step, perhaps an hour before a scheduled guided tour. If everything goes according to plan, you'll have plenty of time for photography before the group catches up with you; if you get lost or something happens to you, you can stay put or retrace your steps and wait for the guided tour.

Photo advice: during the hike inside the Fiery Furnace, don't bother with anything else than a wide-angle! Follow the advice given in the Introduction chapter about photographing in slot canyons—even though there is often quite a bit more light inside the Furnace. If you don't have time to do the guided walk, you can descend for a short distance towards the fins to photograph them with a medium or long telephoto lens and compress the perspective. This works better from late afternoon till sunset.

Sand Dune Arch & Broken Arch

Don't miss the short walk to Sand Dune Arch. It's a peculiar sight and you'll be rewarded on the way by a great shot of a group of symmetrical fins, especially in late afternoon. Broken Arch is also nice and it's an easy flat walk. Consider continuing on the 2-mile loop trail, going through the campground and passing through narrow joints between the fins.

Fins near Sand Dune Arch

The Devil's Garden

Located at the end of the scenic road, the Devil's Garden loop is a real pleasure, arguably one of the most rewarding half-day hikes of the Colorado Plateau. It's a moderate, but spectacular, walk. On your way to superb Double-O Arch, you'll be passing by Landscape Arch, Pine Tree Arch, Partition Arch and Navajo Arch. Past Navajo Arch, you'll climb high on a narrow ridge providing excellent views of the fins below.

At the very end of the trail, you'll come to Dark Angel—a solitary monolith overlooking Salt Valley. From Double-O Arch you can retrace your steps to the trailhead or return by the more difficult Primitive Trail, which is beautiful and less crowded. The Primitive Trail passes through canyons formed by fins and slabs of sandstone, with some sections on steeply slanted ground (slippery when wet). The whole loop, including all the side trails and returning via the Primitive

Trail, is 7.2 miles round-trip. You can shorten your hike by one mile by return-ing the way you came. Take hiking boots, a hat and lot of water on this trail. You should begin the hike early in the morning to capture the best light on Landscape Arch and avoid the extreme heat of the day, especially in summer when it's really cooking. If you do it in the afternoon, however, you'll have the advantage of good light on the most beautiful side of Double-O Arch.

Photo advice: the best season to photograph Landscape Arch is in late spring and early summer, when there are no shadows on the arch in early morning. The view in complete sunshine is only available in mid-morning during the rest of the year and a moderate warming filter will help restore the rich color saturation of the sandstone. In 1991, a large block of rock fell from the 306-foot long span of Landscape Arch, causing the National Park Service to close the trail under the arch. The fence, which was put up to prevent people from venturing under the arch, severely limits your composition in framing Landscape Arch artistically. The best vantage point to photograph the arch against a background of sky is at the end of the short spur. Pine Tree Arch allows interesting compositions by shooting directly from below the arch. Double-O Arch is one of the most spec-tacular arches in the Southwest. To photograph it, pass through the lower open-ing of the arch and climb the little hill on the other side until you find a suitable location. A wide-angle lens is necessary. Remember that this side is in the shade in the morning. The Devil's Garden fins are also best lit in the afternoon.

Double-O Arch

Pine Tree Arch

The Klondike Bluffs

The Klondike Bluffs area offers a nice easy hiking experience coupled with some great sights and photography, away from the increasing stream of visitors. Outside of the season, it is entirely possible to spend a couple of hours in the Klondike Bluffs and never see a soul.

Although massive Tower Arch gets most of the attention, the most striking landmark in the Klondike Bluffs area is the formation group known as the Marching Men, consisting of spires of various thickness and height aligned one behind another, very much like a soldier troop on the go. The loop from the trailhead near Salt Valley Road is 3.4 miles round-trip and takes at least two hours depending on the time you devote to photography.

Photo advice: photography inside the Klondike Bluffs is generally best in late afternoon. If you want to shoot the bluffs from the Salt Valley Road or US 191, morning will also be good. To photograph the Marching Men in the best possible light, plan on returning from Tower Arch about 45 minutes before Sunset and find a suitable location at the top of the sand dune where all the Marching Men appear in your line of sight from a slightly dominant position. This location requires a short telephoto. Alternately, you can walk down toward the middle of the last sand dune and photograph the group from below with a moderate wide-angle to standard lens.

Getting there: the easiest and most common way is to come via Salt Valley road; its turnoff is on the park road, one mile before the Devil's Garden area. The road is usually in good condition, although it can be quite sandy in places or even impassable after a rain. After 7.7 miles, you see a first spur road to your left. This sandy 4WD road leads in about 3 miles to a car park very close to Tower Arch; there is a nasty ramp that needs to be negotiated around mile one. Also, if you use this road, you'll miss the hike though the beautiful scenery of the Bluffs—including the Marching Men. Instead, take the second 2WD road on the left,

The Marching Men

leading in 1.3 miles to the main trailhead. After visiting the Klondike Bluffs, you can take your chances and return to the park road, opposite Balanced Rock, by way of the Willow Flats 4WD road; this is a very sandy and difficult road and every year visitors get stuck on it and have to be pulled out. From the car park near the main trailhead, it's relatively easy to leave the park (and also to enter) by continuing on Salt Creek Road to the north until the intersection with Thomson Road. Turning to the left, you'll then reach US 191 in less than a mile. I have driven this road in a 4WD vehicle and feel it would present no difficulties for a high-clearance vehicle in dry weather. As always, get directions in town or at the Visitor Center to find out the exact condition of the road. Finally, if you feel adventurous and have a 4WD, you can also take the BLM road leaving from US 191 just before you reach the Moab airfield and driving directly toward the bluffs. There is a BLM sign on the gate and a fairly large parking area. Close the gate behind you and proceed on the well-maintained dirt road. Things worsen at the sandy wash crossing and the road becomes very narrow and poorly maintained after that. Drive as far as you feel comfortable, then park and walk toward the bluffs. ❁

Contemplating Canyonlands

Chapter 12
CANYONLANDS — ISLAND IN THE SKY

Dead Horse Point at sunrise

CANYONLANDS — ISLAND IN THE SKY

I heartily recommend Canyonlands Nat'l Park to those who love sweeping canyon panoramas, river goosenecks, outstanding rock formations and who wish to escape the Grand Canyon crowds. I have recommended and continue to recommend this park to innumerable visitors. They return unanimous in their opinion that the views are as vast and impressive as those of Grand Canyon.

Just twenty years ago this park received only 10,000 visitors a year, who had to drive on dirt roads. Today, though not as heavily visited as Arches, it's become the destination of choice for tourists, 4x4 enthusiasts, mountain bikers, hikers and certainly for photographers. Unfortunately, Madison Avenue and Hollywood have also discovered it, and you can see it in more and more movies, TV ads and music videos. This may have a very negative impact on the park in the near future.

Canyonlands Nat'l Park consists of three districts separated by the two rivers merging in its center: the Colorado River and the Green River. Each district has its own distinct flavor of landscape and human activity: to the north, Island In the Sky and Dead Horse Point form a vast peninsula overlooking the canyons and is easy to visit. To the east and south, the Needles district is particularly remarkable for the diversity of its geological features—pinnacles, arches, grabens and canyons—requiring a lot of hiking or 4-wheel driving. To the west, the Maze is wild and desolate and visiting its intricate network of canyons and mesas is only for the most adventurous.

Lacking bridges on the rivers, these three sections are separated by hours of driving. Just to get a glimpse of the three sections one needs several days; several trips are a more realistic approach to enjoy some of the many trails. To gain a true perspective of the vastness of the park and understand its geography, geology and diversity, you would need to fly over it. Given the extreme temperatures that affect this region, the best time to visit is undoubtedly spring and the first part of autumn.

Island in the Sky is the most accessible—and also the most visited—of the three districts of the park. A scenic road provides easy access to expansive views from a high mesa top (reaching 6000 feet of elevation) overlooking dozens of miles of canyon country. This paved road is SR 313, heading southwest about 11 miles north of Moab on Hwy 191. The Visitor Center is located 22 miles past the junction and the road continues for another 12 miles until it dead-ends at Grand Viewpoint Overlook.

Dead Horse Point State Park

Even if you do not have much time, don't miss Dead Horse Point State Park for an outstanding panorama of the area. This small park, administered by the State of Utah, offers the prototypical view of the American West canyons, as pictured in ads and movies.

Photo advice: the best location is at Dead Horse Point Overlook, just past the narrow neck, which offers two panoramas: the bend of the Colorado River with its superb mesa at the center and, on the opposite side, a view of the canyons with the Manti La Sal Mountains in the background. From the parking lot, the choice of views is limited. Walk on the Rim Trail around the viewpoint and pick a foreground you like, which will best show the depth of the canyon and the immensity of the terrain. A 28 to 35mm lens is ideal for the river bend. For the panorama of the canyon and the La Sal Mountains, you can give free rein to your imagination if you have a zoom. Any focal length will highlight something different. The bend is best photographed in the early morning, with the sun rising on the left, but sunset is equally beautiful. In fact, the subject is so awe-inspiring that even mid-day photos can be impressive. It's possible to photograph the bend before sunrise or after sunset using a warming filter to avoid a bluish tint on the mesa. On the other hand, for the panorama of the canyons, a morning or evening light is essential to best render depth and contrast. With a bit of luck and patience, the high clouds will be basking in the last gleams of sunset and the snowy peaks of the La Sal Mountains will be a vivid pink. For a slightly different view of the eastern canyons, you can also go to Basin Overlook, about halfway between Dead Horse Point Overlook and the Visitor Center.

Getting there: the turnoff to Dead Horse Point State Park is on UT 313, 14.5 miles from Hwy 191 and before the entrance to Canyonlands. From the turnoff, drive 8 miles to Dead Horse Point Overlook at the very end of the road. If you have a 4x4 vehicle, you can go back down by way of Long Canyon and SB 279.

Time required: about 1-1/2 hour round-trip to get there from Moab and 1 hour on location. However, you will most likely want to visit this place at the same time as Island in the Sky. The complete circuit—to Grandview Point, including the side roads—can be done in a long half day at a hurried pace, though that will mean sacrificing taking pictures at either sunrise and/or sunset.

Mesa Arch sunrise

Mesa Arch

Mesa Arch, located about 6 miles south of the Island in the Sky Visitor Center, offers an outstanding photographic opportunity, which has become a "classic" from the Southwest. If you go during the day, you'll see the entire superb spectacle of these immense canyons framed through a magnificent arch perched on the edge of a precipitous drop...really pretty, you say. Yes, but there's better still if you're willing to pay the price: you'll have to get up well before dawn to catch it at its very best for a truly magical photograph.

Start by getting the precise time of sunrise for that day. You can get this information the day before at the Visitor Center or in town. Plan to be at the Mesa Arch parking area about a half-hour before sunrise. From Moab, plan on 45 minutes travel time to get there. Park your car and take the short trail, it's a 15-minute walk. There will still be 15 minutes, plenty of time to find a spot, prepare your equipment and try to visualize in your mind's eye the extraordinary spectacle that will soon be unveiled. Don't rush it, even if the sky is already very light. There will still be plenty of time before the sun actually appears and nothing will happen without its presence.

When the sun makes its appearance, far beyond the canyons, the underside of the arch will glow a vivid red, offering an absolutely sublime spectacle. The sun rises on the left of the arch in summer and on the right in winter. In either case, it's possible to frame it inside one of the arch's pillars.

You'll get the best results by spot metering on the sky just above the arch. As a general rule, a clean northern sky is as neutral as a gray card and can be metered on accurately. Do not meter under the bridge where the light is too intense and would severely underexpose your picture. If your camera doesn't have spot measuring, just trust your metering system and add a half stop overexposure to be safe. I have always obtained the best results either with the normal exposure indicated by the camera or with a half stop of overexposure, but not more. You'll have a good 15-minute window of opportunity to photograph the underside of the arch basking in intense red light, gradually turning orange and yellow on the edges. Work briskly, the first five minutes are the most intense. You'll have a hard time containing your excitement in the face of such a magnificent spectacle. For the grand finale, position yourself so the sun appears masked just behind the edge of the arch and bracket a couple of stops on each side.

You'll get excellent results with lenses ranging from an extreme wide angle to 35mm. A 35mm lens will allow you to get better detail of the canyons through the arch and of the Manti La Sal Mountains in the distance. A tripod is of course indispensable to maximize the depth of field. An artistic blur of the foreground or background would kill the impact of this classic landscape composition.

If you back up about 70 feet, a hillock will let you take shots with an 80 to 105mm lens, compressing the perspective of the canyons and the La Sal Mountains with the incandescent top of the arch.

Mesa Arch can also be photographed successfully at the end of the afternoon with the sun lighting the front of the arch and the canyons in the distance. The accent is then on the contrast between the strongly lit arch and the very blue sky.

Grand Viewpoint, Murphy Point & Green River Overlook

Grand Viewpoint offers a breathtaking panorama and you won't regret the miles you've traveled to get to this spot. From the main vista point, your eye encompasses hundreds of miles of canyon country; you can even improve on this view by taking the easy 2-mile round-trip trail leading to the tip of the plateau. Unfortunately, it's not an easy task to capture this on film, unless you have a truly spectacular sky. Instead I recommend that you drive back on the road for about a mile to the picnic area and hike the 1.5-mile round-trip trail leading, at the right fork, to the lesser-known White Rim Overlook. It's a great early morning photograph and the view over Monument Basin is astounding. This is by far the best morning location on the east side. If you're on the Island toward the end of the afternoon, go to the Green River Overlook or to Murphy Point, set up your tripod and get ready to capture another grandiose vista.

Clouds over Murphy Point (photo by Lynn Radeka)

Upheaval Dome

This geologic phenomenon, which looks more like a crater than a dome, is quite interesting to observe but almost impossible to photograph. However, it would be a shame to miss as there's a paved road leading to it. An easy 2-mile round-trip trail leads to two successive overlooks from the edge of the crater. The various geologic layers of the park are particularly well displayed and easy to observe because of the angle of the walls. It's a perfect opportunity for a little refresher course on the geology of the plateau and to learn to distinguish between the colors and the strata of the various sandstone formations. Driving back a few hundred yards toward the main park road from the parking lot of Upheaval Dome, you can also take the easy 1-mile round-trip trail to the top of Whale Rock, from where you have good views. Less than a mile further, you'll find the trailhead for the Alcove Spring Trail, leading to Upper Taylor Canyon and the Moses and Zeus spires. It's a long 10.8-mile round-trip, passing by a spectacular alcove. Even if you do not hike all the way, it's worth hiking as far as the alcove, which is less than a mile from the trailhead. There is a good picture from the back of the alcove with a very wide-angle lens. You can also reach the Moses and Zeus monoliths by 4WD from the Taylor Canyon Rim Trail, for a view from above, and from the White Rim Road (see White Rim Road section below).

The Shafer Trail

The Shafer Trail lets you descend, amongst superlative views, onto the White Rim plateau a thousand feet below. Originally an old cattle road used by ranchers since the late 1800's, it was enlarged in the fifties during the uranium boom. You can observe its spectacular switchbacks carved right into the flank of the steep canyon cliffs from the Shafer Trail viewpoint, located a few hundred yards past the Visitor Center.

You'll need a 4WD or at least a high-clearance vehicle to descend the scary-looking—but not so difficult—Shafer Trail and get a close-up view of the Colorado River and the famous White Rim Road. Don't attempt it in a passenger car unless you want to experience firsthand the expensive proposition of being hauled out with a tow-truck! If you do not have your own 4WD vehicle, it's easy enough to rent one for the day in Moab. Needless to say, this trail must only be driven in dry weather, very slowly and using low gears.

The Shafer Trail can be easily integrated into a highly scenic loop drive, starting and ending up in Moab. In the course of one day, you can watch the sun rise at Dead Horse Point or Mesa Arch, visit Island in the Sky including some of the short hikes described above, descend the Shafer Trail and spend some time on the White Rim—at least as far as Musselman Arch—before returning to Moab by way of the Potash Road and SB 279, passing Thelma & Louise Point along the way. A memorable day by any standards.

Ancient Kiva (photo by Lynn Radeka)

The White Rim Road

To visit the extraordinary White Rim and Monument Basin in greater depth, you'll have to allow for a multi-day trip to cover the 100 miles of this popular loop. You'll need a 4WD or at least a high-clearance vehicle and you can only take this road in a clockwise direction, beginning at the Potash Road or Shafer Trail and ending at Mineral Road. Most of the time, the road winds along the edge of the rim of the flat plateau halfway between the Island in the Sky mesa and the Colorado and Green rivers. It's an unforgettable trip and, all in all, relatively easy to accomplish.

In spring or early autumn, you can do this trip at a relaxed pace without suffering from summer's heat or icy winter nights. On this arid plateau, where wood fires are no longer allowed, nighttime temperatures drop well below freezing by November and remain so until early March.

Photo advice: there are countless opportunities for photography along the track, starting with the Shafer Trail switchbacks. Musselman Arch is an interesting flat span above the basin below. If you have no fear of heights you can cross it. Lathrop Canyon provides access to the Colorado River.

The most interesting section of the White Rim is without doubt Monument Basin, where photographic opportunities abound. If you have no time for a multi-day trip or if you couldn't obtain a permit, it's still possible to make the round-trip from Moab to Monument Basin in one very long summer day.

The western side of the trail offers outstanding views of the Green River and the great monoliths of the Maze: Ekker Butte, Cleopatra's Chair, Buttes of the Cross, and more. Turk's Head is also a good shot. As you progress further north, you'll come level to the Green at Potato Bottom and reach the spectacular location of the Fort Ruin, smack in the middle of a great gooseneck.

Getting there: there is a quota system established by the National Park Service and you'll have to make reservations several months in advance. Only a few permits are issued every day, depending on the size of the groups. Access is limited by the number of primitive campsites located along the road. Some of these campsites are unique, like that of White Crack, at the southern tip of the trail, which has only a single car site. You will be alone on the edge of the canyon, with Junction Butte in front of you and the long ribbon of the Colorado River quietly flowing a thousand feet below. Island in the Sky is behind you, over a thousand feet higher, and a magnificent starry sky serves as your roof. The immensity and solitude of the surrounding canyons is impressive. The only other human beings for over 40 miles around are the few at the other campsites scattered along the trail. Candlestick, on the western side, is also a great single car campsite.

Time required: 2 to 4 days depending on the season. ✿

Druid Arch

Chapter 13

CANYONLANDS — THE NEEDLES

The fantastic Needles panorama at sunrise

CANYONLANDS — THE NEEDLES

The Needles district is much less visited than Island in the Sky. There are two main reasons for this: one difficulty lies in the distance, as it is in a cul-de-sac with only one way in and out. The other is that there is little to see from the scenic road proper—not even viewpoints like at Island in the Sky. The main attractions of this district can only be explored by day hiking, backpacking and 4-wheel driving. The Needles area has a wonderful network of trails, all well marked at the trailheads and made easier to follow thanks to many cairns along the way. Those with enough time and who are not discouraged by the effort will not regret their visit to the Needles. They'll discover a wide variety of geological features, including colorful spires rising hundreds of feet above the ground, many mushroom-like sandstone formations, massive arches, grabens and canyons, as well as much rock art and alcove dwellings left by the early inhabitants.

The best way to visit the Needles is to camp at Squaw Flat, which fills up quickly during the high season. This will let you photograph these extraordinary needles in the early morning, while the light is at its best, beginning a long and rewarding day of exploration in the area. If you can't camp, you can always resort to staying in a motel in Moab or Monticello, but it makes it considerably harder to be on location during the golden hour.

Moab offers all the advantages of modern civilization as well as a central location for exploring the surrounding parks, but it is 75 miles (about 1-1/2 hours) from the Visitor Center. Monticello can save you time as it is only 49 miles (or 1 hour) away. Also, this small town at the foot of the Abajo Mountains has a bit of an alpine flavor, which is quite pleasant. Regardless of your starting point, you turn off US 191, almost opposite an interesting monolith called Church Rock, for the last 35 miles leading to the Needles' Visitor Center on UT 211. The turnoff is 40 miles south of Moab and 14 miles north of Monticello.

From Monticello, you can also take the paved Harts Draw Road and get some nice but distant views of the park down the northern side of the Abajo Mountains before catching up with UT 211 in the vicinity of Newspaper rock. The Harts Draw Road shaves about 8 miles off the trip. Past Newspaper Rock,

The confluence of the Colorado River and the Green

UT 211 becomes particularly scenic as it follows the superb red cliffs of Indian Creek canyon. Under the right light and windless conditions, there is an interesting photo opportunity of their reflection in a little lake located on the right side of the road, a few miles past Newspaper Rock.

If you get to or from the Needles before sunrise or after sunset in winter, watch out for deer that often cross the road between Newspaper Rock and US 191.

A cornucopia of petroglyphs at Newspaper Rock

Newspaper Rock

After passing by the base of the Abajo Mountains, the road follows the lovely, shallow canyon of Indian Creek, along which you'll stumble upon Newspaper Rock State Park, about 12 miles from US 191. Even if you aren't a fan of Puebloan pictorial art, you really should stop to see these remarkable petroglyphs carved in the rock, very close to the road. A couple of them have been found to be 1,500 years old, but the majority were carved more recently over a period of several hundred years. This is one of the largest panels of petroglyphs you are likely to find on the Colorado plateau. These petroglyphs are very easy to photograph at any time of the day, but are better lit in the afternoon.

Lavender and Davis Canyon

Continuing toward the park entrance on UT 211, you'll leave the Dugout Ranch to your left, continue on for about 9 miles and, as you approach the striking silhouettes of North and South Six-Shooter Peaks, turn left on Davis Canyon road then left again toward Lavender Canyon Road. This well-maintained dirt road passes through private land inside the wide and beautiful canyon. It's about 14 miles to the southern park boundary, where a permit is required for 4-wheel driving past the gate. There, you can photograph some interesting arches. First, you'll pass Natural Arch and Caterpillar Arch; both are encountered to your right shortly after the park boundary. Look for them high on top of the canyon wall. Cleft Arch, a massive arch with beautiful streaks of desert varnish is located 3.5 miles further, near the end of the road. Time permitting, there are more arches to be explored in the upper part of the canyon.

Turning back toward UT 211, make a left at the turnoff to Davis Canyon. Although shorter, this canyon is much less visited than Lavender and the road is rough and quite sandy in places. There are fewer arches, but some Puebloan dwellings and the interesting Five Faces pictograph panel.

The Scenic Drive

The scenic drive winds for about 16 miles round-trip from the Visitor Center through red rock country with some distant views of the spires. The first stop along the road is Roadside Ruin, a nice Ancestral Puebloan granary only a few hundred yards from the road. Further up, after about a mile on a side gravel road leading to the Salt Creek area, you reach Cave Spring. This pleasant and easy trail, only 0.6 mile round-trip, leads to a grotto near a perennial creek where you'll find some rock art and a well-preserved cowboy camp with original items

Six-Shooter Peak and Cloud (photo by Lynn Radeka)

left by the last occupants. The trail passes two ladders and continues on slickrock with good views of the surrounding area.

At the intersection of the Scenic Route and Elephant Hill Road, you'll find a lovely flat prairie. It makes an excellent foreground for the view of the Needles in the morning or to observe them from the road with your binoculars.

Two miles farther, the short Pothole Point loop contains a group of waterholes carved into the rock by erosion. These potholes are quite interesting when they are filled with water and you can see myriads of tiny organisms swimming in them. Nearby, you can see some nice examples of cryptobiotic soil along the trail. Be sure not to step on it, as it literally takes decades to regenerate. Shortly before the end of the road, the 2.4-mile Slickrock Trail makes a loop along the mesa top overlooking the canyon. The best viewpoint is at the end of the trail, where Junction Butte and the Island in the Sky district are in full view. If you don't want to walk all the way, the first viewpoint on the Slickrock Trail—a short half mile from the start of the trail—offers a panoramic view of the cliffs with the Manti La Sal Mountains in the background. If you come at sunset, there are miles of cliffs that glow red while the snowy peaks are tinted pink. Big Spring Canyon Overlook, at the very end of the road, is not spectacular but offers an easy access to a lovely canyon, if you prefer not to do too much walking.

Squaw Flat

For a fantastic view of the Needles at sunrise, take the Big Spring Canyon trail from the Squaw Flat parking lot, close to the campground. In less than a mile,

Sentinels of stone line up the Needles horizon

First light on Needles formations

you'll come to a viewpoint overlooking the Needles. An 80 to 200mm zoom lens would be perfect here, allowing you to get different shots with the rising sun striking the walls. A polarizing filter will help accent the relief and darken the sky a bit so that the needles will stand out perfectly.

After having photographed the sunrise from this viewpoint, you might want to follow the very scenic trail descending into Big Spring. It's an easy walk in a wooded canyon bottom and the scenery is enchanting. A little under 3 miles down the trail, you'll come to a second viewpoint, even closer to the Needles. From there, you can best capture them using an 85 to 135mm lens.

Elephant Hill

A gravel road leads in 2 miles from the scenic road to the base of Elephant Hill. There, you'll find the famous 4x4 track of the same name, as well as the foot trail heading south to Chesler Park and Druid Arch. From the highest point on this road, you can get a beautiful panorama of the Needles district. A few hundred yards after the "blind curve" sign, you'll see a small slickrock hill to the right. You can easily climb on it for an excellent view of the entire area, including the Needles. The view is particularly majestic at sunset with a medium to long tele-photo. Watch out for the cryptobiotic soil, however.

The challenging 4x4 track is only for specially equipped vehicles and carries a substantial risk of vehicle damage. No behemoths there either, the Squeeze Play section is very narrow. This track requires excellent mastery of driving on slickrock and of your vehicle's reactions. Elephant Hill is not the only difficult spot of the trail, SOB Hill has some rock steps that are at least as challenging. On the other hand, you can also go this route on foot or on a mountain bike for a short distance as there are good views of the Needles after you've crossed Elephant Hill. It's also very entertaining to see the 4x4s negotiate the slickrock grades. The Elephant Hill 4WD track leads to the Grabens, Devil's Kitchen and its primitive campground surrounded by huge rocks, the confluence of the Green and Colorado Rivers and also to the west side of Chesler Park near the Joint Trail. To best observe and photograph the Grabens, you should invest in a short flight over the area, as described at the end of the Maze chapter.

Chesler Park

This extraordinary group of spires, with strongly colored horizontal striations, is located beyond the Needles that are visible from the road. The extremely ancient spires of Cedar Mesa sandstone are located in the center of a remarkably verdant basin surrounded by a circle of needles. The tall grasses in the park form a magnificent foreground and a singular contrast with the large spires.

The Chesler Park Viewpoint, located on a saddle at the edge of the basin, can be reached on a beautiful slickrock trail that's not always easy to follow. It's a 6-mile round-trip from the Elephant Hill car park, requiring about 3 hours. The

Exquisite Chesler Park in its tallgrass setting

last 200 yards, nicknamed Fat Man's Misery, are moderately challenging.

If you don't mind adding another 1-1/2 hours to your hike, walk back down Fat Man's Misery and take the nice trail to your left, leading to Devil's Kitchen. This allows you to return to the parking lot by way of the Elephant Hill 4x4 track. If you are considering driving it later, it's a good way to gauge the infamous rock steps and make sure you and your vehicle will able to make it.

However, if you really want to get the most out of Chesler Park and take photos in late afternoon light, you'll have to descend into the "park" from the Viewpoint. From there, walk the 5-mile loop around it, via the Joint Trail—a narrow crack in the rock about 60 feet deep and 0.25-mile long located at the southern tip of the loop. The entire loop from Elephant Hill is about 11 miles, using the shortest route. This may seem a bit long, but once in the "park", you'll progress rapidly over flat ground and the loop can be completed in a 7-hour hike. This leaves enough time for pictures, rest and enjoying the scenery. Watch out for the heat and possible dehydration if you do this hike in summer. Even in late afternoon, the heat is still intense.

Photo advice: best early in the morning for the view of the Needles from the beginning of the trail and from Chesler Park Viewpoint, but afternoon is preferred for photographing the spires from the south. You can get distant pictures of the spires from the viewpoint just before the east entrance of the Joint Trail; follow the cairns on the slickrock and climb on a small ridge overlooking the "park", with some red round rocks on white sandstone making a beautiful foreground. For the closest and best views of Chesler Park, follow the side trail toward backcountry campsites CP1, 2 and 3 until you find a suitable spot.

Nearby location: if you are spending the night at one of Chesler Park's backcountry campsites, you can easily push toward Butler Flats to photograph Horsehoof Arch, located just past the remote campsite of the same name, near Bobby Jo Camp.

Druid Arch

Druid Arch is one of the most striking arches of the Colorado Plateau, definitely worthy of the Top Five. It would definitely be yet another overused icon of the west if it were more accessible. As it is, the 11-mile round-trip hike discourages most visitors... as it does art directors for athletic footwear companies. For those who are ready to put in a moderate effort, however, Druid Arch is a fantastic photo destination. The mostly level walk follows the Chesler Park Viewpoint trail from the Elephant Hill trailhead for 2.1 miles before branching south. It is well marked all the way. Walking in the canyon on sand or slickrock is easy and not much different from any other walks in the Needles area. The upper part of the canyons reveals awesome views as you penetrate deeper inside the needles. There is one easily negotiated dryfall and a fixed iron ladder to be climbed in your final approach to the arch.

Druid Arch from the upper viewpoint

Photo advice: if you get to the arch in the morning, continue on the marked trail until you reach the amphitheater. This is the best vantage point for morning photography of the arch. A moderate wide-angle lens will work best. In the afternoon, the arch is backlit from this point. Retrace your steps, descending to the wash from where you started your final ascent. Follow the wash to the southwest, skirting the arch until you end up on the opposite side. Climbing on the slickrock can lead to good vantage points.

Horse Canyon, Salt Creek and Angel Arch

As of this writing, Salt Creek is closed to vehicular traffic because of the pollution generated in the streambed by petroleum residues from 4x4 vehicles. There is a certain amount of controversy about the issue and there have been rumors that the NPS may tentatively reopen the track for further impact studies. I find it doubtful. Assuming that the track reopens some time soon, you'd need a 4x4 for the 22-mile round-trip to Angel Arch. For now, you'll have to walk. Horse Canyon is open to 4x4 traffic, subject to obtaining a permit first.

The track leaves south of the Cave Spring area (see the Scenic Drive section above). After 2.5 miles, you reach the junction with the Salt Creek Road. Take the left fork for Horse Canyon. The track goes on for 8 miles; it is not very challenging but there are some deep pockets of sand in places. You'll pass below Paul

Bunyan's Potty, an interesting pothole arch with a suggestive streak of desert varnish flowing through and out of it. A short telephoto will capture it perfectly. About 2.5 miles from the junction, a 0.5-mile side trip off the track leads to Tower Ruin, a ruin located under an alcove, high on the cliff. A short trail leads to the base of the ruin where you can catch a better glimpse, but do not climb into the ruin; use a medium telephoto to capture it. Continuing on the main track, you'll end up at Castle Arch and Fortress Arch.

Back at the junction with Salt Creek Road, you can follow the wash south for 1 mile until you reach Peek-a-Boo camp. From this point on, the track has been closed to all vehicular traffic since 1998 and you need to backpack—after obtaining the necessary backcountry permit for at-large camping. The walk is level and easy, with patches of deep sand here and there. You'll be constantly following or crossing the dry bed of Lower Salt Creek. During springtime, shallow water is present in the upper part of the creek. Watch out for the extremely aggressive deerflies that patrol the Salt Creek bed during spring and summer. There are many unmarked ruins, granaries and rock art panels along the way. After hiking 8.5 miles from Peek-a-Boo, take the left fork to Angel Arch and continue 1.5 miles to the arch. You can walk right below the spectacular span for close-up photography. A classic way to photograph Angel Arch is to include Molar Rock—a precariously top heavy rock in the shape of a tooth—in the foreground.

Time required: if the Salt Creek Road ever reopens, both Horse Canyon and Lower Salt Creek can be easily visited by 4WD in one long day. Visiting Angel

Angel Arch in late afternoon (photo by Kerry Thalmann)

Arch on foot requires an overnighter and some at-large camping. This area rarely sees visitors nowadays outside of the season.

Nearby location: after visiting Angel Arch, continuing on Upper Salt Creek requires further backpacking and a car shuttle and is outside the scope of this book. However, you can do an incursion into Upper Salt Creek in one long day from the southern trailhead at Cathedral Butte, 18 miles from UT 211 on a dirt road beginning north of the Dugout Ranch. This 17-mile hike to Upper Jump pool passes by the All-American Man pictograph, numerous small arches and Puebloan ruins. Long Ruin, located on the east side of the trail contains more than thirty rooms and is the largest in the park.

Canyon Rims

To reach the two Canyon Rims viewpoints—Needles Overlook and Anticline Overlook—take the well-marked road about 33 miles south of Moab off US 191. Coming from the south the turnoff is 7 miles north of UT 211. This good paved road reaches the Needles Overlook after 22 miles with little to see along the way. The view from the Overlook is spectacular because it is such an incredibly vast panorama; however, by this very nature it doesn't lend itself well to photography. The Colorado River is not visible and the Needles district is very distant, even with a telephoto. Drive back about 7 miles and turn north on the well-graded dirt road until it dead-ends at the Anticline Overlook. The panorama from the Anticline Overlook provides a closer view to Island in the Sky, the Colorado River and Junction Butte, but I do not rate it very high either for photography. Still, both views are spectacular and worth the 2-1/2 hour detour if time isn't an issue. ✿

The Land of Standing Rocks

Chapter 14

CANYONLANDS — THE MAZE

The Fins and Ernie's Country

CANYONLANDS — THE MAZE

Introduction to The Maze

As the name implies, the Maze is an intricate network of canyons. However, it also contains an amazing variety of fascinating rock formations spread out over a vast, wild and rugged area. As Canyonlands's most remote and difficult to access district, the Maze sees relatively few visitors; if you are looking for solitude and quiet, the Maze is for you. With the exception of the Horseshoe Canyon detached section, which can be visited in one day, you will need at least three days to explore the Maze by 4WD and a lot more if you're backpacking or mountain biking. Spring and autumn are the best seasons to explore the Maze. During wintertime, snow conditions often force closure of strategic access routes, such as the Flint Trail. In summer, the heat can become unbearable and there is no water along the trails. Regardless of the season, avoid rainy weather at all cost; it turns the clay roads into a quagmire and you could get stuck for days on end.

The Maze district of Canyonlands Nat'l Park is arguably one of the most remote areas in the continental United States and visiting it requires careful planning and preparation. First off, you'll need to have a 4WD high-clearance vehicle in tip-top mechanical condition. A short wheelbase with low-departure angle is recommended and so are rugged all-terrain tires with as many plies as possible. Large sport utility vehicles will not do well in the Maze, especially in some difficult sections like Teapot Canyon. They will most likely make it—although the stock tires may not—but you'll risk inflicting serious damage to the undercarriage, bumpers, mud flaps, running boards, etc. For additional security, you'll need a couple of extra tires, a high-lift jack, a tow rope, a shovel, chains for all tires if there is a chance of snow, an extra jerry can of gas, lots of water, topographic maps and other necessities as you see fit for an extended 4WD road trip

The Wall, in the Land of Standing Rocks

requiring total self-sufficiency. Needless to say, you also need good 4-wheel driving skills. A vehicle rescue from the Maze will cost you in the neighborhood of $2,500; not an outlandish figure when you consider that the Doll House is located 88 miles from the road, one-way, on a wretched trail. Oh, and don't you forget to bring your own port-a-potty, as required by the National Park Service.

If you plan to do any kind of hiking inside the Park, especially with photographic equipment, you'll benefit from being in good physical shape, as some of the hikes are long and strenuous. Most are on primitive trails, with exposure to cliff edges and steep routes requiring some scrambling and chimneying. Most anybody in decent shape can do these hikes, but you may experience a lot of discomfort if you are not used to hiking and carrying weight over long distances. A rope or a couple of 20-feet straps are necessary to lower packs in some difficult passages.

Any overnight trip to The Maze requires a backcountry permit, which has to be reserved well in advance if you go in spring or early autumn. During the off-season, you should have no difficulty getting a campsite by checking directly with the Hans Flat Ranger Station. Hans Flat is the official entry to The Maze; if you don't enter the Maze via the Hans Flat Ranger Station, you must have a pre-reserved permit in your possession.

One final piece of advice: bring a friend, preferably in a second vehicle. Do not venture into the Maze alone or without leaving specific details on your whereabouts. If you have neither the vehicle(s) nor the partner(s) for this trip, but have a few hundred dollars or more to spare, you may consider hiring an outfitter to take you into the Maze. Let them wreck their vehicle and enjoy yourself free of concerns in one of the world's great wilderness.

Getting there: the following information is valid for all locations inside the Maze district. There are three access routes to the various landmarks of the Maze.

The most common way is to take US 24 to the Hans Flat turnoff, located 0.6-mile south of Goblin Valley Road (see the San Rafael Reef Chapter). This is about 20 miles north of Hanksville or 25 miles south of I-17 if coming from Green River. Follow the good graded dirt road for 25 miles. At the roofed signpost, follow the right fork for another 21 miles to the Hans Flat Ranger Station. The left fork leads in 7 miles to Horseshoe Canyon. There are often pronghorns visible a short distance from the road in this area. Except after a rain, this road is easily passable by passenger car; however 2.5 miles southeast of Hans Flat (at the North Point Road Junction) a high clearance 4WD becomes necessary, whether going west to Panorama Point or south toward the steep switchbacks of the Flint Trail.

After descending the Flint Trail, you can head northeast to the Maze Overlook or, if you want to visit the Land of Standing Rocks and The Doll House, go south then northeast traversing a very tough section around Teapot Rock. This section is not so technically difficult as extremely hard on tire walls and undercarriage.

An alternate way to visit the southern part of The Maze is to enter from the south on the usually well-maintained county road, leaving from US 95 near Hite. This road is located halfway between the Colorado River bridge and the Dirty Devil River bridge and is easy to miss. It allows you to make good speed for the first thirty miles to Waterhole Flats and to avoid the switchbacks of the Flint Trail. However, this can lead to a false sense of security as it leads you smack into Teapot Canyon where things become suddenly hellish. Teapot Canyon is by far the most infamous portion of the road into the Maze. In my opinion, it would be sad to miss the Flint Trail, which is a road of legend and part of the fun of visiting the Maze, much as the Shafer is part of the White Rim Road. However, even if you enter The Maze from the north by Hans Flat, you can also exit via this southern route. Gas is available at the Hite Marina if your tank doesn't hold much.

A third way into the Maze is from Green River via a graded dirt road heading to Horseshoe Canyon (see section below).

Horseshoe Canyon

Horseshoe Canyon is a detached section of Canyonlands National Park, located northwest of the Maze. It protects a series of outstanding early Fremont pictographs dating back from around 1000 BC and located inside a very scenic

The Great Gallery

canyon. By a strange quirk of history, this canyon which was formerly known as Barrier Canyon, has lost its original name, but instead has lent it to a certain style of pictographs associated with the Fremont culture of the Late Archaic period—prior to the advent of agriculture. The crown jewel of Horseshoe Canyon is a large and well-preserved panel of intricately beautiful human and animal figures known as the Great Gallery, stretching over 120 feet of smooth slickrock wall. Most of the figures are life-size and some of them are over seven feet tall. They have large tapered torsos, no appendages and are quite ghostlike in appearance. A few figures are decorated with various patterns or surrounded by small birds and animals. The debate around the age of the mural has long been the subject of controversy, but most historians now endorse the above estimate, since a fragment was carbon-dated and determined to be approximately three thousand years old. Many have theorized that the figures are depictions of shamans in drug-induced spiritual states. Others believe that they represent visiting space aliens. Regardless of your own interpretation, there is little doubt that the Great Gallery is the most spectacular panel of rock art in North America and an unforgettable experience.

The panel stretches out on a ledge located about 15 feet above ground. The area is cordoned off and you'll need to admire and photograph the panel from a short distance of about 30 feet, which makes it easy to capture either large portions of the panel or to focus on specific figures or groups of figures.

To observe and photograph the figures at close range, you can join a ranger-led hike; such hikes are usually organized from April through October on Saturday and Sunday morning (call the Hans Flat Ranger Station for more information). Upon close examination, you'll notice that some of the figures not only consist of pigment applied onto the rock, but that the rock itself is intricately pecked around the silhouette.

One phenomenon you will easily notice without needing to get close, is the fact that some of the figures are pock-marked, leading some archaeologists to theorize that objects could have been thrown at them during rituals.

The hike from the trailhead at the top of the mesa to the Great Gallery and back is about 7 miles round-trip, but can feel longer than that when the weather is hot. It takes approximately 4 to 5 hours to accomplish, with enough time at the site for rest and photography. By hiking out early in the morning, you'll be able to take advantage of the best lighting conditions at the main panel, as well as avoid the hottest part of the day as you climb back up to the plateau, which lies 750 feet above the Canyon floor. It is a long climb—over a mile—and if you do it in the afternoon, it will be extremely hot. In late afternoon, however, the cliff will be in the shade.

At the bottom of the mesa, the canyon itself is absolutely gorgeous, with many cottonwoods providing shade along the way. You'll definitely relish that shade on a hot day. All through the hike, you'll be following a stream that always seems to run with at least a small trickle of water, although it becomes frozen in winter.

There are other pictograph panels along the way to the Great Gallery. The first

The Great Ghost

one is easily spotted on your left, less than 20 minutes after the descent, and is called the High Gallery; you'll know why when you see it. The canyon is fairly wide and you'll need to cross the stream bed and walk on a trail to the right in order to visit the easily missed Living Site, a bit further up. About a half-mile further, you'll encounter a huge alcove on the right side; it makes for a nice resting spot, especially if you are hiking in the sun. Look for a few small pictographs toward the back of the alcove, unfortunately marred by some graffiti. If you look at the roof of the alcove, you will also note marks that seem to have been made by globs of wet mud thrown at the rock.

Continuing on 1.25-mile upstream, you'll eventually reach the main panel of the Great Gallery, to your right.

Photo advice: as with all other large rock art panels of the Southwest, it's up to you to photograph what you want, from the wide scene encompassing the whole panel to the minutest detail.

Anything from a moderate wide-angle to a short telephoto will work well at the Great Gallery. However, a very wide angle will show the unaesthetic fence. A long telephoto is useful to isolate some particularly interesting anthropomorphs, such as the one with the tiny birds perched on its shoulder. Of course, you will want to photograph the Great Ghost, a large figure with a mysterious, ghostly appearance and intricate detail in the head. You'll find it to the left of the main panel, under a shallow alcove. Many of the other figures on the panel look like tapered mummy-like blobs of pigment with broad shoulders and two spots representing the eyes. On the whole, the "Gallery" gets its impact from the number of figures and size of the panel and moderate focal lengths will work best. Use different angles to impart some variety to your shots.

If you hike-in very early in the morning, you will have the ethereal experience of seeing the figures gradually illuminated by the soft morning light. On the other hand, if you end-up photographing the figures in bright sunlight, you may want to use a polarizing filter to eliminate glare. Also, keep in mind my general recommendation of using low-contrast film for rock art.

Getting there: from either Hanksville or I-17 west of Green River, take UT 24 to the Hans Flat turnoff (0.6-mile south of Goblin Valley road) and turn onto the well graded dirt road. Follow it for 32 miles until your reach the parking lot near the top of the mesa. There is a primitive campsite available. From Green River, there is also a direct 45-mile graded dirt road that leaves from Airport Road, south of town. This won't be any faster than using US 24, but it can add some variety to your trip. If you come all the way from Moab, count on approximately 2-1/2 hours of driving time.

Time required: allow one day for Horseshoe Canyon, including driving time both ways, especially if you come from Moab. If you're not going to explore other parts of the Maze, it's easy to visit Goblin Valley State Park in mid to late-afternoon of the same day (refer to the San Rafael Reef chapter).

Panorama Point

Panorama Point affords a fantastic panoramic view of the northern Maze area and Island in the Sky, as well as close views of the Orange Cliffs. However, much like its Needles Overlook counterpart on the east side, the view is far too distant to make for interesting photography. Telephoto views rarely give any quality results because of the haze that usually blankets the area. If you are pressed for time, you can pass this viewpoint without too much regrets and head toward the Maze Overlook instead—although it's much farther. On the other hand, it is also the easiest way to catch a glimpse of the Maze, as it is only an hour's drive from Hans Flat by 4WD, without any technical sections, such as the Flint Trail or Teapot Canyon, along the way.

Getting there: 2.5 miles south of Hans Flat, take the marked track leading east for 7.5 miles, then follow the right fork for another 2 miles to the overlook. The left fork leads in 2.5 miles to the base of Cleopatra's Chair, a huge monolith dominating the whole area.

The Maze Overlook

This is without question the best vantage point over the Maze. You sit above the extraordinary labyrinths of Cedar Mesa sandstone and are relatively close. The group known as the Chocolate Drops is right in front of you, only a mile or so away—a last remnant of organ-shale rock capping the sandstone and looking

The Chocolate Drops from the Maze Overlook

much like a row of nuclear submarine kiosks. The Land of Standing Rocks can be seen in the distance to the southeast, but close enough to yield good telephoto images with a 200mm. Elaterite and Ekker buttes are also fairly close and spectacular. This is a great spot to camp, relax and admire the Maze at its best. Late afternoon is the best time for photography. Approximately thirty minutes before sunset, you'll loose direct light over the Maze, but you'll get great colors in the sky if you have some clouds to the east. Early morning is very good for shooting in the direction of the Land of Standing Rocks. The side light brings out much detail to the maze of canyons at your feet. Don't wait too long: an hour after sunrise, the Maze will appear flat and the opportunity will be gone.

A very steep trail descends into the canyon bottom, leading to four different backpacking trails. One of these allows you to do a half-day trip to the Harvest Scene (see the following section).

Getting there: about 14 miles south of Hans Flat, go left and down the steep switchbacks of the Flint Trail for the 16-mile drive to the overlook. It takes about 3 hours one way from Hans Flat.

Harvest Scene

The Harvest Scene is one of the largest and most intriguing group of pictographs on the Colorado Plateau. It is also one of the oldest. This Late Archaic panel derives its name from scenes of harvest depicting the life of the early hunter-gatherers who traveled through these canyons, at least that is the official explanation. Altogether, there are about a dozen or so figures, spread over roughly forty feet. They are smaller and less impressive than those of the Great Gallery. One striking difference is the lack of a foreboding ghostlike appearance in these figures. No wide torsos here, but some fairly elongated bodies. The horns on the heads on several figures suggest masks used in some shamanistic ritual. The fact that they have feet—but no arms—also contributes to make them a little bit more human-like.

Photo advice: unfortunately, the panel is quite exposed to sun and wind erosion and the pigments have become very faint, making it difficult to see and photograph. If you are there in the middle of the day and the sun is shining directly on the panel, it will be difficult to bring out much detail, even with a polarizer. To photograph the Harvest Scene under optimum conditions, plan on being there preferably in the afternoon. The best light is late in the day, when the sun is just leaving the panel.

Photographing the panel is up to your imagination, however I would like to draw your attention to the large figure to the left, reminiscent of a telephone pole as well as to the interesting anthropomorph on the far right of the panel. Both isolate well vertically.

Getting there: there are two ways to get to the Harvest Scene. The most interesting way is via the shorter but much more exposed Maze Overlook trail, which winds its way 600 feet down a steep cliff and into the Maze. This trail is mildly technical and requires that you negotiate a series of moki steps and a short chimney. It is not overly difficult if you are normally agile and not afraid of heights. A rope or a couple of 20-foot straps will help greatly to lower your gear if you carry a camera backpack and a tripod. I suggest stashing a water bottle at the bottom of the cliff for later. Once in the Maze, follow the surprisingly verdant canyon to the south (left at the base of the cliff and around the eastern side of the Chocolate Drops) on a well-cairned path. Despite the cairns, do not venture inside the Maze without map and compass. There are several small groups of pictographs visible along the way; some are very high up the canyon walls, so keep looking. I estimate the entire round-trip to be a bit over 5 miles. Starting at daybreak, you can be at the Harvest Scene in 1-1/2 hour. My recommendation, however, is to start in mid-afternoon and come back shortly before sundown, catching good light at the panel and possibly a light breeze on the way back up. Incidentally, you'll find that climbing back up is much easier than coming down.

The other way to get to the Harvest Scene is the longer but more flat 12-mile loop starting from Chimney Rock in the Land of Standing Rocks.

The Land of Standing Rocks

One great way to observe and photograph the vast area known as Ernie's Country is by walking down the Golden Stairs, an easy 2-mile hike down a sheer

The Land of Standing Rocks

cliff composed of many different rock strata, hence the name Golden Stairs. If you're part of a group, you could arrange for your party to drop you at the Golden Stairs picnic area, located at the end of a short spur near the bottom of the Flint Trail. You could then take a leisurely walk down this spectacular path and then onto Land of Standing Rocks Road towards the Fins, where you can rendez-vous with your friends after they have negotiated the infamous segment of road around Teapot Rock.

Walking down the Golden Stairs offers great opportunities to see a formation called the Mother and Child, best photographed from the beginning of the trail in early morning.

The Fins are beautiful and the backdrop of the Needles across the Colorado River make the scene very photogenic from the road, especially in mid-afternoon. Look for Cave Arch, easily located with the naked eye in front of the Fins.

After the jarring of Teapot Canyon or the sheer drop of the Golden Stairs, you'll be happy to enjoy a relatively smooth drive through the Land of Standing Rocks, with its spectacular and photogenic monoliths: the Wall, Lizard Rock, the Plug and Chimney Rock.

Getting there: the Land of the Standing Rocks is about 35 miles from Hans Flat, past the switchbacks of the Flint Trail and the infamous section around Teapot Canyon, so count on 5 hours driving time.

The whimsical Doll House

The Doll House

This is one of the most photogenic area in the Southwest, but also one of the most remote. The Doll House is 88 miles away from UT 24 and 65 miles by boat from Moab. But what a place: it's a bit like the Needles, with a whimsical flair thrown in; rocks on pot, you could say. There are some very scenic camping spots dispersed throughout the Doll House, all pre-assigned at the Hans Flat Ranger Station when they issue your permit. Two of these sites are located a half-mile to the southwest of the Doll House and have a good panoramic view of the rock formations. Just wander amidst the formations and seek inspiration, you won't have difficulty finding it. I strongly recommend the 2-mile round-trip walk to the Granary. It goes through a couple of interesting joints (as in the Joint Trail) before reaching the lovely and aptly-named Surprise Valley, a verdant graben that is a refreshing site in this universe of stone. There are also excellent views from the trail going to Beehive Arch.

Photo advice: the Doll House is best photographed in late afternoon and at sunset. Take a general view from the vicinity of the southwest campsites with a medium telephoto, then wander on foot inside the Doll House proper, you'll be using a wide-angle most of the time. At sunrise, you may want to hike to Surprise Valley and down to the little granary or a short while down the Spanish Bottom trail to be on the sunrise side.

Getting there: the Doll House is located 5 miles past Chimney Rock (see the section above) at the very end of the Land of Standing Rocks Road. It is 42 miles from Hans Flat and about 6 hours driving time. Another common way to come to the Doll House in summer is by boat from Moab. All the organized raft trips bound for Cataract Canyon stop at Spanish Bottom. This is a very easy and convenient way to visit the Doll House. Alternately, you could arrange a private trip with a speed boat dropping you off at Spanish Bottom and picking you up the next day, but you'll have to carry all your water, camping and camera gear up and down the trail, which gains 1,200 feet of elevation in only 1.2-mile on a rocky talus slope... not a fun experience.

Doing the trip in one day from Moab is feasible by jetboat, but the light will be very crude in the middle of the day. The boat will wait for you as you climb to the Doll House for a quick peek. You can hike up and back in 2 to 3 hours. The view down the Spanish Bottom trail is superb, but even more so is the view of the Doll House from the Colorado River as you come within a mile from Spanish Bottom on the jetboat.

The Colorado River: Moab to Cataract Canyon

A boat trip down the Colorado River from Moab via Cataract Canyon is a fantastic experience with world-class whitewater along the way and is rated very highly. It can be arranged either privately or with an organized tour. There are many options, including multi-day rafting trips, but these are a bit outside the scope of this book. An excellent alternative is a jet boat tour. In Summer, you can arrange for a jet boat to take you from Potash to Spanish Bottom and back, a fantastic 100-mile round-trip journey on calm waters through the heart of Canyonlands Nat'l Park. This trip takes a whole day, passing through some of the most remote country in the Continental U.S. It is a wonderful alternative or complement to the White Rim drive (described in the Island in the Sky chapter). On your way to Spanish Bottom, you will marvel at the unbelievable scenery, as you travel through Shafer Basin, Pyramid Butte, the great gooseneck below Dead

Spanish Bottom

Horse Point State Park, Lathrop Canyon, Monument Basin, Junction Butte, the Loop, the Slide and the Confluence with the Green. The trip ends at Spanish Bottom, which provides access to the Doll House (see above section). Soon after that, rafting trips hit the impressive rapids of Cataract Canyon, spread over 14 miles of the Colorado River before the latter turns itself into a quiet arm of Lake Powell. The return trip to Potash is even better in late afternoon, when the canyons turn golden. Such a private trip is better suited to a medium-size group as it is rather pricey. If you are willing to forsake some of the flexibility, you can also ride a jet boat delivering or picking up groups of kayakers or rafters at Spanish Bottom.

Above Canyonlands

Although a scenic flight above Canyonlands Nat'l Park is not limited to the Maze district, I chose to include it in this chapter because for many people it is the only way to get an idea of this highly inaccessible section of the park. A flight can easily be arranged from Monticello or Moab. You can also arrange to be picked up and dropped off on the landing strip adjacent to the Needles Outpost, although I hear that the strip is falling into disrepair. Seen from a small aircraft, the landscape of Canyonlands Nat'l Park is extraordinary. A 1-hour flight is enough to view many parts of the three districts: the Needles, with its amazing Grabens, Chesler Park, Salt Creek, the confluence of the Green and the Colorado Rivers with their strikingly distinct colors, Cataract Canyon, all of the fantastic formations of the Maze described in this chapter, the mesas of Island in the Sky and Dead Horse State Park, and more.

If you only take one small plane trip in the course of your journey through the Southwest, make it this one. You won't regret the money spent. Two or three people are necessary to book the flight. Information on scenic flights can be found in Appendix.

Photo advice: a 28 to 50mm lens is well suited to aerial photography of this area. Little or no depth-of-field is required, but you will of course need to keep the vibrations of the aircraft and your own movements in check. With slow film, an aperture of f/4 or 5.6 and a minimum shutter speed of 1/250 sec. represents the best compromise for sharpness and resolution. If you have a short gyro-stabilized zoom, it will work very well at the low end and give you an additional two stops to compensate for the constant movement. If you shoot slides, use a low-contrast film. Ask the pilot if he'll allow you to have the windows open. If not, place the lens as close as possible to the window. In any case, disengage the autofocus and manually set the focus for infinity. Early morning or the end of the day is ideal for color and relief. Such a trip works very well in winter when the sun is constantly at a low-angle, even close to midday. ✿

Square Tower Ruin at sunset

Chapter 15
AROUND MESA VERDE

Spruce Tree House from the Chapin Museum

MESA VERDE

Mesa Verde National Park is the crown jewel of cliff dwellings of the National Park system. Located on a high plateau towering a thousand feet or more over the surrounding area, the park preserves an extraordinary array of pit and cliff dwelling, as well as multi-storied stone houses spanning several centuries of occupation by the native inhabitants.

There are essentially three areas of interest to the park: the vast rim area from the park entrance to Morefield and Far View; Chapin Mesa, which contains the most popular ruins, as well as the Chapin Museum; and Wetherill Mesa, which preserves another set of Puebloan ruins, also spectacular but more remote and accessible only in summer.

The fires of the summer 2000 closed Mesa Verde Nat'l Park for several weeks. They were essentially concentrated in the Morefield area as well as Wetherill Mesa, where everything burned except the ruins protected by fire crews. Fortunately, Chapin Mesa and vicinity were not affected.

Photo advice: there is one piece of information that may make your photography of Mesa Verde stand out by almost guaranteeing an unobstructed view of the structures: the Park Service's "Rent-a-Ranger" program. This program is only available in the off-season and when the roads and trails are free of snow. You will pay for the Ranger's time by the hour with a one-hour minimum. This program is not advertised by the National Park Service; it is subject to change or Ranger availability, so call ahead to make prior arrangements.

Consider also that your enjoyment of the tour and the quality of the photos

you'll bring back are greatly dependent on two human factors: the Ranger leading the tour and the crowds. Most rangers give great tours, but they don't all
move at the same pace and there is no guarantee that the previous group will have
left the area when you arrive. As for the crowds, they are best avoided by book-
ing an early or late tour.

Getting there: 10 miles east of Cortez and 35 miles west of Durango on US
160 to the park entrance turnoff. From there, it is 15 winding miles to the Far
View Visitor Center and 6 more miles to the Chapin Museum. Count on
approximately 45 minutes from US 160.

Time required: at least a half-day for basic car-based viewing, including a tour
of Cliff Palace; a full day to visit a couple of sites on the main mesa at a relaxed
pace. In summer, a day and a half is necessary to include Wetherill Mesa and the
three ranger-led visits: the first afternoon you'd visit Cliff Palace, the next morning you'd see Balcony House, and the next afternoon Long House; this scenario
affords the best compromise between lighting conditions and park regulations.

Nearby location: adjacent to Mesa Verde, lesser-known Ute Mountain Park
contains a large number of beautiful cliff dwellings, granaries and rock art.

The Rim

As it winds its way south into the heart of the park, the rim road offers many
superlative views of the surrounding area. This road looks even more beautiful
on the way back, especially under the golden light of early evening. It is in excellent condition, but it's also long and winding as well as quite crowded, so take
advantage of the four overlooks to get out of the car, stretch your legs and admire
the distant views.

Mancos Valley Overlook offers a great view to the northeast looking down into
the colorful fields of the Mancos Valley. If you are camping, you'll want to settle
in at the Morefield Campground before proceeding. This vast campground has
lots of spaces, so it is not essential to arrive early.

Some of the fire damage from summer 2000 is clearly visible from the road,
but I have found the recovery to be amazingly swift.

After the Montezuma Valley Overlook, looking down into Cortez, a stop at
Park Point is a must. A short trail leads to a fire lookout, located at 8,750 feet,
with incredibly distant views in all four directions. The last viewpoint before the
Visitor Center is the North Rim Overlook. All these viewpoints are better seen
with the naked eye than photographed.

If you are spending the night at the Far View Lodge, you'll probably be eager
to settle in first, but don't do so before stopping at the nearby Visitor Center.

During the high season, a stop at the Far View Visitor Center is essential to
organize your visit, as reservations are required to visit the three most popular
sites: Cliff Palace and Balcony House on Chapin Mesa, and Long House on
Wetherill Mesa. Tickets can be purchased on a first-come first-served basis;

expect long lines during holidays and busy weekends. At the Visitor Center you will also find helpful trail guides and other booklets that will make your visit of the major ruins much more informative and enjoyable.

If you can afford to spend the night in the Park, take the time to stroll through the Far View ruins complex at sunrise.

Introduction to Chapin Mesa

Chapin Mesa has the highest concentration of cliff dwellings in the park. It also has the highest concentration of visitors. On some summer days, it can be bumper-to-bumper traffic along the roads, particularly in mid-afternoon. There is a minor caveat to visiting the Chapin area cliff dwellings, which I personally find non-objectionable, but which any visitor should be aware of: the main dwellings you will be visiting have been reconstructed to some extent. Most of the work has consisted in stabilizing the structures and the Civilian Conservation Corps have done a masterful job of it, but you don't quite get the same feeling of awe and spiritual awareness as with some less restored and less visited Puebloan sites of the Southwest. If you don't let this bother you, you'll enjoy a fantastic photographic experience at Mesa Verde.

The excellent Chapin Mesa Museum is a good place to start your visit and get acquainted with Mesa Verde and its human and natural history. It can be visited year-round and so is the magnificent Spruce Tree House a short distance from it. Just past the museum, you'll find two 6-mile loop roads: the road to the right—called Mesa Top Drive—takes you to some recently excavated pithouses from the Basketmaker era but, while they are interesting to visit, they don't make for spectacular photography. However, there are also two good viewpoints along this road: the first one overlooks Square Tower House, and the second one—located at Sun Temple—has a distant view of Cliff Palace (a 300mm telephoto is necessary to capture detail). The loop road to the left leads to the main sites of Cliff Palace and Balcony House: Cliff Palace is usually open from early April to early November and Balcony House from mid May to mid October. If you do not intend to visit Wetherill Mesa, which is only open from late May to early September, the Chapin Mesa area is best seen during early autumn or late spring.

There are plenty of excellent and widely available sources to help you visit Chapin Mesa, starting with the National Park Service's own excellent maps and numerous brochures, so let's examine the subject from a photographic perspective. I find the following game plan to be the most effective for someone with limited time. It is based on the best lighting conditions at the sites and the fact that Park regulations do not allow you to visit both Cliff Palace and Balcony House on the same day, although at the end of summer, when the crowds begin to thin out, the staff may let you reserve both tours on the same day.

Start with the Chapin Museum in early afternoon, when light isn't too good for photography, then proceed to the guide tour of Cliff Palace before returning

Soft light illuminates the Great Kiva in late afternoon

to the Museum to photograph Spruce Tree House. Finish on Mesa Top Drive to photograph Square Tower Ruin.

If you're still in the park the following day, visit Balcony House in the morning and, during the high season, Wetherill Mesa in the afternoon.

Cliff Palace

Cliff Palace is the largest cliff dwelling in the park with 217 rooms and 23 kivas. I recommend that you visit this grandiose site on a pre-reserved ranger-led tour in mid-afternoon. Waiting for the beginning of the tour at the Cliff Palace Overlook, you'll want to photograph the ruins, but save most of your shots for later as the light will only get better and strong shadows will be minimized. The tour lasts approximately 1 hour and allows for plenty of opportunities to photograph the ruins. After going down some steep stairs, you'll be seated in the shade with Cliff Palace in full view while the ranger gives you some general but informative explanations about the Ancestral Puebloans.

Cliff Palace from the Overlook

Get your equipment ready. The previous group will still be visible amongst the dwellings, but as everybody moves as a group, they'll soon disappear toward the next spot, freeing more ground to photograph without people intrusion. With a bit of luck and timing, you should be able to get some great pictures from this spot, before you begin your own walkthrough of the cliff house. A graduated neutral density filter is a must if you want to limit the damage from the strong shadow areas that will obscure the top of the structures.

During the walkthrough, you'll want to switch to a wide-angle lens. Almost anything goes. This is the perfect time to use this super wide-angle lens you've been aching to try. Even though you are not allowed to leave your group, you can easily move about and get creative with your angles and bring back some excellent shots. Stay at the tail end of your group so you can shoot the entire complex from its southern end unencumbered, just before exiting.

Back at the Cliff Palace parking after your tour, return to the overlook and take your pictures in the better light. You can photograph from the overlook with a variety of lenses going from wide-angle—to include the entire alcove as well as the overhang and a bit of sky—to medium telephoto to isolate a structure that catches your eye. During a brief moment, the ruins are empty of people; you can shoot just as the first group is exiting while the second group is preparing to enter after the ranger's explanation. Don't linger, however, because you should now move to you next destination, the magnificent Spruce Tree House.

Spruce Tree House

Located just below the Chapin Mesa Archeological Museum, Spruce Tree House is the third largest dwelling in the park, with 114 rooms and 8 kivas. It's normally a self-guided tour, except in winter when you have to join a free ranger-led tour (note: there are only three tours per day).

By late afternoon, Spruce Tree House becomes basked in beautiful warm light and it's easy to photograph it at an angle and get great definition and depth. You are allowed to move about the various structures of the cliff house, as long as you don't step on low walls. Thus, with a little bit of care, you can easily exclude fences, signs or other visitors from your images.

There is a reconstructed kiva you can climb into and photograph with the afternoon light falling on the wooden ladder. It requires a very wide-angle lens.

There is an excellent view of the entire Spruce Tree House complex from behind the Park Headquarters building, immediately to the right of the Museum. There, you'll find an open-air viewing area, sheltered by the roof of the Park Headquarters building. There are benches enticing you to stay and admire the ruin complex while waiting for the best afternoon light. A mid-range zoom is perfect for framing various parts of the structure.

As soon as the warm late-afternoon light begins fading, go back to your car and drive to your next destination: Square Tower Ruin.

If you have a couple of hours available during the afternoon—for instance, if you couldn't get a reservation for Cliff Palace—don't miss the Petroglyph Point Trail, a rewarding 2.8-mile loop beginning between the Chapin Museum and Spruce Tree House. This mostly flat and shady trail winds under a mesa ledge to an interesting petroglyph panel before returning to the plateau through a pinion juniper forest. This uncrowded and pleasant trail is a good introduction to the natural environment of Mesa Verde and provides beautiful views of Navajo and Spruce Canyons. It's better hiked counterclockwise—beginning near Spruce Tree House and ending on the plateau above the ruins—especially if you do it in late afternoon when the lower access gate is locked after Spruce Tree House's visiting hours, as there is no gate for the upper access on the plateau.

Spruce Tree House in the afternoon light

Square Tower Ruin

Beautiful Square Tower House contained up to 80 rooms in its heyday. You can only observe it from above, from an overview located a few hundred yards from Mesa Top Drive. Outside summer, Square Tower ruin remains fully illuminated until the last rays of the sun have disappeared, so you do not need to hurry. Just don't waste time and you'll arrive right in time for an exceptionally rich, warm sunset light basking this beautiful structure; it is best photographed with a standard lens to medium telephoto.

If you can't stay long enough to photograph Square Tower Ruin in the evening, you can also photograph it in mid-afternoon, prior to your Cliff Palace tour. The light won't be quite as spectacular but will be decent enough.

Balcony House

Facing east, Balcony House is still partially in shadow in the early morning, so take a mid-morning pre-reserved tour if you can. The fun factor is high during the 1-hour Balcony House tour. Not only do you have the ladders, but you also have to crawl on your hands and knees through a 12-feet long dark tunnel connecting two sets of dwellings. If you carry a large photo backpack and a tripod, exercise caution. Also, to exit the alcove, you have to climb a fairly steep ladder and it may not be advisable for people with a heart condition or a fear of heights.

Balcony House tends to see more families with kids, because of the above-mentioned fun factor. Kids have a tendency to run around the ruins, making it a challenge to take pictures.

Planning your visit, remember that your window of opportunity for Balcony House (mid-May to mid-October) is a full two months shorter than for Cliff Palace and that you are not allowed to visit both on the same day.

The only viewpoint on Balcony House is a very distant one, close to Soda Canyon Overlook, on a 1.2-mile round-trip trail beginning less than a mile past Balcony House's parking lot.

Wetherill Mesa

Wetherill Mesa is only accessible from Memorial Day to Labor Day, so you'll have to plan accordingly. If you can make the trip to this less crowded area, it is definitely worthwhile especially for the superb Long House Ruin. It is the second largest cliff dwelling in the park, with about 150 rooms and 20 kivas.

Consider visiting Long House in the afternoon of your second day. Contrast is high in the morning and the House is in shadows later in the afternoon, so mid-afternoon is best. Bear in mind, however, that the last visit starts at 4PM.

To visit Long House, you must first make your reservation at the Far View Visitor Center. Upon arrival at the Ranger Contact Station, check-in for the 1-1/2 hour ranger-led walk to the ruin. Before taking the free tram to the ruin, you can visit Step House on your own on a 0.5-mile loop trail located close to the boarding station. After leaving the tram at the Long House stop, it's a short 3/4-mile walk to the cliff dwelling, on a slightly downhill path. Unlike the heavily consolidated Chapin Mesa dwellings, Long House is almost 80% intact. A few walls have been stabilized here and there for the safety of visitors and the roof of the kivas have been rebuilt, but all the structures at the back of the alcove are pretty much untouched. Ladders provide access to a work area and Long House's fresh water spring toward the back.

After visiting Long House, and if you have enough time before Wetherill Mesa closes for visitors, you can walk to the nearby Badger House complex and visit it on your own. It consists of four different exhibits encompassing various stages of human settlement at Mesa Verde: Basketmaker pithouses, which have been dated at around 750 AD, and Puebloan ruins from the thirteenth century. It is very unusual to find sites from both eras concentrated in one location. Badger House also contains a tower connected to a large kiva via a 40-foot tunnel.

Getting there: you'll find the road to Wetherill Mesa just past the Far View Visitor Center. It is a narrower and more winding version of the rim road and it takes at least 35 minutes to negotiate the 12 miles to the Ranger contact station, where you park. You must walk or take one of the frequent free trams leaving for the 4-mile loop tour leading to the ruins.

Time required: half a day.

AROUND MESA VERDE

Hovenweep Nat'l Monument

Located on the expansive Cajon Mesa, which is part of the "Great Sage Plain" of Southwestern Colorado and Southeastern Utah, Hovenweep Nat'l Monument protects some of the most interesting examples of pre-Columbian stone architecture in the Southwest. If you are traveling through the Cortez, Mesa Verde, Farmington area, you should consider the short detour through Hovenweep to photograph its unique "towers".

Hovenweep's photographic interest lies primarily in the rich colors of the sandstone walls of its towers, contrasting with pure blue skies, beautiful fluffy clouds during the Monsoon season, and the snow-capped peaks of Sleeping Ute Mountain in winter. Although the remaining structures are only partially standing—Hovenweep was abandoned circa AD1300—they are all very interesting and well worth photographing.

Howenweep Nat'l Monument consists of five distinct groups of ruins. The Square Tower group, is the largest and most easily accessible and we will concentrate on this one. It is located a stone's throw away from the tiny ranger station cum museum. There is a very easy 1-mile loop around a shallow canyon, appropriately named Tower Point loop. A shortcut in the trail allows you to cut a half-mile off the walk if you have had enough of ruins or are in a big hurry. The first part of the walk takes you past some interesting structures resting atop the canyon walls; these are easily photographed from various vantage points.

Hovenweep Castle is the most visible and photographed landmark, not only because of its proximity to the parking lot, but also for the outstanding masonry work of its remaining walls. The "Castle" was actually part of a larger structure bordering the canyon rim, which is now totally gone.

As you turn around the bend of the canyon, Hovenweep House ruins come into view under an alcove. Further up on the trail is Square Tower. This three-story high tower rests upon a large boulder, which makes it quite unique.

At the Twin Towers, you'll have to decide whether to return to the visitor center or continue on. The Twin Towers loop adds another mile and a half to the walk and leads to quite a few more structures around both sides of the canyon. It is an easy and pleasant stroll, mostly on the canyon rim. The most outstanding landmark on this trail is Stronghold House, so named for its lack of an easy entrance, leading archaeologists to believe that it may have been used for defensive purposes.

The Hovenweep Castle

On the Eastern side of the monument is the Holly Group, once home to an estimated 150 people. This group contains five structures; the most noticeable of which is the two-storied Holly tower, built on a tall, narrow boulder.

Photo advice: for once, I'm not recommending that you be at Hovenweep at sunrise or sunset; it's a good thing because, unless you are camping, it's unlikely that you'll be there at those times considering the distance to the nearest towns. In my opinion you'll get plenty of good angles by moving around the structures in mid-morning or mid-afternoon and by concentrating on the strong detail of the masonry work. I have gotten better pictures this way, rather than by blasting the towers in strong evening light and losing much of the detail to the intense color. I also encourage you to seek snow or clouds to add more interest to your images.

Getting there: Hovenweep is located 28 miles East of the intersection of US 262 with US 191. US 262 is now paved all the way to Aneth. From US 191, there are a couple of intersections, so be sure to follow the signs. It can also be reached via County Road 10 from US 666 if you are travelling between Cortez and Monticello. This dirt road is usually passable by passenger cars, but call ahead to inquire on its condition. This road gives you access to Hovenweep's lesser visited groups of Holly, Horseshoe and Hackberry. A small campground is located inside the monument.

Time required: the detour from US 191 will take you a minimum of 2 hours; this will give you just enough time to stroll down the Tower Point Nature Trail at a pace and photograph the main structures. Add another hour if you want to take your time and walk the 1.5-mile Twin Towers loop. ✿

The Great Sand Dunes

Chapter 16

SOUTHWESTERN COLORADO

Colorado Nat'l Monument in winter

SOUTHWESTERN COLORADO

This chapter covers several spectacular sites located in southwestern Colorado—arguably a bit outside the Southwest. These sites, however, should not be missed if you come to or from Mesa Verde and you are not on a tight schedule. If you are on your way to New Mexico, passing north of Taos, a short detour will lead you to Great Sand Dunes Nat'l Monument. Likewise, if you are going from Mesa Verde to Moab, take fantastic US 550, crossing the San Juan Mountains, and discover Black Canyon of the Gunnison Nat'l Park and Colorado Nat'l Monument.

Great Sand Dunes Nat'l Monument

The Great Sand Dunes of southwestern Colorado are the tallest dunes in North America, reaching heights of nearly 750 feet. I am extremely fond of sand dunes and I have had the good fortune of seeing many on all continents, but one thing sets the Great Sand Dunes apart from the rest: the presence of a creek at their very base during springtime and the beginning of summer. This somewhat incongruous factor creates a unique ecosystem that is unlike any other dune system in the world.

The Great Sand Dunes offer a majestic sight both from afar and at close range. From afar, the tall dunes strike a fantastic profile in front of the oft snow capped peaks of the Sangre de Cristo Mountains and lend themselves to superb telephoto photography. From a short distance, the rich brown sand creates a fantastic contrast with the abundant foliage of Medano Creek's riparian area, which turns golden in early fall. On top of the dunes, you'll be rewarded with the view of a vast field of sand with superb crests and ripples, stretching for what seems forever at the foot of the mountains.

There is one drawback to these dunes, as far as photography is concerned: the crowds. This is an extremely popular place for families with kids, particularly on weekends. You'll find kids climbing and rolling down all over the dunes. Fortunately, there are almost 40 sq. miles of dunes so if you climb high and walk on the dune field, you're guaranteed to find solitude and lack of tracks. Talking about tracks, the Great Sand Dunes usually don't keep them for long. The wind is often blowing and will erase yesterday's tracks as easily as they came.

To climb the dunes, you'll have to be in excellent physical shape, as it is fairly strenuous exertion at an elevation of 8,000 feet. Dunes are never easy to climb in general, but these can be lethal and if you don't pick your way carefully and climb on ridge lines, where the sand is more solid, it will be one step forward, half a step back. Previous climbers' footsteps usually—but not always—reflect the easiest way to climb. Remember that distances are deceiving on the dunes and that your destination is often farther away than it looks. If you hike during hot afternoons, you'll need to drink lots of water.

If you want to be on top of the tallest dune—aptly named High Dune—for sunrise, plan on an early start, allowing about one hour from the Medano Creek crossing. Although it feels good to walk barefoot on the cool sand in the early morning, be sure to use tennis shoes or you'll burn your feet later on when the surface temperature of the sand can reach 140°F. From the top of the dune you'll enjoy an awesome 360° view. It's also a great spot for sunset.

Panoramic view of the Great Sand Dunes in late afternoon light

Footsteps on the sand make for fun pictures

There are plenty of photographic opportunities walking upstream in the Medano Creek riverbed. The creek is wide at the crossing but gets progressively narrower. The water flows in strange waves of varying intensity. Sometimes it stops flowing where you are and the current starts building up just a few feet away. This is due to the sand forming small dams, which periodically give way, causing the water to flow in waves along new paths. Just standing there in the shallow water is a wonderfully relaxing experience.

Beginning at Mosca Creek near the Dunes parking lot, follow the creek for a tad over 2 miles until you reach Castle Creek, passing a ghost forest of dead trees suffocated by newly formed dunes. There, the dunes rise abruptly from the creek bed at impossibly steep angles. To return, follow the Medano Pass 4WD road to the Point of No Return car park and take the Little Medano Trail heading to the Pinyon Flats campground. You'll have great views of the dunes from the trail, especially if you take the spur trail to Dunes Overlook, about half way. From the campground, take the one mile Pinyon Flats trail to return to you car.

If you have limited time, walking downstream at the base of the dunes is also very rewarding. There are few people going in that direction and excellent views of the dunes. During summer, moonlight walks on the dunes are pleasant and you can watch some small animals not visible during the day.

Photographers who don't want to walk or carry heavy or fragile equipment can drive their 4WD vehicle on the 12-mile long Medano Pass primitive road. Medano Pass affords spectacular views of the dunes. Check road conditions at the Visitor Center before going, as deep sand is often present past Point of No Return (it may be necessary to reduce the air pressure in you tires) and creek crossing could be hazardous during snowmelt.

Although the park is open year-round, the best time to visit Great Sand Dunes is from mid-May through mid-June and mid-September through mid-October. Winter and early spring are very cold and sometimes windy. Summer is very hot and brings a high danger of lightning during afternoon thunderstorms, making photography on the dunes hazardous with a tripod. June can be made unpleasant by the myriads of aggressive mosquitoes and biting gnats.

Photo advice: a medium telephoto will work wonders to compress the perspective between the dunes and the Sangre de Cristo. Stop anywhere on the road leading to the park; I suggest about a mile past the private lodge and campground on CO 150. On the dunes, anything goes from extreme wide-angle to short telephoto. In early morning, late afternoon and early evening, the dunes have much better color and interesting shadows. Protect your camera when walking and exercise caution when you shoot, as sand penetrates everything in this often-windy area.

Getting there: most people come from Alamosa, which is 35 miles southwest of the monument and has numerous motels. Unless you take US 160 and CO 150 to the north, I recommend coming on US 17 via Mosca and turning east into 6 Mile Lane—which is actually 16-mile long. This is a more scenic road and the San Luis Lakes State Park is an excellent riparian area with good bird watching during the high season. The Pinion Flats campground is pleasant and convenient and makes a good base for photographers. The private Great Sand Dunes Lodge, just outside the park, is very nice. They have very few rooms available, so be sure to reserve well in advance.

Time required: at least half a day. If you have limited time and stay at the campground or at the lodge just before the entrance, you can arrive in mid-afternoon and leave in mid-morning the next day.

Nearby location: the turnoff to Zapata Falls is on CO 150, less than 8 miles south of the entrance to the monument. Take the 3.5-mile well-graded road up to the parking lot and picnic area. From there, you'll have great views of the San Luis Valley and the distant dune field at the foot of the Sangre de Cristo Mountains. It's a good spot for panoramic shots. Walk about 0.5-mile uphill, with good views along the way, to a creek leading to the falls, which are somewhat hidden from view inside a cavern-shaped narrow gorge. To see the waterfall, you need to wade in the gushing water, with the risk of slipping and falling in the water, so I don't recommend crossing with your camera. Photographically, it's not particularly rewarding in summer, but it can be worth it in winter when the waterfall freezes over, creating a beautiful icy-blue sculpture.

Across the San Juan Mountains

An entire volume such as this one could be devoted to photography in the San Juan Mountains, which is a little bit out of the scope of this guide. Thus, it is with a certain hesitation that I write this section, which covers only a few arbitrarily chosen locations around superb US 550, when there are so many others to choose from. However, should you decide to visit either Mesa Verde, the Great Sand Dunes, the Black Canyon or Colorado Nat'l Monument, I highly recommend that you travel through this magnificent area, which offers one of the most outstanding mountains scenery in the West.

In doing so, you'll probably stop by the somewhat commercial, but nonetheless quite pleasant town of Durango, the main gateway to the region. After days of photographing in deserts and canyon country, wouldn't you be tempted by a day of relaxation with cool mountain air and no driving involved? Durango offers just such perfect opportunity with the extremely popular Durango and Silverton Narrow Gauge Railroad. The railroad was originally built to transport ore from local mines, but has been successfully reconverted into a tourist venture. But make no mistake; this is definitely the greatest little train ride in the West. Each morning, from May through October, the vintage steam-powered train climbs the highly scenic Animas River Canyon on its narrow track, crossing open country along steep cliffs and above sheer drops, passing on spectacular wooden trestles, huffing and puffing its way at the foot of snowy peaks, and following the river so close you can hear it. 3-1/2 hours later, you reach the little mining town of Silverton. After a 2-hour visit of scenic Silverton, you can re-board the train for the return trip; instead, I suggest that you return by bus, which will give you a preview of magnificent US 550 for later. The drive, via Molas Divide, is part of the San Juan Skyway and saves you 1-1/2 hour, allowing you to spend time in Durango later in the day. A bit of advice for photographers: reserve your seats long in advance (see Resources in Appendix). The best seats are the very last on the right side—going toward Silverton—in the last car of the train; the bench seats are like being in an open-air Gondola, with no windows. Be sure to take warm clothes, because it can get very cold. You'll see the best side of the landscape, far from the smoke and smut of the engine and you'll be able to take striking images of the locomotive negotiating curves and bridges, as well as panoramic shots through the three open sides at the back of the rear car.

In late September and early October, it will most certainly be cold in the open carriage, but it's a small price to pay to be able to admire and photograph the incredible fall colors of the high-country. Given the jolting and vibrations generated by the old train, choose a fast film and don't shoot below 1/250 s to avoid blurred images. A gyro-stabilized zoom or a monopod could be useful. If you want to photograph the moving train, pulled by its picturesque engine spewing black smoke on a background of mountain peaks, you can do so easily without even taking the trip: simply note the departure time from Durango and scout for a spot on the east side of the tracks on one of the numerous spur roads you'll find along the first ten miles of US 550, just north of Durango.

The wonderful Durango to Silverton Railroad (photo Philippe Schuler)

Traveling in the San Juans along US 550 and its side roads, the mountains are at their best in summer and early fall particularly along two stretches of road: one known as the Million Dollar Highway between Silverton and the lovely alpine town of Ouray. This stretch of road offers numerous photographic opportunities, notably in the spectacular and aptly named Red Mountain. While descending Red Mountain Pass, you'll see to your right several old mining structures that are extremely picturesque, surrounded as they are by forest and towering summits. The second road I recommend is the Dallas Divide. Take CO 62 off US 550 at Ridgway, then CO 145 to Telluride. If you don't have time to explore some of the 4WD roads discussed later, the Dallas Divide is the most spectacular stretch of asphalted road for photography. In summer, wildflowers abound and create exquisite foregrounds to the high peaks. In early fall, large groves of quaking aspen turn gold and amber alongside the road.

Numerous 4WD roads lead to the heart of the San Juan Mountains, passing magnificent alpine basins full of wildflowers, as well as high-mountain passes as high as 13,000 feet. Among the most renowned is the Alpine Loop, an exhila-

Fall in the San Juan Mountains

rating 65-mile joyride that takes a full day to accomplish. The loop is generally open from June to October, heading east from Silverton to Lake City, before returning west toward Ouray. On this loop, Cinnamon Pass, Engineer Pass and Mineral Road require 4WD but make great mini-adventures, tackled without too much difficulty by SUVs and pick-up trucks. Southwest of Ouray, the popular Yankee Boy Basin road allows 4WD owners to reach quickly and with only moderate difficulty a wonderful alpine landscape of hillsides and open meadows brimming with wildflowers in July and early August. One highly recommended road for those with minimal 4WD driving skills is Red Mountain/Corkscrew Gulch. It leads to spectacular high-mountain scenery on a narrow and moderately difficult road, that any prudent driver should be able to drive with a 4WD vehicle, assuming of course that road and weather conditions are cooperating (check first with the Visitor Center in Silverton). From Silverton, drive about 7 miles north on a gravel road leading to the Gladstone Mine; along the way, check out the creek to your right with its surprising rust color in places, yielding interesting abstract shots. Just before entering the mine, take the track to the left for 1.5-mile, then follow another track climbing west in another 1.5-mile to a saddle located at 12,200 feet. From the saddle, you'll have a spectacular view of the snow-capped mountains all around. Some are startlingly red, which of course looks great on photos. The 4-mile descent has steep switchbacks, but the road is usually not bad and soon rejoins US 550 near the abandoned mine of Ironton.

During the high season, hiking and backpacking opportunities in the region are too numerous to mention. If your are not afraid of heights, are sure-footed and there is no chance of rain to render the ground slippery, I recommend one particular trail, both spectacular and well suited to photography. Its trailhead is located right alongside US 550, only 2 miles south of Ouray at the southern end of the tunnel, so it is easy to get to. After going over the tunnel, the Bear Creek National Recreation Trail follows an old mining route, climbing in a series of steep switchbacks for about a mile, with excellent views of Ouray. The trail levels off as it follows Bear Creek Canyon on a ledge overlooking a sheer cliff. In places, the trail has been carved directly into the rock, several hundred feet above the creek. The hike is very exciting and offers good photographic opportunities. When you finally reach the ruins of Grizzly Bear Mine, you'll ask yourself how miners were able to carry all the heavy and bulky equipment over this trail. Count on about 3 hours round-trip.

Black Canyon of the Gunnison Nat'l Park

The Black Canyon of the Gunnison is both superb and yet uncrowded, but its new National Park status—acquired in October of 1999—is bound to draw more visitors in the future. During each of my visits I have managed to get wild and woolly weather, ending up in powerful evening thunderstorms. I feel that this is when the canyon is at its best, basked with spots of light filtering through a threatening dark gray sky. Unlike its southern neighbors, running through a landscape of sandstone layers, the Black Canyon carved its way through hard bedrock, producing a very steep, rugged gorge. The almost vertical walls are over 2,000 feet deep and at one point only 1,200 feet across; this makes the bottom of the canyon very dark, hence its name. A dozen spectacular viewpoints dot the 7-mile South Rim road, all of which offering different views of the canyon from very short trails. My favorites are the Pulpit Rock overlook, the Cross Fissures view, Chasm and Painted Wall view, and most specially Cedar Point, but it is simply a matter of taste as all the other viewpoints are spectacular in their own way. Cedar Point offers an excellent view of the Painted Wall from two fenced areas at the end of a 2/3-mile round-trip trail. The western end of the road offers less dramatic views of the canyon despite its height at over 8,200 feet.

Hiking to the bottom of the canyon is a challenging experience, which is not particularly rewarding from a photographic standpoint. If you feel the urge to do

Storm on the Black Canyon of the Gunnison

it, you'll need a backcountry permit, even for day use. From the three very steep routes going down 1,800 feet to the river from the South Rim, Gunnison Route is the most popular because it only requires a half-day round-trip. Nevertheless, you must be in excellent physical condition and not to be afraid of heights to descend the not-so-obvious path. Among other challenges, you'll have to contend with loose rock surfaces, some scrambling, chains to aid your progress on steep sections, and poison oak in the river area.

Photo advice: a super wide angle is very useful to capture the depth of the canyon and the Gunnison River below.

Getting there: the South Rim is located 15 miles east of Montrose on US 50 and CO 347. The campground is pleasant. Nearby Montrose has a large number of motels.

Time required: at least 2 hours to enjoy the viewpoints of the south rim.

Nearby location: southeast of Black Canyon of the Gunnison Nat'l Park and along US 50, the adjacent Curecanti Recreation Area provides boating through the upper Black Canyon and on the large Blue Mesa Reservoir. Northwest of the Nat'l Park and accessible from side roads off US 50 between Montrose and Delta, the Gunnison Gorge Nat'l Conservation Area provides hiking and whitewater activities.

Colorado Nat'l Monument

By the time they're done seeing Arches and Canyonlands, most people doing the so-called "Grand Circle" have seen enough red rock and are heading back home. For the visitor with a little more time and a special interest in the Southwest, Colorado Nat'l Monument will prove a worthwhile detour. If you're traveling on I-70, perhaps on your way to the Rockies or Dinosaur National Monument, or if you're coming from Durango on US 550 and 50, you'll pass right by Colorado Nat'l Monument and it would be a shame not to stop and explore it. For the photographer, Colorado Nat'l Monument is a dream come true: no crowds, clean air, highly scenic vistas along the road, with great side light mornings and afternoons and wonderful hikes.

The monument is located only a couple of hours northeast of Moab, at the northern edge of the Uncompahgre plateau. In theory, you could visit it in one day from Moab; however, a brief daytime visit would not do it justice photographically and would almost certainly result in mediocre images as you'd miss the golden hour. Instead, I recommend that you spend the night in lovely Fruita or in Grand Junction and take one afternoon, as well as the next morning, to explore the monument. Another alternative, if you like camping, is to stay at the very nice Saddlehorn campground in the western part of the park, which has spectacular views nearby. In recent years, the Monument has become a favorite of climbers from all over the world, so you may face a bit of competition at the campground in the spring or fall, but it is almost never full.

A 23-mile stretch of road called Rim Rock Drive crosses the Monument. Using South Camp Rd, South Broadway and CO 340, it forms a loop that can be started in either Fruita or Grand Junction. My recommendation is that you start in Fruita to concentrate on the western half of the road.

The road climbs the length of gigantic arms of sandstone, gradually rising to about 2,000 feet above Grand Valley. Spectacular views of the valley can be had from a large number of viewpoints on the rim. The gradient of the various canyon arms jutting down toward the valley floor forms extremely interesting perspectives, creating strong lines starting from the edges of your picture and leading the eye toward the center. There are limitless opportunities for creative, strong compositions involving perspective and you'll have a field day doing so, with very little walking involved.

Monument Basin

Below is a list and short description of the viewpoints, as you will encounter them starting from Fruita.

Balanced Rock is a mid-to-late afternoon long telephoto shot. It is somewhat similar to the beacon rock you can see in Arches' Park Avenue, but not quite as nice and easy to photograph. There is limited parking space at the turnoff and you will not be able to stop if you're coming from Fruita.

Fruita Canyon View offers an excellent morning and mid-afternoon view with a moderate wide-angle to normal lens. It is a good example of the strong compositions you can get playing with the arms of the canyon meeting the valley floor.

Book Cliff View, located on the campground loop road offers a fantastic sunrise view on Monument Canyon with a moderate wide-angle to short telephoto. If you want a slightly broader view, encompassing Sentinel Spire, walk all the way to the end of the Window Rock trail. It's only a 5 to 10-minute walk between the two and you can easily visit both locations. These two locations will yield great photographs and are highly recommended.

Otto's Trail to Pipe Organ is a nice trail offering a good late afternoon view of

Independence Monument, an isolated 450-foot high sandstone tower, but it is somewhat weak photographically.

Independence Monument View offers a splendid late afternoon shot of the huge monolith. This view is very interesting in winter or spring when the Entrada monolith cuts a striking profile on snow or green grass with Grand Junction in the background.

Grand View has a beautiful view looking toward Fruita Canyon with Independence Monument in the foreground. This view is equally as good mornings and afternoons.

Monument Canyon View offers a superlative view of the spires of Monument Canyon, great for both sunrise and late afternoon.

Coke Ovens: a good view can be had from the Coke Ovens Overlook in both morning and late afternoon. There are also a couple of roadside spots, northeast of the overlook going toward Cleopatra's Couch, affording great, but distant, views over the ovens.

The Coke Ovens trail is mildly interesting; it puts you almost on top of the softly rounded monoliths, but you're so close that it's difficult to take a picture from there. So is the Coke Ovens Viewpoint, located south of the ovens, unless you want to catch the top of the ovens glowing in the early morning or late afternoon sun. I find the shape of the Coke Ovens less striking from Artist Point as from the Coke Ovens Overlook, but you may disagree with that.

Monument Canyon Trail: the Monument Canyon trail shares the same trailhead as the Coke Ovens Trail. If you have about three hours available and can arrange a car shuttle to the opposite trailhead on CO 340, this 6-mile trail is highly recommended as it goes past the major monoliths, providing a totally different perspective from the bottom. The walk is easy overall, beginning steeply— you'll lose 600 feet of elevation in less than a mile—before becoming gradual. You'll get a great view of the Coke Ovens at Mile 1. You can isolate them individually with a short telephoto for superb effects. Further down the trail, you'll pass at the base of the majestic monoliths, first the Kissing Couple, then Independence Monument.

As you continue east along the road, you'll encounter Ute Canyon and the very steep but beautiful trail of the same name. It offers solitude and plenty of intimate views, if you have time.

Your next stop is Red Canyon Overlook. Red Canyon is vast and long; it doesn't have the dramatic sloping of the smaller canyons to the west, but it's long parallel walls are spectacular, albeit harder to photograph.

Past Cold Shivers Point, you'll catch a glimpse of the Serpent's Trail. The 2.25-mile trail, sporting more than 50 switchbacks, is actually the old road leading into the Monument. It's is a fun walk down if you can arrange a car shuttle close to the Devil's Kitchen picnic area.

Your visit will end up at the Devil's Kitchen trail, a pleasant and popular 1.5-mile round-trip walk leading to huge upright boulders at the entrance of the No Thoroughfare Canyon. This spot is very photogenic.

The Coke Ovens at sunset

Getting there: the west entrance to the Monument is about 100 miles from Moab. Coming west on I-70, take Exit 19 at Fruita and CO 340 to the west entrance. Coming east on I-70, take Exit 31 at Grand Junction to downtown then Monument Road to the east entrance.

Time required: at least 2-1/2 hours, with brief stops at several viewpoints, if you are in a hurry. An overnight stay with mid- to late-afternoon and early morning drives is highly recommended to get good light.

Nearby locations: Grand Mesa is a huge flat top mountain overlooking Grand Valley, east of Grand Junction. At an average elevation of 10,000 feet, this immense mesa is in stark contrast with the surrounding desert. The top of the mesa is covered with forest, lakes and meadows; it offers mild temperatures in summer and great fall colors. Follow I-17 east for about 20 miles from Grand Junction and, at Exit 49, take Scenic Byway 65 to Cedar Edge Pioneer Town. There are several worthy overlooks along the way. At about halfway, you can escape toward Grand Junction using the good Land's End gravel road.

Rattlesnake Canyon, just west of the Colorado Monument has several spectacular arches of the pothole variety. It is actually the second largest concentration of natural arches in the country. It is definitely worth a stop when in Grand Junction, if only to photograph the unique Hole-in-the-Bridge Arch, which sports a large pothole in the center of its span.✿

APPENDIX

A Glossary of not-so-obvious Terminology

Alcove: a shallow cave formed by the breakup of a sandstone layer weakened by water percolating from the top. Best examples: Zion NP, Escalante river drainage.

Antropomorph: a stylized figure with human-like attributes, as seen on rock art all over the Southwest.

Arch: a natural opening eroded by the action of the wind or rain. Best examples: Arches NP, the Needles, all around Moab, Mystery Valley.

Arroyo: Spanish term used in place of "wash" throughout the Sonoran desert region; see wash. Best examples: Organ Pipe Cactus NM and Saguaro NP.

Badlands: desert terrain forming strongly eroded shale or limestone hills, frequently striped with spectacular colors. A translation of the French "mauvaises terres", as named by French Canadian fur trappers. Best example: Pareah Old Town, Petrified Forest NM, Waterpocket Fold.

Bajada: a slope formed of multiple alluvial fans (fan-shaped deposits of sediments and debris found at the base of stream channels.) Best examples: Organ Pipe Cactus NM and Saguaro NP.

Balanced rock: a rock of hard material resting on top of a softer formation that has been eroded away, leaving the former balanced on top of the latter. Best examples: Arches Nat'l Park, Chiricahua and Colorado Nat'l Monuments.

Bedrock: the solid rock of the earth's crust underlying sandstone layers.

Butte: a small, deeply cut mesa that has been protected from erosion by a hard sedimentary layer on its summit. Best examples: Factory Butte, Monument Valley, Valley of the Gods, Lukachukai Mountains.

Cairn: a human-made conical pile of stones marking a footpath.

Canyon: a deep gorge formed by the course of a river. Found throughout the Southwest. Best examples: Grand Canyon, Canyonlands, Escalante river area.

Cave: a hole in a thick wall of sandstone formed by a spring-seep breaking up the sandstone. Best examples: Double Arch alcove (lower cave), Zion's subway.

Confluence: the points where two rivers or canyons meet. Best examples: Green and Colorado rivers in the Needles District, Buckskin and Paria in Paria Canyon.

Cross-bedding: intricately overlapped layers of sandstone. Best examples: Zion Plateau, Escalante, The Wave.

Cryptobiotic soil: a.k.a. cryptogamic soil or simply "crypto", Greek term for "hidden life", a blackish crust inhabited by micro-organisms whose activity creates a network of fibers holding soil particles together. Unfortunately, crypto is easily crushed by footsteps and car tires and takes decades to regenerate. Best examples: the Needles.

Desert varnish: dark stripy patina on sandstone, formed by iron or manganese oxide processed by micro-organisms. Best examples: Canyon de Chelly, Burr Trail, around Moab.

Diatreme: gaseous eruption during which the shattered rock falls back into the pipe. Magma often flows upward through the weakened crust to create a dike around the diatreme. Also known as volcanic plug or neck. Best examples: Shiprock, Agathla Peak, Church Rock.

Dike: intrusive magma rise created when a crack occurred in the earth's crust. Best examples: Shiprock, Agathla Peak.

Fins: a group of individually eroded rocks similar in shape to the fin of a shark and following vertical fracture lines. Best examples: Arches Nat'l Park, The Fins, Behind the Rocks.

Flash flood: a torrent of water suddenly formed by a violent rainstorm falling on non-porous soil. On the Colorado plateau, these torrents naturally gravitate towards fissures in the rock, forming narrows and slot canyons.

Fold: a rise formed by the irregular uplift of sedimentary layers of rock. See also Monocline. In the Waterpocket Fold, a layer located 6,000 feet deep inside the earth at its eastern end may be exposed as a surface layer in the west. Best examples: Waterpocket Fold, the Cockscomb, Comb Ridge.

Hogan: the traditional Navajo dwelling, built of wooden logs.

Goblin: a variation of the Hoodoo; exclusively in soft sandstone. Evokes images of mythological creatures of a grotesque shape. Best example: Goblin Valley.

Gooseneck: bend in a river in the form of a loop. Best examples: Goosenecks of the San Juan, Dead Horse Point, Horseshoe Bend, Capitol Reef.

Graben: a valley formed by a sinking of the ground between two parallel fault lines. Best examples: the Needles, west of Elephant Hill.

Hoodoo: pillar of eroded rock or sandstone, capped at the top by a more highly resistant layer; also referred to as Goblin. Best examples: Bryce Canyon, Cedar Breaks, The Rimrocks, the White Rocks, Coal Mine Canyon, Tent Rocks.

Kiva: underground ceremonial chamber built by Ancestral Puebloans and other native cultures of the Southwest.

Kokopelli: the ubiquitous anthropomorph, with its hunch back and flute. Common on rock art all over the Southwest.

Laccolith: mountain formed by magma uprisings pushing horizontally and vertically through the thick layers of sandstone. Best examples: all the most prominent mountains of the Colorado Plateau.

Mesa: a flat-top remnant of a plateau rising above the surrounding plain. Its name means "table" in Spanish. Best examples: Monument Valley, Mesa Verde.

Monocline: a spectacular fracture in the ground, resulting in layers of sedimental rock exposed at a steep angle. Also known generically as "Fold" and "hogback" when it's shorter in length. Best examples: Waterpocket Fold, the Cockscomb, Comb Ridge.

Natural Bridge: a natural opening formed by water action piercing through thin rock at the bend of a river. Best examples: Rainbow Bridge, Natural Bridges NM, Capitol Reef.

Narrows: extremely narrow canyon formed by a watercourse that is often dry. Best examples: Virgin Narrows, Paria Narrows, Buckskin Gulch.

Needles: a form of spire of Cedar Mesa sandstone eroded in the form of jagged points along fracture lines, also called minarets. Best examples: the Needles and Maze districts of Canyonlands.

Petrified dunes: ancient sand dunes turned to rock after being buried, then rounded and polished by erosion. Best examples: Arches NP, Boulder, Hite, Round Rock.

Petrified wood: remnant tree trunks from ancient forests submerged by volcanic ash, then exposed by soil erosion. Best examples: Petrified Forest NP, Escalante SP, Wolverine area on Burr trail.

Petroglyph: rock art done by pecking, scratching or carving.

Pictograph: rock art painted on the surface of the stone.

Playa: Spanish for "beach", a dry lakebed formed by evaporation and consisting of dissolved minerals. Best examples: White Sands NM.

Pothole: a.k.a. *Tinaja* in Spanish. A shallow pool formed in slickrock or limestone, sometimes even bedrock, by water dissolving the sand or rock particles, which are then washed away during storms. Best example: the Needles.

Rincon: short abandoned loop in a river gorge or any short tributary in a canyon or valley. Best examples: Escalante river drainage.

Reef: a natural rock barrier in the form of a ridge, formed by an almost vertical uplift of sedimentary layers. Best examples: San Rafael Reef, Capitol Reef.

Sand pipes: columns of light-colored rock of a phallic shape emerging in a haphazard manner from the earth. Best examples: Kodachrome Basin.

Slickrock: generic term used to describe exposed masses of hard sandstone polished by the elements, such as the Slickrock Trail of Moab, a favorite of mountain bikers. This sandstone becomes extremely slippery under rain, ice and snow. Best examples: around Moab, Canyonlands.

Slot canyon: a narrow passage with smooth walls, formed not by constantly flowing water, but by the repeated action of flash floods. Best examples: Antelope Canyon, Peek-a-Boo, Little Wild Horse, Wire Pass, Round Valley Draw.

Spires: rock capped by a hard uppermost slab and eroded by rain into vertical towers. Best examples: Fisher Towers, Monument Valley, Chimney Rock in Capitol Reef, Kodachrome Basin.

Tank: a large pothole. Best examples: Capitol Gorge, Waterpocket Fold.

Travertine: layered calcium carbonate formed by deposition from spring waters or hot springs. Best examples: Havasu Canyon, Subway, Crystal Geyser.

Volcanic plug: see diatreme. Best examples: Shiprock, Agathla Peak.

Wash: a dry watercourse channeling runoff water after thunderstorms.

Window: a hole trough a wall of rock, with edges not quite as defined as an arch. Best examples: Arches NP.

Maps

The maps are classified by scale, beginning with the largest and most general.

Large scale road maps: the best general road map is without doubt the Indian Country Guide published by the American Automobile Association (AAA). This remarkable guide/map is a sheer pleasure to read and use. It contains a surprising amount of dirt and gravel roads, with very accurate mileage and it does an excellent job of referencing little-known locations. Unless you intend to do some heavy-duty hiking or four-wheeling, this map is quite sufficient for an ordinary car-based tour of the "Grand Circle". The only site in the present guide that is not covered by AAA's Indian Country Guide is Colorado Nat'l Monument. The latter is adequately covered by the AAA Utah–Colorado map and park mini-guide. You can obtain these maps from any AAA office and many of the bookstores in the National Parks and Monuments.

Detailed road maps: Southeastern Utah and Southwestern Utah maps are published by the Utah Travel Council. Roads and tracks are indicated in a very precise fashion. These maps can prove very useful when used in conjunction with the Indian Country map, especially to find less important 4WD trails.

National Park and Monument miniguides: these wonderfully concise miniguides are packed with all the essential information about the parks, their history, geology and fauna. You can get them at the park entrances or at Visitor Centers. They will help you find your way around on roads and trails. Grand Staircase-Escalante has adopted a different format with a beautiful, richly illustrated, color map. You'll also benefit greatly from their Grand Staircase-Escalante Numbered Road Map, should you visit some of the backcountry sites featured in this book. This road map introduces a very convenient numbering system that greatly helps identifying and navigating the numerous dirt roads of the area.

National Park topographic maps: if you plan on adventuring along the trails and roads in distant parts of the national parks, the topographic maps of the Illustrated Trails series, printed on waterproof paper, are extremely well made and highly recommended. I always use them for hiking in the parks.

Topo maps on CD-ROM: a fantastic resource to plan your trip beforehand. The maps print spectacularly well and you can mark your intended route. Great to enter way points in your GPS. Delorme, Maptech and National Geographic make topo mapping software on CD-Rom. On the web, topozone.com has downloadable maps.

4x4 topographic maps: Fran Barnes' maps in the Canyon Country series are excellent. They are U.S. Geological Survey topo maps on which are superimposed the numerous and little frequented 4x4 trails. They are extremely practical if your primary purpose if to do some four-wheeling in the Moab area.

Topographic atlas: DeLorme Atlas & Gazetteer Series.

Selected Bibliography - Guidebooks

You have a wide selection of materials from which to choose among the traditional guidebooks. Here are some of my favorites:

National Geographic's Guide to the National Parks of the USA, published by the National Geographic Society, (888) 225-5647; an excellent general reference work, very well illustrated with many photographs.

Journey to the High Southwest by Robert Casey, published by Globe Pequot Press, ISBN 0-7627-0499-3: a remarkably endearing and thoroughly documented travel guide to the Four Corners.

Hiking the Southwest's Canyon Country by Sandra Hinchman, published by The Mountaineers Press, ISBN 0-89886-492-5; an excellent hiking guide to the Southwest, very complete, with great maps.

Canyon Hiking Guide to the Colorado Plateau by Michael Kelsey, published by Michael R. Kelsey Publishing, ISBN 0-944510-16-7; a remarkable resource for fit people wanting to explore canyons and remote places of the Colorado Plateau. To be used responsibly and according to the author's warnings and disclaimer. Hiking times are seriously underestimated for the great majority of people. Use maps with caution and not as your primary source of information.

Hiking and Exploring the Paria River by Michael Kelsey, published by Michael R. Kelsey Publishing, ISBN 0-944510-15-9; the comments for the previous book apply to this one too.

Canyon Country Geology for the Layman and Rockbound by F.A. Barnes, published by Arch Hunter Books, ISBN 1-891858-18-1: one of many highly informative and easy-to-read guidebooks by Mr. Barnes. Highly recommended.

Hiking Grand Staircase-Escalante & the Glen Canyon Region by Ron Adkinson, published by Falcon Guides, ISBN 1-56044-645-5: excellent hiking resource for the whole Escalante region.

Trail Guide to Grand Staircase-Escalante by David Urmann and Kevin Bowditch, published by Gibbs Smith Publisher, ISBN 0-879058-85-4: nice book, with good advice on the rarely-documented Kaiparowits Plateau.

Hiking the Escalante by Rudi Lambrechtse, published by Univ. of Utah Press, ISBN: 0874806313: the book to take if you'll be using the Hole-in-the-Rock road as a staging area for hikes.

A Hiking Guide to Cedar Mesa by Peter Francis Tassoni, published by Univ. of Utah press, ISBN 0874806801; the latest "hot" book to have for discovering seldom seen Puebloan dwellings of the Cedar Mesa area.

Utah's National Parks by Ron Adkinson, published by Wilderness Press, ISBN 0-89997-126-1: a great resource, very thoroughly researched.

Utah Byways by Tony Huegel, published by Wilderness Press, ISBN 0-89997-263-2: nice to have in the glove box for good description of the Scenic Backways.

Hiking Zion and Bryce Canyon NP by Erik Molvar & Tamara Martin, published by Falcon Press, ISBN 1-56044-509-2: excellent hiking guide to these major parks.

Exploring Canyonlands and Arches by Bill Schneider, published by Falcon Press, ISBN 1-56044-510-6: excellent hiking guide.

Scenic Driving Utah by Joe Bensen, published by Falcon Press, ISBN 1-56044-486-X: excellent resource for driving around Utah.

Canyon Country Prehistoric Rock Art by Fran Barnes, published by Arch Hunter Books, ISBN 0-915272-25-3: an excellent introduction to rock art.

Rock Art and Ruins for Beginners and Old Guys by Albert Scholl Jr., published by Rainbow Publishing, ISBN 0-9704688-0-6: a fun guide to the major rock art sites.

Canyon Country Off-Road Vehicle Trails (a collection) by Fran Barnes: a must for off-road driving in the Arches and Canyonlands area.

Selected Bibliography - Other Recommended Reading

I cannot recommend too highly the following works, which I consider quintessential to a good understanding of various ascpects of the Southwest. Reading these books during a trip in the American West reinforces the pleasure of discovery.

Standing Up Country by Gregory Crampton, published by Rio Nuevo Publishers, ISBN 1-887896-15-5: a wonderful resource on the human history of the Colorado Plateau, richly illustrated with outstanding photography.

Desert Solitaire by Edward Abbey, published by Ballantine Books, ISBN 0345326490: the classic among the numerous books by Abbey, the rebel ranger, at once liberal and redneck. Abbey depicts his love of the desert with a fine sensibility. It's the perfect accompaniment for a trip to Arches and Canyonlands.

Mormon Country by Wallace Stegner, published by the University of Nebraska Press, ISBN 0803291256: a fundamental work on the colonization of Utah by the Mormons; impartial, remarkably documented and an easy read. It would be a shame to cross Utah without knowing or understanding the remarkable saga of the Mormon pioneers.

The Southwest Inside Out by Thomas Wiewandt and Maureen Wilks, published by Wild Horizons Publishing, ISBN 1-879728-03-6: a highly-innovative and approachable presentation of the natural features of the Southwest. Remarkably illustrated. Outstanding photography.

Architecture of the Ancient Ones by A. Dudley Gardner and Val Brinkerhoff, published by Gibbs Smith, ISBN 0-87905-955-9: Outstanding photography.

The Exploration of the Colorado River and Its Canyons by John Wesley Powell, published by Penguin USA, ISBN 0140255699: Powell's extraordinary journals of his expedition, prefaced by Wallace Stegner.

The Dark Wind by Tony Hillerman, published by Harper, ISBN 0061000035: a novel with a cool Navajo cop as its reluctant hero. An excellent introduction to Navajo culture in the guise of a lively story. A must-read when crossing the Big Rez! Don't be ashamed of the "white guy" syndrome. If you get hooked on Navajo and Hopi culture, you'll naturally step up to serious works.

Centennial by James Michener, published by Fawcett Books, ISBN 0449214192: a remarkable book, even though it's not really about the Southwest. It's an absolutely fascinating saga of the West and a shock for those who have never read Michener.

Needless to say, there are numerous coffee table books depicting the Southwest. These books by well-known photographers such as Ansel Adams, Jack Dykinga, Joseph Lange, David and Marc Muench, Eliot Porter, Lynn Radeka, Galen Rowell, Anselm Spring, Tom Till, Linde Waidhofer, Art Wolfe and many more are a pleasure to look at. They are also an excellent source of locations as well as a great way to improve your photographic skills through emulation.

On the Go Resources

These resources are intended as a quick way of finding further information while you're on the road, by calling the appropriate agency. The phone numbers have been verified shortly before we went to press; however, phone numbers can change and this information may be obsolete by the time you read it. I hope you'll find this list useful in your travels.

It is just a convenient way to call from the road and I have purposely avoided presenting a formal list of web sites. You'll find a large number of links to interesting websites on www.phototripusa.com.

National Parks & Monuments

Arches NP (435)719-2319 or (435)719-2299
Aztec Ruins NM (505) 334-6174
Black Canyon of the Gunnison NP (970) 641-2337
Bryce Canyon NP (435) 834-5322
Canyonlands NP/Island District (435) 259-4712
Canyonlands NP/Needles District (435) 259-4711
Canyonlands NP/Maze District (435) 259-2652
Capitol Reef NP (435) 425-3791
Cedar Breaks NM (435) 586-9451
Colorado NM (970) 858-3617
Curecanti NRA (970) 641-2337
Glen Canyon NRA (928) 608-6404
Grand Staircase-Escalante NM (435) 826-5499
Great Sand Dunes NM (719) 378-2312
Hovenweep NM (970) 562-4282
Mesa Verde NP (970) 529-4465 or (970) 529-4633

Natural Bridges NM (435)692-1234
Pipe Spring NM (928) 643-7105
Zion NP (435) 772-3256

State Parks
Anasazi SP (435) 335-7308
Coral Pink Sand Dunes SP (435) 648-2800
Dead Horse Point SP (435) 259-2614
Edge of the Cedars SP (435) 678-2238
Escalante Petrified Forest SP (435) 826-4466
Fremont Indian SP (435) 527-4631
Goblin Valley SP (435) 564-3633
Goosenecks SP (435) 678-2238
Kodachrome Basin SP (435) 679-8562

Other Parks & Organizations

Archeology Vandalism Hotline (800) 722-3998
BLM of Kanab (435) 644-4600
BLM of Moab (435) 259-2100
BLM of St.George (435) 688-3200
Bryce Canyon Trail Rides (435) 679 8665
Canyonlands-North Travel region (800) 635-6622
Canyonlands-South Travel region (800) 574-4386
Colorado Road Conditions (303) 639-1234
Color Country Travel region (800) 233-utah
Durango Visitor Information (800) 525-8855
Durango & Silverton Narrow Gauge Railroad (970) 247-2733
Escalante Interagency Visitor Center (435) 826-5499
Grand Mesa Information (970) 874-6600
Hall's Crossing Ferry (435) 684-3087
Moab Information Center (800) 635-MOAB or (800) 635-6622
Navajo Nation Tourism Department (520) 871-6659
Nine Mile Canyon information (435) 637-3009
Ouray Visitor Information (800) 228-1876
Paria Canyon-Vermilion Cliffs Wilderness (435) 688-3246
San Juan Skyway Association (800) 962-2493
San Juan Mountains Association (970) 385-1210
Silverton Visitor Information (800) 752-4494
Utah Road Conditions (800) 492-2400
Utah State Parks and Recreation (800) 322-3770
Utah Travel Council (800) 200-1160

Note: all National Parks and Monuments and most travelers' bureaus will send you free documentation anywhere in the world to prepare your trip.

Permits for the Wave
https://paria.az.blm.gov

Flights Over Canyonlands
Slickrock Air Guides (Moab) (435) 259-6216
Red Tail Aviation (Moab) (435) 259-7421 or (800) 842-9251
Mountain Flying Service (Monticello) (888) 653-7365.
Needles Outpost (435) 979-4007

Equipment for the Narrows of the Virgin and the Subway
Zion Adventure (Springdale) (435) 772-1001

Llamas, horses and hiking Concessionaires
Red Rock n' Llamas (435) 559-7325 or (877) 955-2627
Escalante Canyon Outfitters (435) 335-7311 or (888) 326-4453

4x4 Rentals in Moab
Thrifty Car Rental (435) 259-7317
Slickrock 4X4 Rentals (435) 259-5678
Farabee's Jeep Rentals (435) 259-7494

Colorado River Outfitters
Utah Guides & Outfitters Associations (801) 495-2592
Adrift Adventures Canyonlands (800) 874-4483 or (435) 259-8594
Navtec Expeditions (800) 833-1278 or (435) 259-7983
Tag-A-Long Expeditions (800) 453-3292 or (435) 259-8946
Western River Expeditions (800) 453-7450 or (801) 942-6669
Wild Rivers Expeditions (800) 422-7654 or (435) 672-2244
World Wide River Expeditions (800) 231-2768 or (435) 259-7515

A not so brief blip about the Author

I was born in Paris, France. Thanks to an open-minded family I received my education in Paris, London, Frankfurt, Hamburg, Munich and Barcelona, ending up with degrees in modern languages and international business.

A couple of years after college, I did the best thing a young person can do to widen his or her horizons and gain an understanding of our world and its wonderful diversity: I set out on an 18-month trip around the world, which eventually led to a five year stint in Tokyo, Japan, as an instructor at Sophia University and a freelance photographer.

Circumstances of life brought me to Los Angeles in 1982 and I have made it my home for the past two decades. I am married and have an adult son.

I own Graphie Int'l, Inc., a small software and multimedia consulting firm I founded in 1982. Despite my busy schedule, I try to make time for regular travel all over the world.

In the course of researching *Photographing the Southwest*—the sequel to my previous book *Land of the Canyons*—I have flown dozens of time to Las Vegas, Salt Lake City, Phoenix, Albuquerque and El Paso, renting cars for extended 3 or 4 day weekends. I have followed this routine for more than two years. On longer trips, or trips involving four-wheel driving, I drive my own vehicle. I am usually on my own during intense photography trips, although I also enjoy the company of a partner when one is available. On more relaxed trip, I travel with my wife and dog and sometimes also, our two horses.

I know it sounds corny to say that I wrote this guide to share my love for this photographer's paradise that is the Southwest. I'm saying it nonetheless because that's just a fact.

As a photographer, I prefer the 6x4.5 medium format. I do the majority of my photography with two Fuji 645 cameras; I find these cameras well-suited to my style of photography, with their combination of high resolution and good portability. I also use an Olympus OM-4 for extreme wide-angle and long-telephoto shots. I shoot exclusively on Fuji Velvia and Provia transparency film.

... and how this book came to be

While largely incidental to the purpose of this guide, you may find interesting the following story, which relates how this book came to be.

Back in 1975, while on my non-stop trip around the world, I found myself stuck in the city of Luang Prabang, in the small country of Laos (located just east of Vietnam). Renegade bands of Patet-Lao rebels were still partially controlling the countryside, rejecting the truce negotiated in Vientiane between the higher instances of the Patet-Lao and forces loyal to King Norodom Sihanouk.

My goal was to reach Vientiane by bus or truck, but the last vehicles to try a sortie had been shelled with mortar and nobody was leaving Luang Prabang. I was stuck and remained stuck for about a week.

In those days, Luang Prabang was little more than a big village with two main streets intersecting in the center. What it had, however, was a wonderful American Cultural Center with a well-stocked library. With nothing else to do, I spent numerous hours at the library voraciously reading every book I could find on the National Parks. I had originally planned a traditional whirlwind tour of the U.S., but that week I resolved to do whatever it would take to visit as many National Parks as possible.

A few months later, I landed in San Francisco, bought a used VW van and proceeded to drive 22,000 miles all over the U.S. in the course of the next 5 months, wandering from park to park and photographing those marvelous landscapes.

After I settled in Los Angeles in 1982, I promptly renewed my love affair with the Southwest, always returning there over and over again. I will never forget that week at the American Cultural Center in Luang Prabang. Its impact altered the course of my life in an unforeseen direction and this book wouldn't be in your hands today but for this fortuitous event. ✿

INDEX

!$! SAVE WITH THIS COUPON !$!

If you don't yet own *Photographing the Southwest - Volume 2 (Arizona & New Mexico)*, you're missing on some great information and photography!

Order it separately or as a bundle including the two *CD-ROMs Images of the Southwest - Volumes 1 & 2*. Each CD-ROM is a companion to its respective book (Vol 1. or Vol. 2). You'll get the photos from each book, plus many more—a total of 500+ high-quality images, all in full color, royalty-free for your personal use, arranged by chapters just like in the books. This is an excellent way to "pre-visualize" the sites—an indispensable part of quality photography. The CD-ROMs are Windows/Mac compatible.

Fax or mail this coupon and **save $5 off the regular price of each CD-ROM, or save $10 off both CD-ROMs!**

Qty	Item	Price	Total
	BOOK Photograph. the Southwest -Vol.2	$16.95	
	CD-ROM Images of the Southwest Vol. 1	$~~19.95~~ $14.95	
	CD-ROM Images of the Southwest Vol. 2	$~~19.95~~ $14.95	
	Both CD-ROMs	$~~39.90~~ $29.95	
	SUBTOTAL		
	Sales Tax (CA Residents, add 7.75 %)		
	Shipping ($4 for 1st. item, +$2 per add. item)		
	GRAND TOTAL		

All prices are in U.S. Dollars. Shipping charges are for USA only. Shipping is via Priority Mail.
Shipping to Canada & Mexico: $7 for 1st. item, +$3 per add. Item
Shipping to all other countries $10 for 1st. item, +$3 per add. Item

Payment Form: ___ Check ___ VISA ___ MasterCard
Card Number : _____ Expiration: ___ / ___
Signature : _____

Name on Card: _____
Address: _____
City: _____ State: ___ Zip: _____
Country: _____
Fax: _____ *or* eMail: _____

• Fax or mail this special rebate form to:
PhotoTripUSA
8780 19th St. #199. Alta Loma, CA 91701 USA
Fax: (435) 514-5975   eMail: info@phototripusa.com

• or use our convenient secure store: http://www.phototripusa.com

Offer expires 12/31/2003

NOTES